Eastern Cauldron

# Eastern Cauldron

## Islam, Afghanistan, Palestine, and Iraq in a Marxist Mirror

GILBERT ACHCAR

Translated by PETER DRUCKER

MONTHLY REVIEW PRESS

*New York*

Library of Congress Cataloging-in-Publication Data

   Achcar, Gilbert.
   Eastern cauldron : Islam, Afghanistan, Palestine and Iraq in a Marxist mirror /
Gilbert Achcar.

      p.   cm.

   Includes bibliographical references and index.

   ISBN 1-58367-095-5 (pbk.) — ISBN 1-58367-096-3 (cloth)

   1. Middle East—Foreign relations—United States. 2. United States—
Foreign relations—Middle East. 3. Islamic fundamentalism—Middle East.
4. Afghanistan—History—1989-2001. 5. Afghanistan—History—2001-
6. Iraq War, 2003. 7. Arab-Israeli conflict. I. Title.

   DS63.2.U5A625 2004
   327.73056'09'045—dc22

                     2004001239

   ISBN 1-58367-095-5 (paperback)
   ISBN 1-58367-096-3 (cloth)

MONTHLY REVIEW PRESS
122 West 27th Street
New York, NY 10001

*Printed in Canada*

10 9 8 7 6 5 4 3 2 1

# Contents

# PREFACE

The articles assembled in this collection were written over a long period of time, almost a quarter-century, from 1980 to 2003. They nonetheless share the same continuous inspiration: a persistent attachment to a method inspired by that which Marx used to tell the history of his own time in his articles and works. They can thus be seen as a sort of Marxist chronicle of some key moments in the tumultuous history of the Islamic East during the last two decades of the twentieth century. These moments include the abrupt resurgence of Islamic fundamentalism seen in the 1979 Iranian revolution; its repercussions through the region, in particular the war in Afghanistan that hastened the collapse of the Soviet Union; the unfolding struggle of the Palestinian people beginning with the outbreak in 1987 of the first intifada; and the campaign against Iraq until its invasion by U.S. and British forces in 2003.

This is the tragic story of a region that is permanently in flames, like an active volcano at the junction of two tectonic plates. Not a "clash of civilizations" between "Islam" and "the West," but rather—as I have tried to explain elsewhere—the violent shock brought about by the aggressive intervention of two imperial barbarisms: the capitalist West and its local agents of all religions and sects and the Russo-Soviet empire.[1] This shock has continually provoked other barbarisms in reaction, whose predominant local form has been the fanatical varieties of Islamic fundamentalism.

The decision to cover this particular period and include these particular articles was, however, the result of practical considerations. The main factor was the availability of articles written in French or English. I began writing about current events in this part of the world — the region I come from—in 1970, ten years before the earliest article included in this book. But most of the articles and pamphlets I wrote during the 1970s were in Arabic. This was the case in particular with my writings on the war in Lebanon, where I lived until the year following the 1982 Israeli invasion.

7

Most of the articles chosen for this collection were written after I moved to France in 1983, particularly during the years 1987–92 when I was a regular contributor to the Marxist magazines *Inprecor* (in French) and *International Viewpoint*. With one exception, the articles that I wrote on the first Gulf war (1990–91) have not been included; these had already been published in an earlier collection.[2] The articles reprinted here appear as they were first published, with some minor stylistic corrections and the elimination of a few passages that express too directly my concerns as a political activist at the time of publication. The omissions are indicated by bracketed ellipses and footnotes written for this edition are indicated by brackets. The subheads of the articles published in *International Viewpoint* were added by the editors of the original French versions. These articles originally appeared under a pen name.

Their collection and republication today reflects of course the publisher's judgment, and mine, that they are still relevant and still shed some bright light on very recent events. It goes without saying that only later reading can show whether an immediate analysis of past events has stood the test of time. An analysis that passes this test can even be useful in foreseeing the future, insofar as tendencies at work in the past continue at work for some time to come.

A new article, written as an introduction to this collection, traces the development of U.S. strategy in the Middle East and analyzes its wellsprings. It provides an overall perspective within which the events commented on in the other articles can be understood, thus making it possible to see—in a Marxist mirror—their historical logic.[3]

For this edition, English translations of the articles previously published have been thoroughly checked and corrected by Peter Drucker and me. Peter has in addition translated three articles into English for the first time for this collection. It has been a pleasure for me, as usual, to work with him on this new book, as well as with Andrew Nash, Martin Paddio, and the whole team at Monthly Review Press.

GILBERT ACHCAR
*July 2003*

# U.S. Imperial Strategy in the Middle East

In the beginning was the "open door" to oil: this is how any history of the steadily tightening U.S. hold on the Middle East ought to begin.

It was indeed oil that aroused Washington's intense interest in this region in the aftermath of its late entry into the First World War. The oil-producing areas of the Ottoman imperial domain had been major stakes in the first conflagration that pitted the older British and French imperialist powers against imperialist latecomer Germany. The Ottoman Sublime Porte had allied itself in this war with Germany.[1]

## THE SPOILS OF THE OTTOMAN EMPIRE

The United States, the youngest imperialist power, had already become the most powerful thanks to the world war. But the agreement reached by the European allies at the 1920 San Remo conference, preparing the signature of the Treaty of Sèvres with post-Ottoman Turkey, was a slap in its face. The British and French had agreed earlier on partitioning the territorial spoils of the Ottoman Empire in the 1916 Sykes-Picot agreement. Then at San Remo, hosted by their Italian ally, they reached agreement on exploiting any oil discovered in "Mesopotamia," that is, the new state of Iraq, which the League of Nations had put under a British colonial "mandate."

The San Remo agreement gave the Turkish Petroleum Company (TPC, later to become the Iraq Petroleum Company, IPC) a monopoly on Iraqi oil production. London had managed to secure predominance for British interests in this company, the beneficiary of an Ottoman concession, just before the war. Anglo-Persian Oil (later British Petroleum, BP) held a 50 percent interest in the TPC—Winston Churchill had in turn gotten a

majority interest in Anglo-Persian Oil for the British government—Royal
Dutch/Shell a 25 percent interest, and the Deutsche Bank the remaining 25
percent.[2] After the war the British government confiscated the Deutsche
Bank's share and turned it over to the Compagnie Française des Pétroles
(CFP, French Oil Company, later to become Total).

Under pressure from U.S. oil companies, the "internationalist" Wilson
administration protested vigorously against this violation of the Open Door
principle. This high-sounding name denoted a policy that openly expressed
the will of the young U.S. imperialist power to take its own place in the sun
in the imperialist partition of the world, by opposing exclusive control of
markets by the traditional colonial empires that already had virtually the
whole planet under their thumbs. Formulated at the end of the nineteenth
century by the McKinley administration, which ushered the U.S. a bit late
into the imperialist era, the Open Door policy was originally a challenge to
the exclusive sharing of China among the Europeans and Japanese.

By 1920 U.S. imperialism had a great economic advantage, thanks to a
shift in its status that the First World War had helped bring about. From
now on it would therefore use the Open Door and "free trade" as the slogans of its own imperial policy. A newcomer, richer than the others thanks
to the war, the United States had every interest in seeing that every market
was open to it and that it received equal treatment with other, much longer-
established powers. "Freedom," which the United States has championed
on the world scene, has thus always meant free trade and free enterprise
first and foremost. Political freedom has been a much more variable element of U.S. policy, used opportunistically on a case-by-case basis depending on whether it suits the local requirements of U.S. hegemony.

As Raymond Aron has written, "The economic and political aspects of
the general purpose of American diplomacy are inseparable because this
purpose is by definition freedom of access, a notion which encompasses the
exchange of ideas, investments and goods."[3] We can accept this formulation
to the extent that "freedom of access" means in reality making sure that
other countries have "access" to the "ideas, investments and goods" of the
United States and that the United States has "access" to their markets and
resources as well as their political and cultural space. This is what the Open
Door policy means. The U.S. conception of free access does *not* mean setting up some kind of egalitarian "free trade" suitable to a capitalist utopia.

In any event, the pressure that Washington exerted on London and Paris
was irresistible. In 1928 a new agreement was signed, redistributing four

equal shares in the TPC to Anglo-Persian, Royal Dutch/Shell, the French CFP, and a holding company representing a consortium of U.S. oil companies. At the same time the signatories agreed to reserve for joint exploitation under the aegis of the TPC any oil that any of them might discover in the vast ex-Ottoman regime including Turkey, the Arab lands east of Suez, and the whole Arabian Peninsula except Kuwait (which Britain had already wrested from Ottoman control at the end of the nineteenth century). The U.S. oil companies not included in the TPC/IPC—particularly Standard Oil of California (Socal, later to become Chevron) and Texaco—benefited from having their hands free and went on to penetrate the region on their own. Gulf Oil (subsequently acquired by Chevron), Standard Oil of New Jersey (later Exxon), and Standard Oil of New York (Socony, later Mobil) only managed to cast off the chains of the IPC after the Second World War.[4]

In this way Socal became in 1933 the first company to obtain a concession from the new Saudi kingdom. Ibn Saud had proclaimed his kingdom the year before and was ill-disposed toward British interests and thus to the IPC because of his rivalry with the thoroughly British-backed Hashemite dynasty. Socal, which paid a big advance on royalties under the 1933 contract, was making a big gamble: the first commercially workable oil field in the kingdom was only discovered in 1938. In the meantime Socal and Texaco fused their interests east of Suez, on a basis of equality, in the joint venture Caltex.

## OIL AND COLD WAR

The Second World War, even more than the first, definitively raised oil to the status of the world's main strategic mineral resource. At about the same time the gigantic extent of the oil wealth held by the Saudi dynasty was discovered. The bipolar U.S.-Soviet rivalry that took shape during the war brought the two powers into conflict after the war. These developments made the Arab-Persian Gulf region in general and the Saudi kingdom in particular the area with the highest strategic priority for the United States—after the industrialized regions of Europe and Japan—in the framework of this conflict.[5]

As early as 1943 Washington decided to set up a military base at Dhahran, in the heart of the Saudi oil fields, and signed an agreement to this effect with Ibn Saud.[6] Built between 1944 and 1946, this U.S. Air Force base, the biggest one outside Europe and Japan, was meant to protect and foster U.S. interests in the Gulf region in the context of both Washington's strategic competition with Moscow and U.S. economic competition with the British.

Imposing, consolidating, and extending its hegemony in the Middle East clearly became one of Washington's chief postwar objectives. To paraphrase the famous summary of NATO's goals by Lord Ismay, the organization's first secretary general—NATO was meant "to keep the Americans in, the Russians out, and the Germans down"—one could say that the U.S. aimed in the Middle East to keep the Americans in, the Russians out, and the British (and the French along with them) down.

The Middle East and its oil became one of the central issues around which the Cold War would take shape. Iran, as early as 1946 one of the first theaters in which Washington and Moscow faced off, illustrated Washington's three above-mentioned concerns perfectly. The Shah's government itself shared the three concerns and pushed the United States in this direction. The Shah sought at one and the same time to get rid of the Soviet troops on his territory and the British, and in part Soviet, tutelage over his oil, by calling in the United States to replace them as a protecting power and an oil partner.[7]

On March 12, 1947, President Harry Truman, the main initiator of the Cold War, made his famous speech, baptized the Truman Doctrine, in which he offered U.S. assistance to Greece and Turkey, considered the two big ramparts blocking the spread of Soviet influence on Europe and the Middle East. This was the first public formulation of the policy of "containment" of communism. As Daniel Yergin points out in his monumental history of the oil industry, an agreement was signed that very same day integrating Standard Oil of New Jersey and Socony into the Arabian-American Oil Company (Aramco) formed by Socal and Texaco.[8] This agreement created the consortium of four U.S. oil companies that would share the exploitation of Saudi oil among themselves.

In this first phase of the postwar period, U.S. imperial strategy in the Middle East was aimed at both countering Moscow's interests and undermining London's. The intensity and modalities of these two prongs were of course quite different: Britain remained a key U.S. ally in the Cold War, as it had been in the Second World War. U.S. strategy revolved around Washington's relations with an important new actor on the regional scene: the nationalism of the "middle classes," essentially bourgeois or petit bourgeois, opposed to Western domination and to the social classes and categories that Western domination leaned on in its socially conservative enterprise: the big landowners, "comprador" bourgeoisie, and tribal chiefdoms.

Conscious of Britain's considerable unpopularity in the Middle East, the United States had all the more reason to try to dissociate itself from the

British, so as to encroach on the British interests that had pretty much dominated the area between the wars. But U.S. efforts to co-opt the nationalist movement, seen as an effective bulwark against the Communists, did not get very far. The United States quickly came into conflict with the nationalists, and the conflict grew steadily more acute as Washington took London's place as the main Western power in the region. For Washington as for London, the question of Israel was a major source of hostility toward Western domination. The state of Israel was seen as a beachhead of Western domination in the Arab East. Its creation in 1948 and the ensuing Israeli-Arab war were in themselves powerful catalysts in the rise of nationalism in the region.

Iran was once more the scene of the first confrontation in the complex game among the United States, Britain, USSR, nationalists, and Communists. Mussadiq's rise to power in 1951, with the nationalization of the Iranian oil industry at the cost of the Anglo-Iranian Oil Company (AIOC-BP), was the first major challenge from within the Middle East to Western control of its oil. The prominent role that Iranian Communists played in the political crisis, and Moscow's overtures to the new government, made the threat even worse.

After some initial hesitation in deciding on its attitude toward Mussadiq, Washington ended up orchestrating his military overthrow and the restoration of the Shah's power in 1953.[9] The coup also provided an opportunity to redivide the shares in Iranian oil production. A consortium was formed in which the share of AIOC-BP was cut back to 40 percent, with another 40 percent for five U.S. companies (the four partners in Aramco plus Gulf Oil, each with an 8 percent share) and the remaining 20 percent divided between Royal Dutch/Shell (14 percent) and the French CFP (6 percent).

Meanwhile in July 1952, in the midst of the Iranian crisis, a republican coup d'état organized by nationalist army officers overthrew the main Arab monarchy in Egypt, which had been under British domination. At the beginning the "moderate" General Neguib headed the junta, leading Washington to believe that it could strengthen its ties with them. But once Colonel Nasser took power in 1954, the prospects for Washington became considerably less rosy. Nasser's nationalism, with its dual perspective of defending Egyptian sovereignty and promoting Pan-Arab unity, proved inherently irreconcilable with the U.S. drive for hegemony. Nasser rejected Washington's offers of economic and military aid because of U.S. conditions that would have infringed on Egypt's independence.

Goaded by the Israeli threat, revealed among other incidents by the Israeli raid on the Egyptian-administered Gaza Strip that took the lives of thirty-eight Egyptian soldiers in February 1955,[10] Nasser made the first arms deal the following September that any Arab country had ever made with the Soviet Union.[11] The Egyptian leader joined in shaping Third World nationalism in the era of decolonization at the April 1955 Bandung conference, a conference that made him one of the movement's stars. He tried to assert and promote his country's sovereignty and counterbalance Western influence by calling on the Soviets. In a world much dominated to begin with by the Western powers, nonalignment worked in Moscow's favor, so that Moscow saw many more positive aspects to it than Washington did. Nasser's opposition to the Baghdad Pact, which linked the British-sponsored Iraqi monarchy to Iran, Pakistan, Turkey, and Britain with the U.S. "big brother" as godfather, was only logical in light of his strategy.

Washington reacted in a niggardly way, withdrawing its offer of funds for the Aswan High Dam, one of Nasser's most cherished projects. The move accelerated Nasser's radicalization. In July 1956 he nationalized the Suez Canal. In response Israel, Britain, and France attacked Egypt in October. Washington—still playing a complicated game in which it sought to take its distance from traditional colonialism, supplant London in the Middle East, and at the same time "contain" Communism and compete with Moscow—opposed the tripartite aggression. Moscow responded by trying to outbid the United States in order to strengthen its image as the great ally of Third World liberation struggles.[12]

## ARAB NATIONALISM GROWS MORE RADICAL

The years 1957–61 were a watershed for U.S. regional strategy. Britain, its prestige much weakened by its Egyptian misadventure and with many of its clients and protégés going over to the United States, was less and less a competitor for Washington, more and more an ally in the fight against the growing strength of Communism and anti-Western nationalism. During the same years the ambiguity in Washington's attitude toward Arab nationalism, seen as a hostile force and yet at the same time as at least a potential, objective ally against the Communists, faded away. As the Communists were crushed and the nationalists steadily radicalized, Washington's ambivalence gave way to pure and simple antagonism.

In January 1957, President Eisenhower proclaimed his doctrine of supporting Middle Eastern governments opposed to communism. Nasser's Egypt rejected the Eisenhower Doctrine immediately. For the Egyptians

Israel was the main enemy, not the Communists and still less the USSR. Nonetheless Washington continued in 1957 to count on Nasser to ward off the danger posed by the strong Communist influence in Syria.[13]

The shock wave of 1958 showed the full ambiguity of the situation. Anti-Western Arab nationalism reached new post-Suez heights, galvanized by the proclamation in February that Egypt and Syria were uniting to form the United Arab Republic (UAR). Unrest shook two pro-Western governments that had already fallen under U.S. tutelage, in Jordan and Lebanon. A nationalist, republican coup d'état on July 14 overthrew a third pro-Western government, the Hashemite monarchy in Iraq, centerpiece of the Baghdad Pact (rebaptized CENTO, Central Treaty Organization, after Iraq's defection). The very next day Washington sent troops into Lebanon, while at the same time negotiating a compromise settlement with Cairo rather than supporting pro-Western Lebanese President Camille Chamoun.[14] Meanwhile British troops based in Cyprus intervened in Jordan.

This confrontation did not stop Washington from observing with relief how nationalists brutally crushed the Communists in Syria beginning in 1958–59 and in Iraq from 1959 to 1963. Washington's relief was all the greater because the Communist parties in both Syria and Iraq had grown to the point that they could aim at seizing power. (The Egyptian Communists were also harshly repressed, but had never been as strong.)

At the same time the United States rejoiced at the rise of dissension among nationalists. First there were tensions between, on the one hand, Iraq's pro-UAR Nasserites and Ba'athists, and on the other hand Iraqi General Qasim, who pushed them out of government shortly after the republican coup in Baghdad. Then there were tensions between Nasser's Egypt and its Syrian partners, which led to the breakup of the Egyptian-Syrian union in September 1961 following a coup in Damascus. These dissensions were a serious blow to Nasser's grand design of realizing Arab national unity under his leadership. But he still did not give up this ambition, which was as much of a nightmare for Washington as the idea of a Communist takeover of the Arab region.

Nasser's regime continued to grow more radical. This was the result partly of the Egyptian social dynamic, partly of the logic of his political project for national sovereignty. But it also expressed his desire to weaken the Egyptian commercial bourgeoisie, which in Egypt as in Syria was putting spokes in the wheels of his nationalist ambitions. The backdrop was a red wind blowing for radical Third World nationalism—particularly from

Cuba, where nationalizations began and the First Declaration of Havana was issued in 1960. Washington had seen Arab nationalism as a bulwark against "communism"; now Arab nationalism began to look in Washington's eyes more and more like communism. In July 1961, Nasser promulgated an impressive series of measures bringing the economy under state control, restricting private fortunes and heavily taxing high incomes, as well as measures favoring waged workers. Egypt's radical left turn horrified the Syrian bourgeoisie, thus precipitating Syria's secession from the UAR.

The following year Nasser issued a national charter that defined the regime as "socialist," using a vocabulary borrowed in part from the communist movement. The new "socialist" dimension bore witness to how far Nasser's anti-imperialism was going. His opposition to U.S. interests in the Arab region became still more vehement, while he carried out a spectacular rapprochement with Moscow. His offensive against Arab regimes under Washington's sway, particularly the Saudi, Jordanian, and Libyan monarchies, reached its apogee. Nasser's attacks discomfited the Saudi dynasty—caught as it was in a glaring contradiction between its fanatical Islamic puritanism (Wahhabism) and the presence of non-Muslim troops on its "holy" soil—to the point that it felt compelled to ask the United States in 1961 to evacuate the base at Dhahran. The United States in fact did so the following year.

Having thus succeeded in getting U.S. troops kicked out of the Saudi kingdom, Nasser did not hesitate to send in his troops when there was a republican coup d'état next door to the Saudis in Yemen in September 1962. Egyptian troops arrived in October to give Yemeni republicans a helping hand in the civil war pitting them against the royalists. At the same time Nasser stepped up the pressure for dismantling the other U.S. base in the region, the Wheelus base in Libya.

The increasing radicalism of Nasserism had a powerful impact on nationalist forces throughout the region, from newly independent Algeria to Iraq and Syria, where Ba'athists and other Arab nationalists took power in 1963. Nasser's model of "socialism"—a state-controlled economy, Soviet-style planning and privileged ties with Moscow—caught on in these three countries, in Iraq in 1964, Syria in 1965, and Algeria in 1970. In February 1966 the left wing of the Ba'athist party took power in Damascus, launching Syria on a course that made Washington see it as a second Cuba, even further to the left than Soviet-inspired Nasserism.

Washington was in addition getting bogged down in Vietnam, facing the rise of revolutionary guerilla movements in the Third World, and no longer able to count on its British ally, which was in the process of disengaging from the remnants of its old empire east of Suez. The United States thus felt obliged to revise its strategy for defending its interests in the Middle East, more threatened than they had ever been before. Engaged in a counterinsurgent counteroffensive in Southeast Asia and Latin America, the United States could not do the same in the Arab region. There it would have had to attack governments backed by Moscow in an area where people were fiercely hostile to any form of Western domination.

## THE U.S.-ISRAELI "SPECIAL RELATIONSHIP"

The United States was up against a wall in the Middle East. The strategy it had followed in the postwar years had failed: the Russians were more and more "in," while the Americans themselves were being pushed out. Recognition of this state of affairs was the factor that transformed the state of Israel, long seen as a liability for Washington's Middle East policy, into a strategic trump card of the first order.

Contrary to a projection that portrays Israel in hindsight as a U.S. pseudo-pod from the moment of its creation—not to speak of the phantasmagoric vision of Israel having the United States in its back pocket!—the Zionist state was throughout the 1950s an even more inconvenient ally for the United States than Britain was. Despite President Truman's partiality toward Israel, the United States had respected the embargo on arms deliveries to all the belligerents that it had imposed in 1948.[15] It had not supplied Israel with any weapons or given it any military aid anytime during the 1950s, out of fear of alienating Arab public opinion—the same logic that had led the United States to keep its distance from Britain and France. France was Israel's main arms supplier for more than two decades. Admittedly Washington's economic aid to Tel Aviv financed Israel's arms purchases from other suppliers. But the lack of direct military ties shows clearly the distance maintained between the two countries, under the Eisenhower administration in particular.

Noting the growing closeness between the two countries under Lyndon Johnson, some people believe that this development can be interpreted as a result of the relative weight of Jews, if not the "Jewish lobby," in the Democratic electorate as opposed to the Republican electorate.[16] True, it is a well-known fact that the great majority of the "Jewish vote" in the United States, as with other ethnic minorities, goes to the Democratic Party. But the idea that the pro-Israeli lobby is in command of Washington's foreign policy—

particularly with regard to one of the regions of greatest strategic interest—attributes much more power to it than it really has.[17] It even rates the Israel lobby higher than the oil lobby, which represents the country's weightiest capitalist interests. As Noam Chomsky has quite rightly commented:

> Despite the remarkable level of U.S. support for Israel, it would be an error to assume that Israel represents the major U.S. interest in the Middle East. Rather, the major interest lies in the energy reserves of the region, primarily in the Arabian peninsula. A State Department analysis of 1945 described Saudi Arabia as "a stupendous source of strategic power, and one of the greatest material prizes in world history." The U.S. was committed to win and keep this prize.... A more recent variant of the same theme is that the flow of petrodollars should be largely funneled to the U.S. through military purchases, construction projects, bank deposits, investment in Treasury securities, etc....
>
> Had it not been for Israel's perceived geopolitical role—primarily in the Middle East, but elsewhere as well—it is doubtful that the various pro-Israeli lobbies in the U.S. would have had much influence in policy formation.... Correspondingly, it will very likely erode if Israel comes to be seen as a threat rather than a support to the primary U.S. interest in the Middle East region, which is to maintain control over its energy reserves and the flow of petrodollars.[18]

Israel's geopolitical role became crucial to the United States at a time, beginning in the early 1960s, when the U.S. was facing an expanding, radicalizing Arab nationalism, to the point of being forced to end its direct presence in the heart of a region that it rated as the most strategic. It evacuated the Dhahran base, in the middle of the Saudi oil-producing area, fifteen years after the base was built, just as a gathering storm was threatening the very interests that the base was meant to protect. This gives a sense of what a perilous moment the United States was going through in its project to dominate the Middle East.

Any direct aggression on Washington's part at the time would have inevitably made Arab popular feeling hostile to U.S. interests flare up even more. Add to all this the defensive handicap due to the absence of U.S. troops on Saudi soil in the event of an attack on the kingdom from without (Yemen) or threats from within, and Israel emerged clearly as a priceless strategic asset.

Israel's value to the United States had two complementary aspects. On the one hand Israel played a military role as watchdog of imperialist interests in the region. On the other hand, Washington derived political benefits in Arab countries' eyes by showing that it had a grip on the watchdog's leash. These two considerations combined to lead Washington to replace Paris as designated purveyor of weapons to the Zionist state. Israel's military dependence on the United States that was thus created came on top of its already existing economic dependence, given the amount of public and private aid to Israel coming from the United States.

The rise of U.S. military credits to Israel speaks volumes on this subject. Nonexistent from the creation of the Israeli state in 1948 until 1958, they were quite low in 1959 ($400,000) and 1960 ($500,000), then reached $13.2 million in 1962, $13.3 million in 1963, and $12.9 million in 1965, before leaping up to $90 million in 1966, the year before Israel launched its attack on Egypt, Syria, and Jordan.[19] Cheryl Rubenberg has described this development well:

> When Kennedy assumed office in 1961, he initially took the position that peace in the Middle East was dependent on a balance of military power between Israel and the Arabs; however, he shortly began to perceive certain advantages in the idea of an Israeli Sparta acting as a U.S. surrogate. Kennedy thus initiated the concept of a "special relationship" with Israel and began the policy of providing the Jewish state with sophisticated American weapons. France had been supplying Israel with arms since the early 1950s under the terms of a secret Franco-Israeli arms arrangement (in violation of the Tripartite agreement, but with American support and encouragement). However, after Charles de Gaulle's ascension to power in 1958, the French reoriented their policy toward the Middle East and by the early 1960s the supply of French arms to Israel began to diminish. This decline, combined with the Soviet Union's provision to Egypt of MIG-21s and TU-16s (in the aftermath of Israel's 1956 invasion) and in the context of the emerging perception regarding Israel's potential usefulness to the United States, induced Kennedy to respond favorably to Israel's insistent demand for American arms. In September 1962 Washington agreed to sell Israel short-range Hawk missiles. That sale was followed by tanks in 1964 (under the Johnson administration) and Skyhawk planes in 1966. These sales marked the beginning of Washington's commitment to assure the absolute regional military superiority of Israel, which has continued to be a cornerstone of U.S.-Israeli relations and of American policy in the Middle East.[20]

The different composition of the Republican and Democratic electorates—in other words, the Jewish vote—is not the factor that explains the "special relationship" between the United States and Israel. Although

this relationship grew up in the early 1960s under a Democratic administration, it was perpetuated and even became much tighter under the
Republican administrations of Nixon (Kissinger), Reagan, and George W.
Bush. This shows that the reasons for the relationship are the ones given
here. The U.S. turn toward using Israel as an auxiliary force in the Middle
East would prove itself an excellent investment when it culminated in
1967. The United States has maintained it at a very high level ever since.

The quantitative and qualitative increase of U.S. military supplies to the
Zionist state in 1966 (adding planes to the package) is highly significant. The
United States wanted its Israeli ally to inflict a decisive military defeat on the
Egyptian and Syrian regimes, both of which it considered major threats to
U.S. interests in the region. Rubenberg has summed up the reasons well:

> The argument for "unleashing" the Israelis included the likelihood that it would
> serve to discredit Nasser and possibly bring about his downfall; it would end
> Egyptian participation in the civil war in Yemen, facilitating a Royalist victory; it
> would embarrass the Soviets by crushing the armies of states that they had been
> heavily arming; it would weaken and destabilize the Ba'ath regime in Syria; it
> would provide the United States with information about Soviet weapons sys-
> tems; and it would leave Israel in such a powerful position that it could act as an
> instrument for the extension of American dominance in the region.[21]

## THE JUNE 1967 WAR

The Israeli aggression of June 5, 1967, was the first war that Israel waged in
collusion with the United States. It revealed both the new complicity that
had been established between the two countries and the ongoing differences
between their respective goals. While their immediate interests converged,
their plans partially diverged. Strong in its awareness of Washington's guarantee and backing, the Zionist state struck a decisive blow to Egypt and
Syria, the two bastions of radicalized Arab nationalism. At the same time
Israel pursued a goal that was strictly its own: completing its conquest of the
whole of Palestine west of the river Jordan and occupying the West Bank, in
a war against the Jordanian kingdom that had no place at all in Washington's plans. The Six-Day War thus concealed two wars in one: one war in the
interests of the United States as well as Israel's interest against Arab nationalism, their common enemy; and another war exclusively in Israel's interest
against Jordan, in order to fulfill the Zionist project.

The June 1967 offensive was victorious far beyond Israeli and U.S. expectations. It confirmed in Washington's eyes the soundness of its new strategic orientation in the Middle East, and at the same time ensured its resolute, generous support to its new surrogate. U.S. public aid to Israel— by far the largest amount of aid that Washington gives to any other country—gives Washington a high return on its investment. The military value of the Israeli surrogate force is much greater than what the same expenditure could produce if it were added each year to the U.S. military budget. In other words, the "marginal utility" of this amount if added to U.S. direct military spending would be incomparably less than the utility of its investment in supporting the state of Israel's activities as a U.S. strategic ally. All the more so since the military yield of each dollar invested in the Israeli army is several times greater than the same dollar invested in the U.S. army, if one compares the relative efficiency of the two armies' budgets.

Nevertheless, despite the crushing Israeli victory in June 1967, its effects in speeding up popular radicalization in the region delayed any political benefit that might have been reaped. Nasser, the main target of the aggression, did submit his resignation on June 9, but a genuine outpouring of popular support in the streets of Cairo made him withdraw it. A strong wind of radicalization picked up in all the Arab countries, affecting young people in particular and flowing into the worldwide wave of radicalization that culminated in 1968. The most visible sign of this radicalization in the Middle East was the rapid growth of armed struggle organizations among Palestinian refugees, first of all in Trans-Jordan,[22] and their success in taking over the PLO, which had originally been subordinated to the Arab governments.[23]

The Syrian regime was able to stay in power, even increasing the radicalism of its rhetoric. Meanwhile there was yet another nationalist, republican coup d'état in the region in September 1969, in Libya. The junta led by Qaddafi obliged the United States to evacuate its Wheelus Air Force Base the following year. The success of the Israeli strike thus had the paradoxical result of still further decreasing U.S. direct military presence in the region, which by the same token raised the strategic importance of the Zionist state even more in Washington's eyes. In addition the Marxists of the South Yemen National Liberation Front took power in Aden in 1970, inaugurating the most radical revolutionary experience in Arab history to date, though with an impact limited by the country's extreme poverty.

Overall Israel's 1967 victory had contradictory short-term results. Nasser withdrew his troops from North Yemen shortly after his defeat in the

Sinai, foreshadowing the overthrow of his Yemeni emulator in November. In July 1968 a coup d'état by the right wing of Ba'athism overthrew the Nasserite-leaning government in Baghdad. It installed a climate of counter-revolutionary terror while crushing the Iraqi version of Middle Eastern radicalization—the most politically advanced version, originating as it did from the country's major communist tradition.

The year 1970 in any case saw Arab nationalism finished off politically, so that the 1967 attack attained its political objectives with a three-year lag. This required crushing the other most advanced, most spectacular spearhead of the radicalization of the popular movement, which had temporarily counter-balanced the military victory of the U.S.-Israeli alliance. In September 1970 ("Black September") the Jordanian army drowned in blood the alternative, quasi-state power that the bloc of Palestinian armed organizations had built. On September 28 Nasser died, succeeded by Anwar al-Sadat. The very next month Hafez al-Assad ventured a trial of strength against the radical team in power in Syria, and succeeded in ousting it for good in November.

Thus 1970 was the year of the final rout of radical Arab nationalism. Sadat would distinguish himself as the gravedigger of Nasser's legacy in the name of *infitah* ("opening," mainly in the sense of economic liberalization). The policy's name amounted symbolically to a way of accommodating U.S. demands for an "Open Door." Assad did not delay in following Sadat's example in the name of the same *infitah*, though very cautiously. The last avatar of Arab military nationalism, the "Libyan revolution," proved to be the farce that marked the all too real end of this tragic historical phenomenon. Similarly, the "federation" between Egypt, Syria, and Libya proclaimed in 1971 as well as the repeatedly announced union between Egypt and Libya beginning in 1972 were caricatures of the 1958 United Arab Republic and its aftermath.

Other than these grotesque remnants, nothing remained of radical Arab nationalism but a demagogic, sinister imitation, which the Iraqi Ba'athist regime incarnated in its foreign policy. Baghdad seized the opportunity provided by the defection of the traditional Egyptian and Syrian bastions of nationalism in order to spread itself in more-nationalist-than-thou rhetoric. Given its hypocrisy, Iraqi Ba'athist swaggering did not carry much conviction. It was a thousand leagues removed from the popularity that Nasser enjoyed from 1956 to 1967, or even until his death.

In 1971 Sadat gave his backing to Ga'afar an-Numeiry's military dictatorship as it crushed the Communists in Sudan, thus decimating the Arab world's last big, independent Communist Party. In 1972 the same Sadat expelled his Soviet military advisers and seized the premises that they had on Egyptian soil. Thus the most populous Arab country and the one that had until then played the most important role in regional politics, left the Soviet orbit. Sadat's switch compensated the U.S. for its losses elsewhere in the region, as well as—in advance—for its withdrawal from Indochina the following year.

True, Baghdad wanted to occupy the space that Sadat vacated in this way as well, by improving its ties with Moscow. But the Iraqi regime always remained independent from the USSR politically. Iraq's role as a Soviet client state remained essentially commercial, as did, by the way, Moscow's relations with Libya. Since both countries were oil exporters, they were both independent and solvent. Their relations with the Soviet Union were thus very different than Egypt's and Syria's, two countries that cost the USSR a great deal in aid—until 1972 in Egypt's case, until the Soviet collapse in Syria's.

## THE OCTOBER 1973 WAR

The October 1973 war, though launched against the United States' strategic partner, suited the U.S. well. By giving Sadat a nationalist exploit that he could boast of—having dared to take the initiative of an offensive against Israeli occupation troops—the war made him a much more useful ally for the United States than a discredited Egypt would have been. It also created the political conditions that would at last allow Washington to play the role of "honest broker" between the Arabs and Israelis, moving ahead toward a Pax Americana in the Middle East. By the next year, against the backdrop of the accelerating infitah, Nixon made a triumphal visit to Cairo.

The October 1973 war also provided the occasion for an Arab oil embargo that led to a spectacular hike in oil prices, which the deterioration of world terms of trade to the advantage of the industrialized countries had held down for too long. This spurt in oil prices—and thus in oil revenues—benefited the United States in more ways than one. It increased the income of its own oil companies as well as the petrodollar holdings of its protégés on the Arabian peninsula, from which it was able to draw great advantages. At the same time it diminished the competitiveness of the rival German and Japanese economies, which are much more dependent than the United States on oil imports; and it considerably strengthened the position of the Saudi kingdom, Washington's main client and ally in the Middle East.[24]

The real military outcome of the 1973 war—a remarkable military recovery by Israel, thanks to an airlift of U.S. military supplies, after it had teetered on the brink of catastrophe—also confirmed that the Zionist state was invincible as long as it had active support from Washington. Israel's dependence on the United States for its security increased greatly thanks to this "Yom Kippur War," while it demonstrated its formidable military efficiency to its Arab neighbors once more. Washington gained on both counts.

In addition, the jump in oil revenues enabled the shah of Iran to acquire sophisticated weaponry, supplying the U.S. military-industrial complex with big profits. He thus affirmed his role as Washington's Middle Eastern surrogate on the eastern flank of the Arabian Peninsula, complementing the other regional surrogates: Israel on the western flank—soon to be joined by Egypt—and Turkey on the northern flank. The "Nixon Doctrine" enunciated in 1969 thus pointed to a plethora of actors in the Middle East. A response to the U.S. quagmire in Vietnam and the general U.S. decline, the doctrine foresaw a greater role for U.S. allies—whether imperialist powers themselves or Washington's regional surrogates—in defending the world imperialist system.

U.S. fortunes in the Middle East thus revived spectacularly in the first half of the 1970s. Its regional recovery formed a stark contrast with the decline in its global imperial hegemony in the course of the same decade: the dollar crisis, withdrawal from Vietnam, an ideological and moral crisis with the Watergate scandal as its backdrop, the final Communist victory in Indochina, Soviet advances in Africa, etc. The Middle East became the privileged area for Washington's global counteroffensive; the other priority area was Latin America, where Pinochet struck a blow for the U.S. counteroffensive with his bloody 1973 coup in Chile.

The only major U.S. setback in the Middle East in 1970–75 resulted from the rise of Third World economic nationalism, a corollary to the decline of U.S. hegemony. Washington and its oil companies could not stop regional producers from nationalizing oil production. Saudi Oil Minister Ahmad Zaki Yamani floated the idea of "participation" as an alternative to nationalization, with the national share rising from 20 percent to 51 percent over the course of ten years, but to no avail.[25] In these difficult straits the oil companies fell back on pushing for the highest possible compensation from the most docile governments and for guarantees for their role downstream in refining and distribution.

Washington's political priority in the Middle East during the 1970s was demonstrating its capacity to establish a regional Pax Americana. In other words, it wanted to show that it could extract enough concessions from Israel so that the countries ready to accept U.S. tutelage could escape from the ongoing state of war, which was eating up their resources, without losing face. The strategy that Henry Kissinger thought up consisted of working toward a series of separate settlements, beginning with an Egyptian-Israeli settlement. He hoped in this way to prevent Arab governments from outbidding each other in nationalist fervor in joint negotiations, as he had experienced in Geneva in the aftermath of the October 1973 war. The procedure had the added advantage of keeping Moscow out of the operation.

Washington quickly reached the conclusion that in order to achieve its objective it needed to crush the PLO, the main obstacle to a U.S.-sponsored settlement to the Arab-Israeli conflict. The PLO had fallen back on Lebanon, where it had established a new alternative quasi-state power to make up for the one it had lost in Jordan. Washington's Lebanese Christian allies attempted to provoke a situation in 1975 in which the Lebanese army would intervene Jordanian-style to checkmate the Palestinians. The attempt failed, leading to a fifteen-year civil war. In the war's first phase the Lebanese army fell apart, and the U.S. allies were defeated in 1976. The Syrian army then came to their rescue, with a green light from Washington and Israel.

In 1977 the Likud succeeded in winning the Israeli elections for the first time in the history of the Zionist state. The situation seemed to be a stalemate, until Sadat took the spectacular initiative of traveling to Israel, breaking the Arab boycott that had been in effect since Israel's creation. Sadat's initiative showed his readiness to gamble everything on loyalty to Washington and alliance with Israel. It led first to the 1978 Camp David accords and then to the 1979 Israeli-Egyptian peace treaty.

The United States could be seen as at the pinnacle of its influence in the Middle East. This was far from the truth. Its allies' defeat in Lebanon and the fact that they had to resort to help from Damascus meant that the other actors that were still independent of Washington and necessary for an Arab-Israeli settlement—the Palestinians and Syrians, the former bottled up by the latter in Lebanon—were still in a strong position. Admittedly, Sadat had gone the last mile in supporting a Pax Americana. But his fellow Arab leaders denounced him as a traitor for having chosen to play the Lone Ranger. He became a pariah in the Arab world, forfeiting the prestige he had won in 1973.

## ISLAMIC REVOLUTION IN IRAN

In February 1979, the month before the Israeli-Egyptian peace treaty was signed, the United States suffered the most serious setback in the history of its presence in the Middle East: Ayatollah Khomeini's arrival in power in Iran. Just as the Communist threat seemed to have gone forever and nationalism seemed to have reached the end of its rope in the Middle East, an ideological current that Washington had grown accustomed to seeing as its instrument of choice in its anti-Communist crusade—Islamic fundamentalism—burst on the scene with impressive power and dynamism. It proved so protean that it could mutate into the chief enemy of the United States throughout the Islamic world

What the strategists in Washington had failed to grasp was that the Communists' destruction and nationalists' historic failure meant nothing more than the elimination of two particular channels through which people expressed their anti-imperialist resentment but did not mean in any way—far from it—that the resentment itself had been eliminated. The resentment flowed (back) quickly into the old-new channel of fundamentalism, which Washington and its Saudi allies had been using against the two other channels for more than three decades. Islamic fundamentalism could mutate because it could easily oppose the West with as much vehemence and fanaticism as it had opposed communists and progressive nationalists. The Janus face of contemporary Islamic fundamentalism had been inscribed on its birth certificate: the Muslim Brothers movement had been born in Egypt, a half-century before the Iran Islamic revolution, from a double hostility to British domination and its Egyptian myrmidons on one side and the Left on the other.[26]

The overthrow of the shah of Iran was a serious strategic loss for the United States. Not only did it lose a regional surrogate, it also lost one of its best economic clients. The nature of the monarchy's successors—a "mullahrchy" determined to make the U.S. "Great Satan" pay for having backed the shah, and presenting itself as Washington's sworn enemy throughout the Muslim world—further aggravated the loss. The long (444 days!) captivity of the U.S. embassy staff, held hostage in Teheran beginning in November 1979, bore witness both to the great intensity of anti-Americanism among Khomeini's followers and to the general U.S. decline. The United States proved powerless in face of this huge provocation, particularly after experiencing a humiliating fiasco during its abortive attempt to rescue the hostages.

A whole series of regional setbacks further amplified the feeling of powerlessness that the Iranian revolution evoked in the United States. Gary
Sick, a member of the National Security Council and adviser to President
Carter on Iranian affairs, summed up well the reaction at the moment of
the shah's overthrow:

> This blow was compounded in February 1979 by reports of an incipient invasion
> of North Yemen by its avowedly Marxist neighbor to the south. This event, com-
> ing in the wake of the Marxist coup in Afghanistan in April 1978, the conclusion of
> the Ethiopian-Soviet treaty in November 1978, the fall of the shah, and the assas-
> sination of U.S. Ambassador Adolph Dubs in Kabul in February 1979, created the
> impression that the United States had lost any capacity to influence regional
> events. That impression was strengthened when Turkey and Pakistan followed
> Iran in withdrawing from the Central Treaty Organization in March.[27]

Washington's only consolation was knowing that the rise of Iranian-style
Islamic fundamentalism alarmed Moscow every bit as much if not more,
given the size of the Muslim population shut up in the Soviet "prison of peoples" that had been inherited from czarist Russia. Seized with panic in reaction to Khomeini's revolution, the rulers in the Kremlin made the fatal error
of invading Afghanistan. The Soviet version of the domino theory which
inspired them struck the fear that Islamic fundamentalism might win a second victory along the USSR's borders and that the bacillus would spread
even further. Washington reaped great benefit from Moscow's mistake.

At the beginning of the 1980s Washington faced a dual threat to its
positions in the Middle East: the danger that Khomeini would export his
revolution and the Soviet army's first military thrust into the Middle East
since its 1946 withdrawal from Iran. The United States entered the decade
at the nadir of its imperial decline. It was incapable of intervening directly
in Iran because of the "Vietnam syndrome"; had been incapable of dissuading Moscow from invading Afghanistan; and had no regional surrogate
capable of reacting in either case. The United States chose to counter these
two threats by relying on forces that acted in complicity with Washington
without being under its tutelage. These two forces would ultimately turn,
wholly or partially, against Washington.

Against the Soviet troops in Afghanistan, working together with its
Saudi and Pakistani allies, the United States chose to support Afghan
Islamic resistance forces, supplemented by a loose assortment of Islamic

fundamentalists from the four corners of the Muslim world, financially and militarily. By now we know the tragic sequel to this story all too well. Washington's fatal mistake was to believe, or convince itself, that violent hostility to the United States among Islamic fundamentalists was a peculiarity of Shiite Islam, and that Sunni and particularly Wahhabi variants of Islamic fundamentalism were inherently inclined to ally with the West.

Against Iran, the United States counted on Saddam Hussein's Iraq. Contrary to a simplistic though widespread perception when the Iran-Iraq war began, Washington never wanted Baghdad to win. It could not forget that the Ba'athist regime had repeatedly outdone its Arab rivals in the virulence of its anti-American and anti-Israeli stance. Baghdad had distinguished itself quite recently by its eagerness to take the lead of the Arab opposition to Sadat after Sadat's defection. Washington knew for a fact that the Iraqi regime, whose regional ambitions were dictated by Saddam Hussein's megalomania, would never tie itself to U.S. apron strings. How could it, when up until the end its preferred partners and arms suppliers were the USSR in first place and France in second place?

U.S. policy toward the war between Iraq and Iran consisted, in the purest Machiavellian tradition, in prolonging the war as long as possible and making sure that neither of the two belligerents decisively defeated the other. On occasion, if need be, the United States came to the assistance of the side that was losing, so as to right the balance on the battlefield. The United States stuck to this policy through the first five years of the war, all the more serenely inasmuch as oil markets accommodated to it perfectly. Moreover, the fall in Iraqi and Iranian oil exports increased the role of the Saudi kingdom in OPEC.

But when the war got out of hand and threatened sea traffic in the Arab-Persian Gulf beginning in 1986, the United States decided it was better to end it. Iran was winning, so the big powers gave Baghdad a green light—de facto if not explicitly—to use chemical weapons in order to push Iranian troops out of Iraqi territory. These war crimes enabled Baghdad to recuperate its territory and persuaded Iran in July 1988 to accept the cease-fire that it had previously rejected. The cease-fire took effect the following month.

Two wars ended at the same time: the Iran-Iraq war and the Soviet army's war in Afghanistan.[28] Washington could be content with the result: its three adversaries had been bled white by the conflicts. First of all, the Soviet Union's Afghan adventure accelerated its final crisis and decomposition. This outcome surpassed all the United States' hopes. However tragic the consequences were of al-Qaeda's later turn against its U.S. sponsor, the immediate result—the implosion of the USSR and the fall of Communism—undeniably justified the policy the United States had followed, in the minds of U.S. policy makers (all the more because Bin Laden's defection could have been avoided).

## THE 1991 GULF WAR

What of the other two adversaries, Iran and Iraq? The problem was that while Iraq had been bled white economically, it came out of the war with a disproportionately large army, battle-hardened by eight years of merciless warfare. Saddam Hussein had to choose between drastically cutting military spending to save the economy and rushing into a new war. His neighbors and funders' stingy, greedy behavior, beginning with Kuwait, inspired him to revive Iraq's historical claim to the emirate, which the British had created at Iraq's expense. On August 2, 1990, Saddam Hussein's troops invaded Kuwait. This is exactly what Washington wanted.

The United States was looking for a pretext to kill two birds with one stone. On the one hand, it wanted to radically cut back Iraqi strength, which it considered too threatening to the nearby oil-producing monarchies. (The security of the oil states, the Saudi kingdom's in particular, not Israel's, was the main motive for U.S. intervention.) On the other hand, it was looking for an opportunity to reestablish the direct military presence of U.S. armed forces in the Arabian peninsula, over a quarter-century after their withdrawal. Saddam Hussein handed it the pretext on a silver platter.

The "Gulf war" allowed Washington to destroy two-thirds of Iraq's military potential. It also enabled the U.S. military to reinstall itself in the Saudi kingdom and then to install itself in Kuwait and other Gulf emirates after the operations ended. Meanwhile in the background the Soviet Union was going through its death agony, drastically decreasing its influence in the region before its final implosion. Its influence had sunk so deeply that even the Syrian regime, Moscow's traditional client, joined the coalition against Iraq led by Washington. The Gulf war thus inaugurated the period when U.S. hegemony in the Middle East reached its climax.

This war was above all Washington's chance to make clear that the Cold War had ended in a victory for the United States, left standing alone in the arena as the world cop, rather than in a new era of peace founded on disarmament. By giving a stunning demonstration of its formidable military might, the United States let the rest of the world know that it was "the indispensable nation," as Madeleine Albright later put it. The United States was "indispensable" in defending the world system against new threats to its security and its oil supplies that would be arising soon enough, as the Iraqi case illustrated.

By restoring a U.S. presence in the Arabian Peninsula, the Gulf war also simultaneously restored its strategic primacy as guardian of the sources of oil, which its European and Japanese partners are more dependent on than it is. The billions of dollars paid to finance the war effort in the Gulf, not only by the oil monarchies themselves but by Germany and Japan as well, consecrated the United States as it were in its role of lord protector. At the same time Washington guaranteed that it would keep and increase its lion's share in the worldwide exploitation of oil and petrodollars.

The U.S. war in the Gulf was the first demonstration of U.S. "hyperpower," but at the same time emphasized the limits of this "hyperpower," which is far from omnipotence. The chief limit to U.S. power derives from the relationship between the government in Washington and the people of the United States, either mediated by elected officials or expressed directly in the streets. This relationship is crucial, inasmuch as the United States is—luckily—a capitalist democracy, not a dictatorship. George H. W. Bush had considerable difficulty in getting a green light from Congress in 1990 for his war to "liberate Kuwait." He could not afford in any way to exceed his mandate and occupy Iraq.

Unable to take control of the Iraqi government by installing U.S. armed forces in Baghdad, therefore, Washington preferred not to take the risk of overthrowing the Ba'athist regime, which would have led to a chaotic situation and threatened the stability of the whole region. The risk was particularly great in March 1991 since Iraq was going through a popular uprising. The fall of the regime in these circumstances would have inevitably led to a revolutionary situation, which the United States and its Middle Eastern allies feared much more than the ongoing rule of a much weakened Saddam Hussein.[29] The United States thus authorized Hussein to bloodily suppress the popular uprising.

## THE 1990S

In the decade following the Gulf war (1991–2000), U.S. strategy in the Middle East revolved around two major axes: "dual containment" of Iraq and Iran and the search for a settlement to the Israeli-Palestinian conflict. "Dual containment" was a strategic choice dictated by two simultaneous considerations. First, both Iraq and Iran had been bled white and were therefore incapable of mounting any serious military threat to their neighbors, especially given the very expensive lesson Washington had inflicted on Baghdad. It sufficed to keep a close watch on both countries—and in Iraq's case to maintain such a tight embargo that it had consequences of genocidal proportions. (The embargo caused 90,000 deaths annually during the almost twelve years of the embargo according to UN agency estimates: more than a million deaths.) The United States also banned U.S. companies from making heavy investments in Iran, particularly in the oil sector.

The second consideration that made "dual containment" feasible was the state of the world oil market. Just as it had made it possible to adapt to eight years of war between Iraq and Iran, it also made it possible to adapt to twelve years of embargo against Iraq, which kept the country's production at about half the level of its prewar output and a third of its production capacity. Production remained this low even after the limitation that had been imposed was lifted, because the embargo stopped oil infrastructure from being repaired and above all stopped it from being modernized. Oil prices had peaked at the beginning of the Iran-Iraq war, then gone down again. From that point on a structural surplus of supply over demand characterized the oil market. Sharpened competition among exports kept prices down, even lower than they had been at the start of the big oil boom after the October 1973 war and Arab oil boycott.

On the Israeli-Arab front, Washington noted that the "peace process" launched by the Israeli-Egyptian accords had come to a standstill in the early 1980s. It responded by "unleashing" its Israeli regional surrogate to attack the PLO, which it saw as the main obstacle to a Pax Americana. At this point the Vietnamese trauma was still keeping the United States severely paralyzed, so that it was at the nadir of its imperial power.

Israel's 1982 invasion of Lebanon succeeded in striking a decisive blow against the PLO, forcing it to evacuate most of its troops and command centers from the country. This fifth Israeli-Arab war even provided the opportunity for the first return of U.S. troops to the Middle East since the marines' landing in Lebanon in 1958 and the evacuation of the U.S. bases in Dhahran (1962) and Wheelus (1970). That was in the framework of a "multilateral interposition force" made up in reality of NATO troops.

But the U.S. intervention ended in a double disaster. First, the suicide bombings directed against the United States forced it to withdraw its troops precipitously from Lebanon, adding a "Beirut syndrome" on top of its "Vietnam syndrome." Second, for the first time the Israeli army had to retreat unconditionally from an occupied territory, a territory conquered in its most unpopular war ever—including inside Israel itself. The Israeli retreat took place in two phases. First in 1985 Israel retreated to a fairly narrow "security zone" in southern Lebanon; then in 2000—under pressure from the armed attacks of the Lebanese resistance led by Hezbollah—from virtually the whole country, abandoning the occupation army's local auxiliaries.[30]

The U.S. retreat, followed by successive Israeli retreats, considerably increased the prestige of the Islamic fundamentalist current as a whole. It was a great inspiration to Palestinian fundamentalists, inciting them to take up this form of violent action in their struggle against Israeli occupation and settlement of their land. Violent action became all the more popular after the Palestinian popular struggle reached the high point of the intifada in 1988 only to be scuttled by a combination of Israeli repression and co-optation by the PLO bureaucracy.[31]

The intifada had nonetheless put the Palestinian struggle back in the center of the Arab political scene, to the point that the Reagan administration had officially opened negotiations with the PLO in 1988, though without reaching an agreement. After the spectacular comeback of U.S. hegemony in the Middle East thanks to the Gulf war, Washington found itself compelled to turn its attention to the Israeli-Palestinian issue once more. It felt it had to jump-start the stalled advance toward a Pax Americana, which had become more necessary to it than ever, at a moment when U.S. hegemony was at its height and it absolutely had to consolidate it by stabilizing the situation.

A few months after the official end of the Iraq war, George H.W. Bush opened an Israeli-Arab peace conference in Madrid: the first one since the 1974 Geneva conference to include all of the countries involved. Washington had to twist Likud Prime Minister Yitzhak Shamir's arm to achieve this, since Shamir was unenthusiastic at the idea of taking part in a conference meant to reach a regional settlement. He knew in advance that he would have to reject the minimal requirements for any such settlement, since he favored the de facto if not de jure annexation of the Palestinian and Syrian territories occupied in 1967. The Bush administration got the Israeli prime minister to Madrid by threatening to withhold the promised U.S. guarantee for a $10 billion loan. The Shamir government needed this money badly to finance absorbing Russian-Jewish immigrants to Israel—who were crucial for both Likud's expansionist plans and consolidating its electoral preeminence.

By contrast with previous years, this episode of U.S.-Israel tension showed that the strategic value of the Zionist state had decreased in Washington's eyes. In fact, just as a weaker U.S. position in the Middle East had increased the strategic importance of its alliance with Israel in the early 1960s, the massive direct presence of U.S. armed forces in the region since 1990 tends to make Israel much less essential for defending U.S. interests. It therefore tends to increase U.S. demands on its Zionist ally.

Even the Israeli Labor Party's return to power in 1992 did not prevent the Madrid conference from bogging down. Betting all his chips on one roll of the dice, just as Sadat had in 1977, PLO leader Arafat agreed to negotiate secretly with the Rabin-Peres government behind the back of the PLO's own executive committee. The talks led to the famous Oslo accords. Their signature, in a ceremony on the White House lawn in September 1993, opened the way to the Israeli-Jordanian peace treaty in 1994. But Oslo was essentially a sucker's deal for Arafat. It revived the Allon Plan for Palestinian enclaves in territories under Israeli military and settler control. In return Arafat was fooled into accepting the mirage of an "independent" state, which was never promised or mentioned in any document. He failed even to get a guaranteed settlement freeze.[32]

The 1993 accords enabled Israel to carry out in seven years as much as it had achieved in applying the Allon Plan in the quarter-century between 1967 and 1993. From 1993 to 2000 Israel doubled the number of settlers and intensified the buildup of its strategic network (roads, etc.) in the territories it had occupied in 1967. Meanwhile the Palestinians, mystified or kept in check by Palestinian Authority apparatuses, kept relatively quiet—until they gradually realized how they had been swindled and tried to react by any available means. Their reaction became more and more exasperated, then desperate, as Israel increased the brutality of its repression and strangled the territories with blockades. Israel was deliberately trying to increase tensions as much as possible, in order to compel the Arafat leadership to carry out its assigned task of repressing its own people.

Finally the moment came for a "definitive settlement" of the Israeli-Palestinian conflict—that is, the Clinton administration and Israeli Barak government decided that the moment had come. They were disappointed at Camp David in July 2000 to see that the Arafat leadership, having pocketed an impressive series of affronts and made a record number of capitulations, was not ready to make its final surrender. It was not prepared to liquidate the Palestinian people's historic rights in broad daylight. As a

quasi-state apparatus in search of territory on which to fulfill its bureaucratic calling, it had been aspiring to an "independent state" for some thirty
years. It refused to settle for mere Bantustans.[33]

### THE YEAR 2000: STRATEGIC TURNING POINT

U.S. Middle Eastern strategy for the decade 1991–2000 had thus run up
against its limits on both of its main fronts. On the Israeli-Palestinian
front, it had become clear that the "peace process" had run aground. Only a
major concession by one of the two sides could set it afloat again, given that
their divergences concerned issues that were fundamental for both. From
Ehud Barak's point of view, which Clinton supported, the Palestinian leadership had to accept the "generous offer" that Barak had made at Camp
David. In the absence of any broad consensus on the Israeli or Palestinian
side, Barak's offer corresponded to a version of a "settlement" that Washington considered satisfactory.

The direct inspiration for Barak's offer was the agreement negotiated in
October 1995, just before Yitzhak Rabin's assassination, by the two men principally responsible for negotiating the Oslo accords: Yossi Beilin, at the time
working under Shimon Peres at the Israeli foreign ministry, and Mahmoud
Abbas, alias Abu Mazen, a member of the Palestinian leadership. Their
agreement foresaw that Israel would keep settlements in the territories occupied in 1967, both in an area that Israel would annex and in the remaining
Palestinian area. The territory of the "Palestinian state" would be cut up into
separate enclaves controlled by the Israeli army, which would maintain strategic positions there. Israel would keep the part of Jerusalem that it had
annexed in 1967, while the Palestinian capital would be in the Jerusalem sub-
urb of Abu Dis. Finally, Palestinian refugees would receive international
compensation and a "right to return" to the "Palestinian state."[34]

At Camp David Arafat had argued, rightly, that he could never make the
base of his own Fatah organization, let alone the Palestinian people as a
whole, accept this kind of "settlement." Both Washington and the Israeli
Labor Party drew the conclusion that the way out of the impasse was to
reduce Palestinian resistance and demands by force. This conclusion
induced Barak to authorize Ariel Sharon to commit his provocation at
Jerusalem's Haram al-Sharif on September 28, 2000, thus provoking a
Palestinian uprising. The violence of the repression with which Israel
responded to this second intifada—at Barak's orders—tended to radicalize

it, in such a way as to create the conditions for its brutal suppression. This was supposed to make the Palestinians give in and accept the Camp David conditions. The Palestinians for their part, poorly led by an autocrat at the end of his tether surrounded by corrupt bureaucrats, fell into the trap of "militarizing" the intifada.

A broad front thus took shape, including Washington as well as all the major Israeli political currents, that agreed on the goal of drowning the Palestinian rebellion in blood. With this as the task, no one was better suited to carry it out than Sharon, a general with an impressive record as a war criminal. Something that had seemed unthinkable only a few years earlier happened: one of Israel's most extremist politicians, a man whose fanaticism had managed to exasperate Menachem Begin himself, took over the leadership of Likud and won the Israeli elections in February 2001. Sharon settled down to the task of breaking the Palestinians' spirit of resistance, with the more fundamental goal of provoking them to leave their territories en masse. To this end he worked to make Palestinians' living conditions unbearable for as long as possible. He thus resorted systematically to provocations, in the spirit that had brought him to power, notably by carrying out "extrajudicial executions" of leaders of the Palestinian groups that were most determined to react: the Islamic fundamentalists.

For Sharon the Oslo accords as well as the Beilin-Abu Mazen accords, including the version presented at Camp David, were all unacceptable. His own vision of a settlement swings back and forth between his optimal solution of "transfer" and the maximum that he is prepared to accept. "Transfer" is the Israeli euphemism for expelling the Palestinians from their territories, that is, a new edition of what happened in 1948. This is what Sharon, like his extreme-right coalition partners, fervently desires. But if necessary he would be willing to accept a less "ideal" solution, consisting in reducing the Allon option to three separate, tightly controlled Palestinian enclaves—three Palestinian concentration camps, in short—including a total of only 42 percent of the West Bank land occupied in 1967. This option, which Sharon laid out when his party came to power in 1977, would in fact go together with a massive but less than total "transfer." The so-called security wall, whose construction Sharon began in June 2002 after his predecessors had threatened to do so, fits in very clearly with this sinister perspective.[35]

Yet this same Sharon—who has never hidden his ideas—presided over a coalition government including the Labor Party until November 2002, a coalition responsible for the worst episodes of the brutal war waged on the

Palestinians.[36] This same Sharon benefited from the "benign neglect" of George W. Bush's administration, inaugurated only one month before Sharon's own election. The connivance among the three parties—the Likud under Sharon, the Zionist Labor Party, and the U.S. administration—was a clear expression of their convergence toward a common objective: crushing any spirit of Palestinian resistance. Their divergences were put off to a later date, after the common objective had been reached.

In the Arab-Persian Gulf, the other major front in U.S. Middle East strategy, or rather on a part of this front, another strategic shift occurred in 2001. "Double containment" was replaced with single containment, directed at Iran. Washington hoped—encouraged by the rise of popular protest—that the Iranian regime would crumble the way the Eastern European regimes had. In the case of Iraq containment gave way to military overthrow, designated by the euphemism "regime change."

George W. Bush's team had entered office in January 2001 with the firm intention of overthrowing the regime in Baghdad. Bush had expressed this intention himself during his presidential campaign. Several members and coworkers of his administration agreed with him, to the point of jointly petitioning Bush's predecessor Clinton in January 1998 to this effect. The petition was organized by the Project for the New American Century, a reactionary think tank whose influence on the Bush administration has been widely noted. The fact that eleven out of eighteen signers of the petition that called on Clinton to overthrow the Iraqi regime by military force later found themselves associated with the Bush administration,[37] at the Pentagon in particular, could easily have given the impression of a conspiracy, had their project not been proclaimed so openly.

George W. Bush's administration, like his father's administration that waged the first U.S. war against Iraq, is as tightly linked to the oil industry as any administration in history. At the risk of annoying those who react to any explanation of U.S. foreign policy in terms of economic interests, and oil interests in particular, with cries of "reductionism," the oil lobby has traditionally played a key role in formulating U.S. foreign policy, at the very least since the Second World War.[38]

Some administrations are more sensitive than others to oil company influence, however. The administration of Bush Junior, whose presidential campaign had all the oil and gas industry's chief companies (including, of course, ExxonMobil, BP Amoco, El Paso, Chevron, etc.) among its main donors, is certainly one of the most sensitive. Besides his own personal and family ties to the industry, Bush appointed people with equally close or closer ties to it to key posts in his administration, including Vice President Dick Cheney (Halliburton) and National Security Adviser Condoleezza Rice (Chevron).

As it happens there was a sharp rise in oil prices (and in gas prices at the pump in the U.S.) during the presidential campaign year 2000. Since the imposition of the embargo on Iraq and throughout the years 1991–99, nominal prices of crude oil had stayed under their 1990 level ($22.26 a barrel),[39] which was in turn 35 percent below the 1974 price when adjusted for inflation.[40] The situation turned around in 2000, with a jump in nominal prices from $17.47 a barrel in 1999 to $27.60 a barrel (though even this price was lower in real terms than the 1990 price).[41]

More important, Bush's team shared the U.S. ruling class's general concern about the future of the oil market and the prospect that hydrocarbon sources will gradually dry up.[42] The influential Center for Strategic and International Studies (CSIS) in Washington expressed this concern most clearly in a November 2000 report made public in February 2001 under the title *The Geopolitics of Energy into the 21st Century*. According to this report, world energy demand should increase by over 50 percent during the first two decades of the twenty-first century.

> The Persian Gulf will remain the key marginal supplier of oil to the world market, with Saudi Arabia in the unchallenged lead. Indeed, if estimates of future demand are reasonably correct, the Persian Gulf must expand oil production by almost 80 percent during 2000–2020, achievable perhaps if foreign investment is allowed to participate and if Iran and Iraq are free of sanctions.[43]

The report underscored the "fundamental contradiction" between this need and Washington's policies:

> Oil and gas exports from Iran, Iraq, and Libya—three nations that have had sanctions imposed by the United States or international organizations—are expected to play an increasingly important role in meeting growing global demand, especially to avoid increasing competition for energy with and within Asia [meaning sudden, sharp price hikes]. Where the United States imposes unilateral sanctions (Iran and Libya), investments will take place without U.S. participation [meaning we had better get rid of these sanctions if we don't want to help our competitors]. Iraq, subjected to multilateral sanctions, may be constrained from building in a timely way the infrastructure necessary to meet the upward curve in energy

demand. If global oil demand estimated for 2020 is reasonably correct and is to
be satisfied, these three exporters should by then be producing at their full potential if other supplies have not been developed.[44]

For the Bush administration, as for U.S. capitalism as a whole, the need to put
an end to the embargo imposed on Iraq was becoming urgent. It was time to
make possible reconstruction and modernization of Iraq's oil infrastructure—meaning several years of investments and work. Iraq sits on the second
largest oil reserves in the world after the Saudi kingdom; Washington's goal
was to allow Iraq to double and then triple its production (up to its estimated
capacity) during the first decade of the new century, so as to ward off an oil crisis during the following decade. Underlying this concern was the principle
that a substantial margin of flexibility in Saudi production—a margin of safety between the kingdom's actual production and its production capacity—
must be maintained.[45] This is crucial to the stability of the world oil market
under U.S. supervision, and constitutes "the cornerstone of its oil policy."[46]

### SEPTEMBER 11: BUSH'S WINDFALL

It was thus becoming urgent to create the conditions for lifting the embargo on Iraq. There were essentially two preconditions. First, Saddam Hussein had to be overthrown and replaced by a government under U.S.
control. Without this "regime change" Washington would not contemplate
moving to lift the embargo. Paris and Moscow had been calling for some
time to lift the embargo on the Ba'athist regime, precisely because it was in
their interests and contrary to Washington's.

Baghdad had granted its two privileged partners—which France and
Russia had always been—major oil concessions whose implementation
depended on ending the embargo. Given the magnitude of what was at
stake in Iraq—the huge market for rebuilding the country, devastated as it
was by twenty years of war and embargo, on top of its gigantic oil
resources—it was out of the question for Washington, backed by London
for identical reasons, to hand it all on a silver platter to Paris and Moscow.

The Bush administration's only options—like the Clinton administration's before it—were either maintaining the embargo or securing U.S.
control of Iraq. To make this last, more and more pressing option possible,
another condition had to be fulfilled, however: it had to be politically possible, essentially in terms of U.S. domestic politics, to invade Iraq and keep

the country under direct U.S. occupation and tutelage. In truth, the one and only sure guarantee of keeping Iraq under Uncle Sam's thumb is ruling the country directly from Washington.

The reason is that Iraq is not located in Eastern Europe, but rather in the one part of the world where popular feeling is most hostile to the United States. In the absence of any U.S. ideological hegemony that would ensure Iraq's ongoing guaranteed dependence on the United States, the country had to be placed under some original form of trusteeship. Since Bush Senior had been politically incapable of achieving this, he had preferred to let Saddam Hussein bloodily repress the March 1991 popular rebellion rather than allowing the triumph of an Iraqi revolution that would not have been under Washington's control. Clinton, constrained by the Republican opposition's exploitation of the Lewinsky scandal, was certainly not able to invade and occupy Iraq either when the crisis around the UN inspectors provided him with a suitable pretext in 1998.

In this context, September 11, 2001, came as a terrific windfall for the Bush administration. As with Saddam Hussein in 1990, one could say that if Osama bin Laden had not existed he would have had to be invented—for Washington's benefit. The spectacular blow struck by Islamic fundamentalists, former U.S. allies who had become its sworn enemies, created such a huge political trauma in the United States that the Bush administration thought it was possible at last, for the first time, to break once and for all with the "Vietnam syndrome" and return to the unbridled military interventionism of the first Cold War decades.

We know from investigative reports and interviews that some members of Bush's team wanted to seize the occasion immediately to go after Iraq, although they knew full well—whatever they claimed—that Baghdad had nothing to do with the men who had attacked the World Trade Center and Pentagon. There was a debate inside the administration between proponents of the "Iraq first" option (like Donald Rumsfeld) and the "Afghanistan first, Iraq later" option (like Colin Powell). The principle of invading Iraq eventually had long been a point of consensus. For obvious political reasons, the president chose the second option.

The invasion of Afghanistan was also a chance for the Bush administration to carry out a project it had cherished since the final collapse of the USSR. But establishing a direct U.S. military presence in the heart of ex-Soviet Central Asia had seemed even more improbable than a U.S. occupation of Iraq.[47] A military presence in the heart of the Eurasian continental mass joining Russia to China—two countries tempted to ally with each other in order to resist U.S. hegemonic pressure more effectively, or even to ally with Iran as well—had evident geostrategic value.[48] Besides, a U.S. military presence in Central Asia and the Caspian Basin (in Uzbekistan, Kyrgyzstan, Georgia, and so on) fit into its global and Middle Eastern strategy of taking control of sources of oil, supplemented in this particular case by natural gas.

In fact, the previously cited CSIS report, while noting that Caspian oil would be "important at the margin but not pivotal," indicated that foreseeable increased demand for natural gas would raise the strategic value of this energy resource in years to come.[49] The region made up of Eastern Europe and the whole of the former Soviet Union holds only a bit more than 6 percent of the world's proved oil reserves, even if estimated reserves are sometimes believed to be much greater. By contrast, the region holds more than 30 percent of the world's proved natural gas reserves.[50]

The central objective of the Afghanistan war, besides destroying the al-Qaeda network, was in fact U.S. strategic implantation in Central Asia and on the shores of the Caspian Sea. This explains the low level of interest in Washington in controlling the Afghan interior or in building the promised "modern" state, to be led by its loyal vassal Hamid Karzai. The United States knows quite well in any event that the stakes are too small in Afghanistan to justify the enormous financial and military investment that would be needed to try to control this country in reality—without any guarantee of success. Afghanistan's reputation as indomitable destines it to be the prey of the warlords Washington relied on to "liberate" it.[51] The war against the Taliban–al-Qaeda alliance actually provided the opportunity, along with Vladimir Putin's miscalculations and illusions, that allowed the U.S. government to softly accomplish this ultimate extension of its imperial military network behind the back of U.S. public opinion.

Once the Afghan operation had been more or less completed, the Bush administration turned to the main course: Iraq. In this case, given how much is at stake, Washington has definitely decided to make a huge effort in order to rebuild an Iraqi state that would be its loyal vassal and capable of ensuring neocolonial order under U.S. supervision and the protection of U.S. troops. This perspective was even the sine qua non for invading the country and overthrowing Saddam Hussein, as we have already explained. The Bush administration's curt attitude toward Paris in particular expressed its determination to exclude France from any share in the booty. Washington knew that France had some major trump cards in its rivalry with the United States: its long experience with the Iraqi market and its standing among Arab peoples, which contrasts sharply with the general hostility to the U.S.-British tandem.

### THE "QUAGMIRE"

The Bush administration, and above all Rumsfeld's team at the Pentagon, committed the monumental error, however, of underestimating the great difficulty of the task and overestimating the means that they really had at their disposal. These difficulties were entirely predictable, and many people—including the present author—had predicted them.[52] Resentment of the U.S.-British occupation of Iraq, which the great mass of the country's Arab population is expressing in an increasingly visible and lethal way, is impelling Washington to speed up its search for solutions that can slow down the situation's slide into a "quagmire." This quagmire would resemble the Israeli army's quagmire in Lebanon more closely than Uncle Sam's old quagmire in Vietnam, incidentally. Washington is obviously improvising, in a way that the Bush administration's political adversaries are criticizing harshly. The result is already a decline in the artificial, inflated popularity that Bush had enjoyed since September 11, 2001.

The United States may have the world's most formidable army and be able to dispose of any other army. But the Bush-Rumsfeld team is discovering to its cost that its "smart" or even "brilliant" bombs, its robots and other remote-controlled or electronically programmed drones are useless when it comes to controlling masses of people. The problem is not that the United States is short of settlers or "imperialists," meaning candidates among the population of the occupying power who are prepared to live in the conquered country and administer it, as in the glory days of the Raj. Niall Ferguson, the author of a bestseller on the defunct British empire who made this argument in the *New York Times Magazine*, was reasoning by analogy.[53] However, he failed to see the big difference between the British imperial epoch and our own time—a difference that explains, by the way, the other difference he mentioned about would-be colonial settlers.

When the population of an occupied country today is hostile to an occupying force and sees it as such, it is incomparably more dangerous for the occupiers than in the nineteenth or even the first half of the twentieth century. A century ago the great bulk of colonized peoples was often resigned to their subjugation. Since then people have taken note of the national liberation struggles that characterized the era of decolonization. In addition, levels of education and therefore of national consciousness are now at a qualitatively higher level.

Israel was able to occupy the West Bank and Gaza without too much difficulty during the two decades after 1967—before the outbreak of the first intifada turned the occupation into a nightmare for the Zionist army— because its occupation of the 1967 territories was and remains a genuine military occupation. Zionist colonialism is a form of settler-colonialism intended to evict the autochthonous population. The settlers are isolated from the Palestinians for security reasons and have little in common with the colonial administrators of former times. Only the quantitative strength of Israeli occupation troops relative to the population of the occupied territories, made possible by the size of the territories and the fact that the occupiers' territory adjoins them, has enabled Israel to keep the situation under control for so long.

These conditions are virtually the opposite of the conditions that the occupying powers confront in Iraq, where they face a substantial population of almost 20 million people (counting only Arabs). The U.S. problem is that it does not have enough soldiers to control Iraq and at the same time maintain its imperial role in relation to the rest of the world. This is why Rumsfeld now plans to ask Congress to authorize a considerable increase in the total numbers of the U.S. armed forces, whose personnel has been much reduced since the end of the Cold War and the technological "revolution in military affairs."[54] In light of the Iraqi people's hostility and nationalist touchiness, the essential form of U.S. presence in Iraq can only be military. U.S. civilians in Iraq are seen as the political and economic arm of an armed occupation, and therefore require military protection.

Washington is trying to extricate itself from the quagmire that its troops are sinking into by exploring the possibility of using forces from other countries, Muslim countries in particular. But the problem will not be solved as long as the troops, wherever they are from, act as auxiliaries of U.S. troops. Washington's dilemma is that changing the Iraqi population's perception of the occupying forces would require no longer using them to oversee the culling of Iraqi resources by the U.S. and its British allies. But that is exactly why Washington set out to occupy the country in the first place!

The myth that Washington wants to endow Iraq with a democratic government that would be a model for the whole region, the myth that the United States is replaying in Iraq the tape of Germany and Japan's post-1945 democratization, will not stand up for long to the test of events. In the two big countries defeated in the Second World War, sizable capitalist classes with ideological hegemony over their societies were ready to collaborate with the U.S. occupier and rebuild their countries under its tutelage and with its aid—all the more willingly because they lived in terror of the "communist" threat. While allied with the United States, they were still capable of governing on the basis of genuine electoral majorities.

Nothing comparable exists in Iraq today. The effects of the Iraqi bourgeoisie's long confinement in the iron collar of an omnipotent, semi-fascist state apparatus further aggravate the structural weakness characteristic of Third World bourgeoisies in general. There are no reliable U.S. allies in Iraq with any real credibility among, not to speak of ideological hegemony over, the great Arab majority of the population. Iraq, like other Middle Eastern countries, thus only confirms what Samuel Huntington called "the democracy paradox: adoption by non-Western societies of Western democratic institutions encourages and gives access to power to nativist and anti-Western political movements."[55]

This is a "paradox" in any event only in the eyes of those who believe that democracy goes hand in hand with submission to the West. Anti-U.S. resentment among Muslim peoples, which is even more deeply felt than among other peoples of the Third World, is the result of a long history of oppression. The fact that Western domination is identified with the hated despotic regimes that it depends on, and with the state of Israel, has kept this resentment alive up to the present day.[56] So it is entirely natural that if the majority of the people could express itself freely and truthfully at the ballot box in Muslim countries, it would elect governments hostile to Western domination.

Iraq is no exception to this rule, quite the contrary. Consequently there are only two possibilities. Either Washington will keep the country under its rule by brute force, exercised directly or through the mediation of puppets despised by the people and "legitimized" by a travesty of democracy, on the model of what it is doing in Afghanistan; or the Iraqis will democratically choose their own government and elect leaders hostile to continuing U.S.-British control of their country's resources. The "democratic" ideological delirium of a few "neoconservatives" in the United States will not count for much next to the economic interests that are at stake in Iraq—even if these "neo-cons" really do naively believe in their own ideological discourse, which is very far from certain.

Events on the Israeli-Palestinian front since the official end of the war in Iraq strikingly confirm the rule laid out above. In the Palestinian case,

Washington is not directing its "democratic" reproaches at a bloody tyrant but at Yassir Arafat, the only man in the Arab world with a status comparable to that of a head of state who has been elected through a process that was relatively democratic and enjoys the real support of a majority of his own people. The United States' "democratic reform" has consisted in imposing on the Palestinians and their elected president a "prime minister" whom the overwhelming majority of Palestinians rejected as a new Quisling. This "prime minister" was—surprise!—Mahmoud Abbas, alias Abu Mazen, the same one who accepted the 1993 Oslo Accords and the 1995 agreement with Yossi Beilin.

The second Bush administration, like the first, needs to stabilize U.S. regional hegemony by clearing all obstacles out of the way to establishing a Pax Americana in the Middle East. It therefore needs, like its predecessor, to move toward a settlement of the Israeli-Palestinian conflict. To this end it has published its "road map" and made clear to everyone in the region that it means to impose it. Strengthened by its new, direct hold on the region from occupied Iraq, the U.S. administration, more even than in 1991, has declared itself ready to put strong pressure on its Israeli ally.

But Sharon is stalling, as Shamir did in 1991. He pretends to yield to Washington's demands by making minor or purely formal concessions while continuing to provoke the Palestinians. He is counting on the fact that 2004 is a presidential election year in the United States, and U.S. administrations are generally not much inclined to put strong pressure on Israel during election years. Furthermore, the more the U.S. occupation of Iraq turns into a quagmire, the more the Bush administration will see dealing with Iraq as its top priority; it will thus be tempted to give up on chasing two Middle Eastern hares at once.

So what remains of the prospects for "democracy" in the Middle East? The term "democracy" has increasingly made way in official U.S. statements for the term "freedom," the term that was used, by the way, to name the invasion of Iraq, Iraqi Freedom. But what kind of "freedom" is this? George W. Bush has not delayed passing on the good news to the peoples of the Middle East: in a speech on May 9, 2003, he proposed to them "the establishment of a U.S.-Middle East free trade area within a decade."[57]

Meanwhile the mission of overseeing the restructuring of the Iraqi oil industry has been assigned to Philip Carroll, former CEO of the U.S. branch of Royal Dutch/Shell. It would be hard to think of a better symbol of the U.S.-British alliance. Carroll's job will consist of carrying out the decisions made at a hush-hush meeting held in London by the U.S. State Department with the designated future heads of the Iraqi oil industry on April 5, just before the fall of Baghdad.[58] Central to the London decisions were the "production sharing agreements" that U.S. and British oil companies mean to impose on Iraq. The agreements will be a model—real, not mythical, this one—for agreements with other Middle Eastern countries. The goal is to go back to the "participation" that the Saudi oil minister proposed thirty years ago as an alternative to nationalizations!

In the beginning was the "open door" to oil. ...

JULY 23, 2003

# PART I

# The Resurgence of Islamic Fundamentalism

## CHAPTER ONE

# Eleven Theses on the Current Resurgence of Islamic Fundamentalism

*These "theses" have been circulated widely and translated into many languages since their first publication in 1981. Their success was due to their Marxist analysis of a phenomenon that was then still relatively new. The current resurgence of Islamic fundamentalism dates from the 1970s, and reached its first crescendo, after years of underground activity, with the Iranian revolution of 1979.*

1

The extent and diversity of the forms taken by the resurgence of Islamic fundamentalism, which has marked the beginning of the last quarter of the twentieth century, preclude any hasty, generalized conjectures about it. It would be totally mistaken to equate the Catholicism of the Polish workers with that of Franco's reaction, though this should not make us overlook the common features of the agrarian histories of Spain and Poland or the political and ideological content that their respective forms of Catholicism share. Similarly, elementary analytical caution forbids putting such diverse phenomena as the resurgence of Muslim clerical and/or political movements in Egypt, Syria, Tunisia, Turkey, Pakistan, Indonesia, or Senegal, Zia Ul-Haq's military dictatorship in Pakistan or Qaddafi's in Libya, the seizure of power by Iranian Shiite clergy or by Afghan guerrillas, etc., all into the same category.[1] Even phenomena that on the surface appear clearly identical, such as the progress made by the same movement, the "Muslim Brotherhood," in Egypt and Syria, have different underlying political content and functions, determined by their different *immediate* objectives.

Beneath their agreement on otherworldly matters, beyond their agreement on problems of everyday life, when they do agree on such issues, and notwithstanding their similar, even identical, denominations and organizational forms, Muslim movements remain essentially political movements. They are thus the expression of specific sociopolitical interests that are very much of this world.

2

There has been no eruption of Islam into politics. Islam and politics have always been inseparable, as Islam is a *political* religion in the etymological sense of the word. Thus, *the demand for the separation of religion and state in Muslim countries is more than secularist: it is openly antireligious.* This helps explain why none of the major currents of bourgeois or petit bourgeois nationalism on Islamic soil, with the exception of Kemalism in Turkey, have called for secularism. What is an elementary democratic task elsewhere—separation of religion and state—is so radical in Muslim countries, especially the Middle East, that even the "dictatorship of the proletariat" will find it a difficult task to complete. It is beyond the scope of other classes.

Furthermore, the democratic classes of Muslim societies have on the whole shown no interest, or almost none, in challenging their own religion. In fact, Islam has not been perceived in the twentieth century as the ideological cement of an outmoded feudal or semifeudal class structure in these societies. It has been seen instead as a basic element of national identity jeered at by the foreign Christian (or even atheist) oppressor. It is no accident that Turkey is the only Muslim society not to have been subjected to direct foreign domination in the twentieth century. Mustafa Kemal too was exceptional among his peers. He waged his main battle not against colonialism or imperialism but against the Sultanate, a combination of temporal and spiritual power (the Caliphate). On the other hand, Nasser, however radical a bourgeois nationalist, had every interest in identifying with Islam in his main combat against imperialism; all the more so because this was a cheap way for him to protect his left and right flanks.

3

The following theses do not deal with Islam as one element among others, albeit a fundamental element, in the ideology of nationalist currents. That kind of Islam's time has passed, as with the currents that identify with it. More generally, we shall distinguish between Islam used as one means among others of shaping and asserting a national, or communal, or even sectarian identity, on the one hand, and Islam considered as an end in itself, a *total, general objective,* a unique, exclusive program, on the other. "The Koran is our constitution," declared Hassan al-Banna, founder of the Muslim Brotherhood in 1928. The Islam that interests us here is Islam elevated to an absolute principle, to which every demand, struggle, and reform is subordinated—the Islam of the Muslim Brotherhood, of the Jamaat-i-Islami, of the different ulemas' associations and of the movement of Iranian ayatollahs whose organized expression is the Islamic Republican Party.

The common denominator of these different movements is *Islamic fundamentalism,* that is, the wish to *return to Islam,* the aspiration to an Islamic utopia, which incidentally cannot be limited to a single nation but must encompass all Muslim peoples if not the whole world. In this spirit, Bani-Sadr declared to the Beirut daily *An-Nahar* in 1979 that "Ayatollah Khomeini is an internationalist; he is opposed to Islamic Stalinists who want to build Islam in one country" (*sic!*). This "internationalism" is also visible in the way that all these movements go beyond the borders of their countries of origin and/or maintain more or less close relations with one another. They all reject nationalism in the narrow sense, and consider nationalist currents—even those that claim to be Islamic—rivals if not adversaries. They oppose foreign oppression or the national enemy in the name of Islam, not in defense of the "nation." The United States is thus not so much "imperialism" for Khomeini as the "Great Satan"; Saddam Hussein is above all an "atheist," an "infidel." For all the movements in question, Israel is not so much a Zionist usurper of Palestinian land as "the Jewish usurper of an Islamic holy land."

4

However progressive, national, and/or democratic the objective significance of certain  struggles carried on by various Islamic fundamentalist currents, it cannot mask the fact that their ideology and their program are essentially, by definition, *reactionary.* What sort of program aims to construct an Islamic state, faithfully modeled on the seventh century of the Christian era, if not a reactionary utopia? What sort of ideology aims to restore a thirteen-century-old order, if not an eminently reactionary ideology? Thus it is wrong and even absurd to define Islamic fundamentalist movements as bourgeois, whatever the extent to which some struggles they wage align them with all or part of their countries' bourgeoisies. It is just as wrong to define them as revolutionary when they happen to come into conflict with these same bourgeoisies.

*In terms of the nature of their program and ideology, their social composition, and even the social origins of their founders, Islamic fundamentalist movements are petit bourgeois.* They do not hide their hatred of representatives of big capital any more than of representatives of the working class, or their hatred of imperialist countries any more than of "communist" countries. They are hostile to the two poles of industrial society that threaten them: the bourgeoisie and the proletariat. They correspond to those layers of the petit bourgeoisie described in the *Communist Manifesto*:

> The lower middle class, the manufacturer, the shopkeeper, the artisan, the peasant, all these fight against the bourgeoisie to save from extinction their existence as fractions of the middle class. They are therefore not revolutionary, but conservative. Nay more, they are reactionary, for they try to roll back the wheel of history.[2]

Petit bourgeois Islamic reaction finds its ideologues and leading elements among the "traditional intellectuals" of Muslim societies, ulemas, and the like, as well as among the lower echelons of the bourgeoisie's "organic intellectuals," those coming from the petit bourgeoisie and condemned to stay there: teachers and office workers in particular. In a period of ascendancy Islamic fundamentalism recruits widely at universities and other institutions that produce "intellectuals," where they are still more conditioned by their social origins than by a hypothetical and often doubtful future.

5

In countries where Islamic fundamentalist reaction has been able to become a mass movement and where it now has the wind in its sails, the labor force includes a relatively high proportion of middle classes, according to the *Communist Manifesto* definition: manufacturers, shopkeepers, artisans, and peasants. Nevertheless, any outbreak of Islamic fundamentalism mobilizes not only a larger or smaller layer of these middle classes, but also layers of other classes newly spawned by the middle classes under the impact of capitalist primitive accumulation and impoverishment. Thus parts of the proletariat whose proletarianization is recent, and above all

parts of the subproletariat that capitalism has dragged down from their former petit bourgeois level, are particularly receptive to fundamentalist agitation and susceptible to being caught up in it.

This is Islamic fundamentalism's social base, its mass base. *But this
base is not the natural preserve of religious reaction*, the way that the bourgeoisie relates to its own program. *Whatever the strength of religious feeling
among the masses, even if the religion in question is Islam, there is a qualitative
leap from sharing this feeling to seeing religion as an earthly utopia.* In order for
the opiate of the masses to become an effective stimulant once more in this
age of automation, the people must truly have no other choice left but to
throw themselves on God's mercy. The least one can say about Islam is that
its immediate relevance is not obvious!

Indeed, Islamic fundamentalism poses more problems than it solves.
Although Islamic law is several centuries younger than Roman law, it was
produced by a society considerably more backward than ancient Rome. (The
Koran was largely inspired by the Torah, just as the Arabs' way of life was fairly similar to the Hebrews'.) And besides the problem of updating a thirteen-
century-old civil code, there is also the question of completing it. In other
words, the most orthodox Muslim fundamentalist is incapable of responding
to the problems posed by modern society with exegetical contortions alone,
unless the contortions become totally arbitrary and therefore a source of endless disagreements among the exegetes. There are thus as many interpreta-
tions of Islam as there are interpreters. The core of the Islamic religion,
which all Muslims agree on, in no way satisfies the pressing material needs
of the petit bourgeoisie, quite apart from whether it can satisfy their spiritual
needs. *Islamic fundamentalism in itself is in no way the most appropriate program for satisfying the aspirations of the social layers to which it appeals.*

6

The social base described above is notable for its political versatility. The quo-
tation from the *Communist Manifesto* above does not describe a fixed attitude
of the middle classes, but only the real content of their fight against the bourgeoisie when there is a fight, when they turn against the bourgeoisie. Before
fighting against the bourgeoisie, the middle classes were its allies in the fight
against feudalism; before seeking to reverse the course of history they contributed to advancing it. *The middle classes are first and foremost the social base
of the democratic revolution and the national struggle.* In backward, dependent

societies such as Muslim societies the middle classes still play this role as long as the tasks of the national and democratic revolution are still more or less uncompleted and on the agenda. They are the most ardent fans of any bourgeois leadership (and even more of any petit bourgeois leadership) that champions these tasks. The middle classes are the social base par excellence of the Bonapartism of the ascendant bourgeoisie; they are the social base of all bourgeois Bonapartism. So the only time when large sections of the middle classes strike off on their own and seek other paths is when bourgeois or petit bourgeois leaderships that have taken on national and democratic tasks run up against their own limits and lose their credibility.

Of course, as long as capitalism on the rise seems to open up prospects of upward social mobility for the middle classes, as long as their conditions of existence are improving, they do not question the established order. Even when depoliticized or unenthusiastic, they normally play the role of "silent majority" in the bourgeois order. But if ever the capitalist evolution of society weighs on them with all its force—the weight of national and/or international competition, inflation, and debt—then the middle classes become a formidable reservoir of opposition to the powers that be. Then they are free of any bourgeois control, and all the more formidable because the violence and rage of the petit bourgeois in distress are unparalleled.

7

Even then the reactionary option is not unavoidable for the petit bourgeoisie, downtrodden though it is by capitalist society and disillusioned with bourgeois and petit bourgeois democratic-nationalist leaderships. There is always another option, at least in theory. The middle classes are faced with the choice between *reaction and revolution*. They can join the revolutionary struggle against the bourgeoisie, as the *Communist Manifesto* foresaw:

> If by chance [the middle classes] are revolutionary, they are so only in view of their impending transfer into the proletariat, they thus defend not their present, but their future interests, they desert their own standpoint to place themselves at that of the proletariat.[3]

In the backward and dependent societies that the *Communist Manifesto* did not take into account, the middle classes have absolutely no need to abandon their own viewpoint in order to place themselves under proletarian leadership.[4] Quite the contrary, *by taking up the middle classes' aspirations, notably national and democratic tasks, the proletariat can manage to win them over to its side.* But for the proletariat to win the middle classes' confidence, it must first of all have a credible leadership itself, a leadership that has proved itself politically and practically. If on the other hand a leadership with a majority in the working class has discredited itself on the level of national democratic political struggles (while maintaining its majority position because of its trade union positions or simply the lack of an alternative), if it proves politically flabby in face of the established order, or if, even worse, it supports the established order, then the middle classes will really have no choice but to lend their ears to petit bourgeois reaction—even if it is as inscrutable as Islamic reaction—and possibly respond to its calls.

8

In all the countries where Islamic fundamentalism has gained considerable ground, particularly in Egypt, Syria, Iran, and Pakistan, all the conditions described above exist.[5] In all these countries middle-class living standards have manifestly deteriorated over the last few years. Although some of these countries are even oil exporters themselves, the only effect the massive oil price increases have had on most of their middle classes has been unbridled inflation. In addition, bourgeois and petit bourgeois democratic-nationalist leaderships are generally discredited in these countries. In all four, democratic-nationalist leaderships have undergone the test of state power. All of these leaderships had had virtually unanimous middle-class support at certain moments in their history as they were trying to implement their national democratic programs. Some went a long way in this direction, notably Egypt and countries under Egyptian influence, where Nasser towered over the political landscape. Nationalists were able to stay in power for a long time, or are still in power—in the latter cases because they owe their power to the army.

In Iran and Pakistan, where the nationalists formed civilian governments, the army soon swept them away; Mossadegh and Bhutto came to sad ends.[6] In all four countries, in any case, the progress made so far in carrying out the national democratic program, even within the framework and limits of a bourgeois state, ranges from very little to almost none. Even in Iran where the Mossadegh experience was a short one, the Shah took it on himself (on his U.S. tutors' advice) to bring about with his own pseudo-

Bismarckian methods what the combined efforts of Robespierres and Bonapartes accomplished elsewhere.

On the other hand, the only noteworthy working-class political organizations in the whole region are Stalinist parties. These, when they amount to anything, have totally discredited themselves with a long history of selling out popular struggles and making deals with the powers that be. So when middle-class discontent began to surface these past few years in the four countries mentioned, no working-class or bourgeois or petit bourgeois nationalist organization was able to capitalize on it. The way was wide open for petit bourgeois Islamic fundamentalist reaction.

By contrast, in Algeria, Libya, and Iraq, where the enlightened despotism of a bourgeois or petit bourgeois nationalist bureaucracy allowed broad middle-class layers to benefit from the oil manna, Islamic fundamentalism could be contained.[7]

## 9

While Islamic fundamentalism has made notable gains in Egypt and Syria as well as Iran and Pakistan, the forms and extent of its gains differ greatly from one country to another, as do its political content and function.[8] In Syria, the fundamentalist movement is the main opposition to the declining Bonapartism of the Ba'athist bourgeois bureaucracy and is engaged in a life-and-death struggle against it. Syrian fundamentalists have profited from the fact that the Ba'athist ruling elite belongs to a minority faith (Alawi). The outrageously, purely reactionary nature of the Syrian fundamentalist movement's program reduces its possibilities of seizing power on its own to almost nothing. It cannot on its own, on the basis of such a program, mobilize the forces needed to overthrow the Ba'athist dictatorship. Still less can it run, alone, a country whose economic and political problems are as thorny as Syria's. The Syrian fundamentalist movement is thus condemned to cooperate with the Syrian propertied classes (bourgeois and landowners). It is not, and cannot be, any more than their spearhead.

In Egypt too, for the same reasons, the possibility of an independent seizure of power by the fundamentalist movement is limited, all the more so because it has less influence there than in Syria. In both these countries a long struggle against progressive regimes has hardened the fundamentalist movement, thus highlighting its reactionary character. Moreover, the very scope of Egypt's economic problems makes the fundamentalists' bid for power even less credible. The Egyptian bourgeoisie is perfectly aware of this and is thus very obliging toward the fundamentalist movement. The fundamentalists constitute in its eyes an ideal "fifth column" inside the mass movement—a particularly effective "antibody" to the left. That is why the Egyptian bourgeoisie is not at all worried about the fundamentalist movement's trying to outbid the Left on the Left's two favorite issues: the national question and the social question; any gains made by Islamic reaction on these two issues mean equivalent losses for the Left.[9] The Egyptian bourgeoisie's attitude toward the fundamentalist movement resembles that of any bourgeoisie faced with a deep social crisis toward the far right and fascism.

Pakistan is different from Egypt in that the Pakistani fundamentalist movement has consolidated itself mainly under reactionary regimes. It has therefore been able to reclaim some elements of the national democratic program for long periods of time and thus form a credible opposition to the established order. But during these same long periods, bourgeois democratic- nationalist tendencies were in opposition, and more credible and thus more influential than the fundamentalists were. Only when Bhutto, skipping the stages of a Nasser-type evolution in an impressive historical shortcut, rapidly alienated the masses by getting entangled in his own contradictions was the way opened up for the extreme right dominated by the fundamentalist movement (given that the Pakistani far left was insignificant). Bhutto's bankruptcy was so glaring that the fundamentalists managed to mobilize a huge mass movement against him. The army's coup d'état was meant to forestall the "anarchy" that could have resulted had this mobilization led to Bhutto's overthrow (as in Iran). To win the fundamentalists' sympathy, Zia Ul-Haq's reactionary bourgeois military dictatorship took over their projects for Islamic reforms and used them to its own advantage. Today it is counting on the fundamentalist movement to neutralize any "progressive" opposition to its regime, including the late Bhutto's party.

In the three cases analyzed above, the fundamentalist movement has proved itself to be nothing but an *auxiliary for the reactionary bourgeoisie*. But Iran is different.

10

In Iran the fundamentalist movement, represented mainly by the fundamentalists among the Shiite clergy, was forged in a long and bitter struggle against the Shah's eminently reactionary imperialist-backed regime. The sad historical bankruptcy of Iranian bourgeois nationalism and Stalinism is too well known to describe here. Because of this exceptional combination of historical circumstances, the Iranian fundamentalist movement managed to become the sole spearhead of the two immediate tasks of the national democratic revolution in Iran: overthrowing the Shah and severing the ties with U.S. imperialism. This situation was all the more possible because the two tasks in question were in perfect harmony with the generally reactionary program of Islamic fundamentalism. So as the social crisis matured in Iran to the point of creating the preconditions for a revolutionary overthrow of the Shah, as the middle classes' resentment of him reached fever pitch, the fundamentalist movement personified by Khomeini managed to harness the immense power of the embattled middle classes and subproletariat and deal the regime a series of body blows. The fundamentalists were almost suicidal in their determination to remain unarmed, a feat of which only a mystical movement is capable. The Iranian fundamentalist movement managed to carry out the first stage of a national democratic revolution in Iran. But its fundamentalist character quickly got the upper hand.

In a sense, the Iranian revolution is a *permanent revolution in reverse.* Starting with the national democratic revolution, it could under proletarian leadership have "grown over" into a socialist transformation. Its fundamentalist petit bourgeois leadership prevented that, on the contrary pushing it in the direction of a *reactionary regression.* The February 1979 revolution was astonishingly similar to February 1917—two identical points of departure ushering in diametrically opposite processes. While October 1917 enabled the Russian democratic revolution to go to its logical conclusion, in Iran the fundamentalist leadership betrayed the revolution's democratic content. The Russian Bolsheviks replaced the Constituent Assembly, after having struggled to have it elected, with the eminently democratic power of the soviets; the ayatollahs replaced the Constituent Assembly, which they too had placed at the head of their demands but never allowed to see the light of day, with a reactionary caricature: the Muslim "Assembly of Experts." The fate of this demand common to the two revolutions eloquently sums up the counterposed natures of the leaderships, and thus the opposite directions they took.

As for the democratic forms of organization that arose in the course of the Iranian February, the Islamic leadership co-opted them. The *shoras* were a far cry from the soviets! On the national question, while the Bolsheviks' proletarian internationalism made possible the emancipation of the

Russian empire's oppressed nationalities, the ayatollahs' Islamic "internationalism" turned out to be a pious pretext for bloody repression of the Persian empire's oppressed nationalities. The fate of women in the two revolutions is just as well-known.

The fundamentalist Iranian leadership only remained faithful to the national democratic program on one point: the struggle against U.S. imperialism. But it stayed true to this struggle in its own peculiar way. Describing the enemy not as imperialism but as the "West" if not the "Great Satan," Khomeini called for throwing out the baby with the bathwater, or rather the baby before the bathwater. He attributed all the political and social gains of the bourgeois revolution, including democracy and even Marxism, which he considered (correctly) a product of (supposedly "Western") industrial civilization, to the hated "West." He called on Iranians to rid their society of these plagues, while neglecting the main links between Iran and imperialism: the economic links. The U.S. embassy affair, the way it was managed, gained Iran nothing. In the final analysis it proved very expensive, profitable in the last analysis to U.S. banks. However the fundamentalist dictatorship evolves in Iran from now on, it has already proved to be a major obstacle to the development of the Iranian revolution.

Moreover, its evolution is problematic. Beyond the exceptional combination of circumstances described above, there is a fundamental difference between Iran and the three other countries mentioned earlier: Iran can afford the "luxury" of an experiment with an autonomous, petit bourgeois, fundamentalist regime. Its oil wealth is the guarantee of a positive balance of payments and budget. But at what price and for how long? The economic balance sheet of two years of fundamentalism in power is already negative compared with earlier years. On the other hand, the inconsistency of the fundamentalist "program" and the great variety of social layers that identify with it and interpret it according to their own lights are manifest in a *plurality of rival and antagonistic centers of powers*. Only Khomeini's authority has made it possible so far for them to keep up a facade of unity.

11

Islamic fundamentalism is one of the most dangerous enemies of the revolutionary proletariat. It is absolutely and under all circumstances necessary to fight against its "reactionary and medieval influence," as the "Theses on the National and Colonial Question" adopted at the Second Congress of the

Communist International said many years ago. Even in cases such as Iran, where the fundamentalist movement takes on national-democratic tasks for a time, the duty of revolutionary socialists is to fight intransigently against the spell it casts on the struggling masses. If not, if they do not free themselves in time, the masses will surely pay the price. While striking together at the common enemy, revolutionary socialists must warn working people against any attempt to divert their struggle in a reactionary direction. Any failure in these elementary tasks is not only a fundamental weakness but can also lead to opportunist wrong turns.

On the other hand, even in cases where Islamic fundamentalism takes purely reactionary forms, revolutionary socialists must use tactical caution in their fight against it. In particular they must avoid falling into the fundamentalists' trap of fighting about religious issues. They should stick firmly to the national, democratic, and social issues. They must not lose sight of the fact that a part, often a big part, of the masses under Islamic fundamentalist influence can and must be pulled out of its orbit and won to the workers' cause. At the same time revolutionary socialists must nevertheless declare themselves unequivocally for a *secular* society, which is a basic element of the democratic program. They can play down their atheism, but never their secularism, unless they wish to replace Marx outright with Mohammed!

FEBRUARY 1, 1981; first published in English in *International Marxist Review* 2, no. 3 (Summer 1987).

## CHAPTER TWO

# The Swan Song of Khomeini's Revolution

*Khomeini's death in June 1989 provided an occasion to give a social explanation of the revolution he had led and the regime he established, in keeping with the analysis made eight years earlier and reprinted in the previous chapter. My diagnosis emphasized at this early date that Khomeini's movement as it had emerged from the February 1979 revolution was at an end, exhausted by its own socioeconomic and political failures. My prognosis was that factional battles would intensify inside the Iranian regime, with Rafsanjani playing a winning hand.*

Millions and millions of Iranians, forming a gigantic sea of humanity, took part in the funeral of Ayatollah Khomeini, "guide of the Islamic revolution," who died on June 3. Idolized by millions, hated by millions of others, the name of this visionary leader of the Iranian "mullahrchy" must be added for good to the rolls of historic figures who called forth the most violently contradictory passions during their lifetimes.

The impressive breadth of the mourning for Khomeini's death nonetheless surprised many people. It was a resounding refutation of claims by many Iranian oppositionists of both right and left that the "Islamic" regime had lost any mass base and was clinging to power itself by terror alone. Many people around the world who—for good or bad reasons—were looking forward to the end of Khomeini's regime had joined in this wishful thinking. The outburst of feeling in Tehran was a bitter disappointment to them all.

Of course, the scenes of collective hysteria prompted by the Imam's funeral show clearly that the event was in large measure a phenomenon of mass psychology.[1] But if we are to avoid falling into the primitive form of idealism represented by the psychological conception of history, we cannot

attribute the grief expressed by a large part of the Iranian population simply to a fanaticism that it fell prey to out of ignorance and backwardness.

## TEN YEARS LATER

Psychological, ideological, and religious factors are real forces in determining history. However, they do not operate on masses that can be manipulat-
ed at will, susceptible to any kind of brainwashing. In order to turn masses
of people into fanatics, you have to convince them that you are offering
them a reliable road toward improving their lives and attaining greater dignity. In order to turn them into fanatics in a lasting way, you have to be able
to offer them tangible progress along that road.

The most amazing thing about the mass outbursts of June 4, 5, and 6 in
Tehran is that they happened over ten years after the extraordinary mobilization that greeted Khomeini on his return from exile to the same city on
February 1, 1979. During those ten years the Iranian population has been
able to get a good idea of what the Islamic regime means in reality. Hundreds of thousands of Iranians have paid with their lives during those ten
years for the demented pigheadedness of the octogenarian from Qum (the
holy city where he lived) in the war against Iraq, while almost two million
people chose exile and tens of thousands fell victim to the Khomeini
regime's terror. Yet ten years later millions of Iranians were still ready to
weep for the Imam.

A correct analysis of the process set in motion in Iran in 1979 can provide the key to this apparent paradox. In this respect, moreover, the ayatollah's funeral was highly revealing. It contradicted the interpretation that
saw Khomeini as a usurper of the February 1979 revolution, the leader of a
Thermidorian reaction or even a counterrevolution. According to this interpretation, the establishment of the "Islamic" dictatorship was a break, a
reversal of the process initiated in 1979, to the point that the situation
became worse for the Iranian population as a whole under Khomeini than
it had been under the shah.

The undeniable fact that the millions who poured out to mourn in
Tehran this month are the same ones who formed the majority of the popular mobilizations ten years earlier, especially in the capital, clearly invali-
dates this view. It confirms by contrast the interpretation that stressed the
continuity of the Iranian process, which was predictable from the outset;
the uninterrupted retrogression constituted by a revolution that began with

national and democratic demands, but was led from the start by a profoundly reactionary network of mullahs and fundamentalist activists—a sort of permanent revolution in reverse.[2]

From this standpoint, there was admittedly a series of breaks in the Iranian process, as its leadership broke with one or another category of people who had converged with it in its twofold opposition to the shah and his U.S. guardians. Nonetheless, the establishment of the "Islamic" dictatorship in no way constituted a break in the process itself, but was rather its natural culmination.

### IMPOVERISHED MASSES

The shah's regime was hated as few regimes have ever been. It put on its megalomaniacal shows of conspicuous consumption before the eyes of impoverished masses, whose numbers were constantly swelling as a result of the brutal and distorted capitalist development that the regime promoted from the early 1960s on. These masses, in particular those in the sinkholes of Tehran society, who come from the peasantry or traditional petit bourgeoisie of the countryside or towns, formed a gigantic, highly explosive reservoir of forces ready to move into action against the regime.

The historic failure of Iranian modernist bourgeois nationalism, revealed by Mussadiq's fall in 1953; the discrediting of Stalinism represented by the Tudeh party in the wake of Mussadiq's fall; and the deficiencies of the revolutionary Left following guerrilla-type models left the field open for another candidate to overthrow the shah—the fundamentalist faction of the Shiite clergy with Khomeini as its standard-bearer.

Through its social welfare activity, helping the poor in the name of Islamic charity, the substantial network of the Iranian clergy—with 120,000 members in 1979 or one in 300 of the country's population!— provided a kind of cadre for the impoverished masses. It offered them the ideological refuge of a religion that, in its Shiite version in particular, exalts the oppressed, the *mustazafeen* ("downtrodden"), holding out the prospect of ideal social justice in the framework of an Islamic utopia.

Based on the idea of a return to a mythical early Islam, this utopia is eminently reactionary by its very nature. Theocracy, patriarchy, and obscurantism are the three pillars common to all varieties of Islamic fundamentalism. It can nonetheless serve to mobilize masses of people suffering the horrors of dependent capitalism and feeling nostalgia for the past. The

more illiterate the masses are and the lower their level of political awareness because of stifling of civil liberties, the more vulnerable they are to
this "opium of the people," which has the peculiar property of being capable of becoming a stimulant.

The *mustazafeen*, organized by the mullahs and the lay missionaries of
Islamic fundamentalism and led by "supreme guide" Ayatollah Khomeini,
thus formed the spearhead of the 1979 Iranian revolution. Flocking by
hundreds of thousands into the various apparatuses and institutions of
the new regime, they had the illusion, after toppling the throne of a seem-
ingly all-powerful ruler, that they had been transformed overnight from
pariahs to a new ruling class. At the time of the hostage-taking at the U.S.
embassy in Tehran in 1979–80, the feeling that they had launched a challenge that the United States, the superpower that had dominated Iran and
protected the shah, had been unable to meet intensified this fabulous psychological lift even more.

## THE WAR AGAINST IRAQ

On top of this twofold exaltation came the exaltation of Iranian patriotism,
or even Persian chauvinism, in the war against the Iraqi invasion from September 1980 on. For seven years, this war became the main theme in the
mullahs' ideological mobilization of the people. During these seven years
Iran moved from containing the invaders to the counteroffensive, pushed
them back to the border in 1982, and then began a slow but real advance
into Iraqi territory, with the declared aim of reaching Baghdad and overthrowing the Saddam Hussein regime.

From 1982 on the war against Iraq became a giant escape hatch for the
Khomeini regime. Without this, it would have been forced to confront
grave socioeconomic problems and worsening internal dissensions. The
military mobilization and the slaughter caused by the war enabled it partially to absorb potentially enormous unemployment. The priority given to
the war effort justified its economic setbacks and simplified its choices.
National unity against the enemy called for putting a damper on differences within the regime, under Khomeini's presiding sprit.

At the same time, the "Islamic" regime continued to minister to the
needs of its clientele. Institutions like the Jihad for Reconstruction or the
Martyrs' Foundation (in charge of the families of war victims) allotted public
housing and distributed food, goods, and other sorts of subsidies. Material

interests thus combined with political and ideological mobilization and emotional excitement to assure the regime a rather comfortable popular base.

What enabled the Iranian mullahs' regime to finance both warfare and welfare for its social clientele was not manna from heaven but manna from underground: oil. Waging a war of a very low capital intensity, resorting to a large extent to "human waves," Iran managed the feat of avoiding going into debt. Oil revenues were sufficient, just barely to be sure, to keep the regime afloat. Without the oil factor the ten years of the Khomeini regime would have been impossible; the demands of capitalist economic rationality would have clashed with the economically "irresponsible" or "irrational" character of the Khomeini regime's social and political policies. By pumping up the state budget, oil gave the regime a wide margin of maneuver and autonomy.

Nonetheless, Iran is not a rich country, if you compare its oil revenues with the size of its population. Oil has only cushioned the inexorable downward slide in the country's economic and social conditions, dragged down by the combined weight of the war and waste. Unemployment and poverty swelled against a backdrop of galloping inflation, far exceeding the regime's capacities for social assistance. The way the Iranian forces bogged down in Iraq from 1987 on, after four years of slow advances at a high cost in human life, compounded the regime's difficulties. The wind began to shift in Iran itself, where signs multiplied of the whole population's growing disaffection with the regime.

### "POISON"

In 1988, Iraq regained the upper hand in the war. It managed in its turn not only to push Iranian troops out of its territory but also to begin to nibble again at Iran's territory. Khomeini was forced to abandon his dream, and in July he accepted the cease-fire declared by the UN Security Council a year before. In his own words, this decision was "more painful than swallowing poison." It was the beginning of his political death agony. He tried again to find a safety valve for the passions of his social base in the person of Salman Rushdie. But this time the target was too small and too far away to serve as a real target for mobilization.

On June 3, Khomeini died at the age of eighty-nine in his hospital bed, after sending a million teenagers and men in the prime of life to be slaughtered in a senseless war. In a final outburst, his social base mobilized for his funeral. But there should be no mistake. This last farewell mobilization—

equal to if not greater than the one for his return in 1979—was the swan song of Khomeini's movement. The best evidence of this, paradoxically, is the intensity of the grief and distress shown by the black-clad masses. It was distress at the collapse of a fantasy world that is disappearing with the death of its inspirer, distress of a people who had been abandoned, facing a difficult present and a highly uncertain future. It is distress at the great void left by Khomeini, which none of his epigones is capable of filling.

The battle to determine the Imam's successor has already begun. With no one to fill the role of arbiter that he played, it promises to be a stormy one. At this stage, the four main actors in the drama are the incumbent president of the republic (whose term expires in October), Hojatoleslam Ali Khamenei, who was appointed on June 4 to succeed the Imam as supreme guide and promoted at the same time to the rank of ayatollah; Hojatoleslam Ali Akbar Hashemi Rafsanjani, the present speaker of parliament, who has just announced his candidacy for the presidency of the republic in the elections scheduled for August; Ahmed Khomeini, the Imam's son, whose role depended until now entirely on the fact that he controlled access to his father and seemed to exercise a growing influence over his decisions; and, finally, Ayatollah Hussein Ali Montazeri, who was named the Imam's successor in 1985 and then ousted last March 27.

In addition to these four figures, there is a gaggle of ayatollahs and mullahs who can claim power or hold a piece of it, generally in the context of special alliances with one of the men mentioned above. The struggle for power in Iran revolves around theological and clerical differences as well as political ones. What looks on the surface like competing personal ambitions nonetheless reflects a clash of differing sociopolitical projects.

## HETEROGENEOUS CLERGY

Although the Shiite clergy is definitely the backbone of the Iranian Islamic regime, it is not a homogeneous social layer. The Shiite clergy is an estate divided into ascending ranks and directly woven into the social fabric on which it depends. It cannot be equated to a Bonapartist bureaucracy, whose special feature is precisely that it is detached from civil society. Like the French clergy during the revolution at the end of the eighteenth century, for example, the Iranian clergy reflects the divisions in society. Within it the lower clergy must be distinguished from the higher, and various social attitudes and affiliations must be distinguished inside each hierarchical subcategory.[3]

The great majority of the clergy was welded together around Khomeini. All the clerics have profited from the "Islamic revolution" that propelled them into power. But when it came to exercising this power, the options were as manifold and divergent as the social and political factors at work. A faction of the clergy, notably at the top, is linked to the traditional wealthy classes in the towns (rich bazaar merchants) or the countryside (big landowners). But the greater part of the clergy, especially the lower strata, belongs socially and politically to a gamut of urban and rural petit bourgeois layers ranging from the poorest to the most well off. Its political behavior corresponds to that of its particular layer, including its characteristic oscillation.

This is the source of the great confusion and heterogeneity, against a background of instability, that typifies the Iranian mullahs' regime. The dominant fundamentalist ideology is too vague and imprecise with respect to the problems of modern society to be a source of cohesion and consensus. It is modulated to suit the real social aspirations of the various actors. These range from a populist fundamentalism with radical, anti-plutocratic tones to an ultraconservative fundamentalism favoring unbridled free enterprise. All of these positions are backed up with verses from the Koran and quotations from the Prophet and his cousin and son-in-law Ali (whose disciples the Shiites are, unlike the Sunnis).

Ayatollah Montazeri is the main figure in the populist fundamentalist current. In that sense, he is the most faithful to Khomeini's tradition of 1979–80. Up until 1987, Montazeri enjoyed the confidence of the Imam, who designated him his successor. He was a natural choice, in particular since he alone among the politically active clerics had the theological qualifications required for the job according to the 1979 constitution.

Some people close to Montazeri provoked a break with Khomeini in 1986 by exposing Rafsanjani's secret dealings with Washington and setting off the Irangate scandal. The severe repression against those close to Montazeri in 1987 marked the beginning of a period in which he and his followers had a rough time of it. Clearly, the Imam was unhappy because, addled by his desire to finish off Saddam Hussein, he had secretly given Rafsanjani the green light.

Ahmed, the Imam's son, who had previously been an ally of Montazeri, went over to Rafsanjani. The latter, a notable opportunist, great demagogue, and fabulously wealthy landowner, is the main representative of those who favor stabilizing Iran on a course of capitalist development open to the outside world and especially to the imperialist countries. Since 1987 he has steadily gained ground in his advance toward taking over the government in Tehran. Appointed head of the regime's armed forces by the Imam in June 1988, he convinced Khomeini to accept the cease-fire in July.

With Ahmed Khomeini's complicity, he managed to get the Imam to kick out Montazeri in March and then set up a commission to reform the constitution. The reform limited the temporal powers of the religious "guide," a title that Rafsanjani cannot pretend to and does not aspire to. Following the U.S. model, it also considerably increased the powers of the presidency of the republic, which he intended to run for.

The alliance between Khomeini junior and Rafsanjani made possible Ali Khamenei's appointment as "supreme guide" after Khomeini's death. Khamenei, a colorless figure and weak character, entirely suits the redefinition of the role of guide that Rafsanjani, still speaker of parliament, wants. Of course, the new ayatollah may have some surprises in store. But for the moment he is hardly capable of putting Rafsanjani in the shade, while Rafsanjani has already launched the final phase of his conquest of power.

## BATTLE FOR POWER

Montazeri himself, who is fully qualified to challenge the unconstitutional appointment of Khamenei and claim the post of "guide" for himself, also went into action after the Imam's death. He may choose to announce his candidacy for the presidency of the republic against his adversary Rafsanjani. In this looming battle, Montazeri has the support of a major part of the regime's activist base, including the Pasdaran, or Revolutionary Guards. Since being put in a minority in the regime, he has allied himself with the liberals around Mehdi Bazargan and become a champion of restoring democratic rights and liberties, thereby gaining further popularity.[4]

Rafsanjani for his part is counting on the aspiration for stability and opening up to the outside world that he embodies. He is relying on the support of the technocratic and administrative apparatus and, of course, the support of the wealthy classes. Finally and perhaps above all, he is counting on the military hierarchy, which he has been able to link himself to thanks to his position as interim chief of the armed forces since June 1988. But the late Khomeini has left Rafsanjani with a time bomb: his will sets out a foreign policy line totally contrary to Rafsanjani's, and calls for choosing a man of humble origins as leader of the country!

The existence of several power centers has characterized Iran since 1979. Can a centralized, stable bourgeois regime around Rafsanjani emerge from this? That is not very likely. Will the battling factions blow up the regime? Will the conflict degenerate into civil war? Several scenarios are possible: notably, if there is a descent into chaos, intervention by the regular army in Tehran, or even the establishment of an Islamic military regime similar to the one Zia ul-Haq installed in Pakistan.

The Iranian Left, unfortunately, is too weakened today to have an impact on the situation in the country. Let us hope that Khomeini's death will offer it an opportunity to rebuild itself on new bases, drawing the lessons from its serious errors in the past.

JUNE 11, 1989; first published in English in *International Viewpoint*, no. 166 (June 26, 1989).

CHAPTER THREE

# CHAPTER THREE

# The Arab Despotic Exception

*Three themes in this text are worthy of note: the fundamental responsibility of Western domination for "the Arab despotic exception" (the article's original title, replaced in the June 1997* Le Monde Diplomatique *by "The Arab World: Absence of Democracy"); the central role of the Saudi monarchy in determining this Western attitude; and the disastrous character of the Saudi-U.S. gamble on the Sunni fundamentalist current—many elements of this current turned against the West with the 1990 Gulf crisis, after having been longtime Western allies in the fight against communism and the Soviet Union. All three of these themes are at the heart of the discussions that arose after September 11, 2001.*

Six years after the end of the Gulf War, the Arab world seems strangely static. Everywhere else the "liberal" parliamentary model has triumphed, yet in the Middle East and North Africa authoritarian regimes just keep going without any major reforms. This "Arab exception" does not result from some "cultural specificity"; rather, it is in part the product of Western policies. The West, anxious to guarantee its access at low cost to the region's oil resources, is worried mainly by the rise of fundamentalist opposition groups.

In these times, when people take globalization as going hand in hand with democratization and the free market is generally linked to a political liberalism, presented as its natural counterpart, the Arab world presents something of an anomaly. Not only is it the only geopolitical area of the world still subject as a whole to various forms of absolutism, but the Western powers also seem happy with this state of affairs.

The Arab world is the only geopolitical region in which a relative reduction of the state's influence on the economy, though inaugurated by Anwar al-Sadat in Egypt as long ago as the early 1970s, has not seen an accompanying reduction in its control over politics. It is also the only one where civil society has been unable to wrest political expression from bureaucratic or despotic state control. The political regimes in the Arab world range from monarchies that are absolute de jure to republics that are absolutist de facto. In those Arab countries that lay claim to democracy, free elections are a fiction and, even in the best of cases, the freedoms granted are parsimonious, selective, and closely supervised.

What makes matters worse is that there is no glimmer of hope on the horizon. Advances were made in Algeria, Jordan, and Yemen in particular at the height of the worldwide drive for democracy in the late 1980s, but this progress was thrown into reverse by the repercussions of the Gulf war.[1] Even Lebanon, which until recently had relatively credible electoral and parliamentary institutions and real freedom of expression—albeit still subject to the fiat of its Syrian overlords—is in the course of being brought to heel again.[2]

How are we to explain this Arab exception? And, more important, why is it so blatantly tolerated by those same big powers that preach democracy to the rest of the planet? The West chose to shut its eyes on the occasion of the abrupt suspension of elections in Algeria in 1992, just as it closes its eyes to the depths of tyranny to which the Tunisian regime has sunk. The Emir of Kuwait, who owes his throne to U.S. military power, has been left free nevertheless to pursue his career as a potentate. And Saddam Hussein's appalling dictatorship has been preserved in the name of noninterference in the internal affairs of Iraq. The Palestinian Authority that Yassir Arafat was allowed to set up, far from drawing inspiration from the liberal political model of Israel under whose colonial diktat it labors, bears a striking resemblance to the state structures of its Arab neighbors.

Is it fair to assume that this can all be explained by some particular characteristic of Arab or Muslim culture? In 1992, Amos Perlmutter, a leading light in U.S. foreign policy, had no hesitation in writing in the *Washington Post,* "Is Islam, fundamentalist or otherwise, compatible with liberal, human rights-oriented, Western-style, representative democracy? The answer is clearly no."[3]

The culturalist line of argument smacks of barely disguised racism. Moreover, it does not stand up to comparative analysis: several Muslim countries have no cause to envy their Third World peers when it comes to democratic evolution, without having repudiated Islam. But the real function of the culturalist thesis is political. It makes it possible to justify the West's complicity with the worst Muslim tyrannies (without asking any democratic concessions of them, on the grounds that we must respect their "cultural specificity") as well as a dictatorial suppression of militant Islamic movements in the name of democracy. The essence of the argument is that if there has to be dictatorship, at least let it be pro-Western. It was in this vein that Amos Perlmutter's article went on to justify the Algerian military junta's cancellation of the freest elections that the Arab world has ever known.

## THE CURSE OF OIL

Two basic factors explain the Arab despotic exception. The first is the curse of oil; the second is the nature of political opposition in the region, led by Islamic movements.

Western sponsors' perpetuation, and in some cases establishment, of archaic tribal dynasties in the oil states of the Arabian peninsula contrasted strongly with colonialism's project of overturning traditional structures in other parts of the world and setting up models emulating political modernity. The West's "civilizing mission" in establishing state institutions did not apply to the oil states. Here, on the contrary, its project was to consolidate backwardness in order to guarantee the tutelary powers' unfettered exploitation of hydrocarbon resources. This was particularly the case in the Saudi kingdom.

Because the Saudi kingdom has the largest oil reserves in the world, it is one of the countries to which Washington attaches the greatest importance. The United States has long directly controlled the kingdom's economic and security affairs, and maintained a structure of maximum social rigidity in order to foreclose any possibility of popular disorder. Special attention has been given to ensuring that no indigenous working class develops. The formula—identical to that applied in other oil states, but particularly absurd in Saudi Arabia given the size of the population—has been to favor the development of a privileged middle class among Saudi nationals, while relying essentially in the area of industrial production and manual labor on an immigrant workforce that is rigidly controlled and relatively restricted in numbers, thanks to the country's irrational recourse to the most advanced production technologies.

The structure of the Saudi army follows the same logic. Relatively small in number, in order to minimize the domestic risk of a republican coup d'état of the kind that brought down monarchies in Egypt, Iraq, and Libya, it is impressively armed with equipment bought at prohibitive prices in what has proved to be a bonanza for Western cannon merchants. Thus, for a population four times the size of that of neighboring Jordan, the Saudi kingdom has barely twice as many personnel in its armed forces, but it spends thirty-three times what the Hashemite kingdom spends on its own military budget.[4]

The Saudi army and National Guard, which are modeled on the country's tribal structures, are essentially a praetorian guard for the monarchy. Their effectiveness against external threats is doubtful, and in any event is quite out of proportion to their costs, which are two and a half times greater than those of Israel's army. Much of Riyadh's most advanced weaponry is "pre-positioned" so as to be available for eventual use by U.S. troops—a formula much favored by the Pentagon after the enormous logistical efforts required of it in the months following the Iraqi invasion of Kuwait in August 1990. It is an open secret that the huge airport at Jeddah is not designed merely for the transit of pilgrims to Mecca.

Saudi Arabia's decision, revealed in a recent article in the *Washington Post*, to order 102 F-16 aircraft from Lockheed Martin for a mere $15 billion ($3 billion for the aircraft themselves and $12 billion for fitting them out and maintaining them and training their pilots) speaks volumes about the scale of Saudi spending. Leaving aside the usual Israeli objections, generally aimed at squeezing more military largesse out of Washington by way of compensation (in this instance F-22 "Stealth" bombers), the *Post* treats us to an instructive polemic within the U.S. establishment itself. One part of the administration (within the State Department) would prefer that the money be used for social projects geared at maintaining the kingdom's domestic stability; others (in the Pentagon) would prefer that the Saudis modernize their land army rather than adding to the hardware of their already overequipped air force.[5]

This kingdom, so closely allied to the United States that U.S. officials feel free to debate its budgetary policy, is the antithesis of democracy. It is a kingdom where the Koran and Sharia are the only basic law, run by ultra-orthodox Wahhabis. It is undoubtedly the most fundamentalist state in the world, the most totalitarian in political and cultural terms, and the most oppressive of the female half of the population. It makes Iranian society look relatively liberal, pluralist, and freedom-loving toward its women by comparison.

Here we see the hypocrisy of those who are perfectly ready to condemn fundamentalism in the name of secularism and democracy whenever it takes on an anti-Western tinge, but who are equally happy to enjoy and exploit their lucrative friendship with the Saudis. One can easily see why the peoples of the Arab world saw the proclamations of the anti-Iraq coalition during the Gulf war as mendacious and inadmissible, given that this same coalition, with the United States at its head, was trumpeting its defense of democratic values from bases in the Saudi kingdom and with Saudi help.

So one of the basic reasons for the despotic exception in the Arab world is that the West could not promote democratic values in the Arab world—even if only in words—without running the risk of damaging its protégés in the Gulf.

But there is also a second fundamental reason: the burgeoning growth of the other, Iranian-style, radically anti-Western face of fundamentalism. Here the West is reaping what it helped to sow. For more than three decades its fight against progressive nationalism (as typified by Nasser's model backed by the USSR) went hand in glove with the Islamic propaganda emanating from the Saudi monarchy, a sworn enemy of the Egyptian regime. With a view to supporting the Muslim Brotherhood against Egypt's President Gamal Abdel Nasser, Riyadh, with the aid of the CIA, financed and provided a haven for a sizable section of the hazy international groupings of Islamic fundamentalism.

When Nasser's movement disintegrated, the regimes that carried out the "pro-Western restoration" reproduced this same alliance as a means of combating the Left and the supporters of the former regime. Remember what happened to Anwar al-Sadat; the tale is reminiscent of the sorcerer's apprentice. In the early days of his presidency he greatly contributed to freeing and strengthening Islamic fundamentalist activities, in order to outflank his leftist opposition. He ended up being assassinated in the name of Islam. In the meantime, to the great surprise of Washington and Riyadh, the 1979 Iranian revolution revealed a new face of militant opposition to Western domination.

After so many years of anti-communist and anti-nationalist struggle conducted under the banner of Islam rather than liberal democracy, bankrupt nationalism and an impotent Left have left the door wide open to Islamic fundamentalism. Riyadh and Washington had thoroughly greased the slippery slope of religion, thus lending itself most readily therefore to nationalist and social popular challenges.

There followed a long period of hesitancy, during which the Saudi rulers and their U.S. advisers imagined that the contagion could be contained by playing up the specifically Shiite nature of Iran, and by playing off "Sunni moderates" against "Shiite extremists." Riyadh continued to play godfather to Sunni fundamentalist movements, in particular the currents emerging from the Muslim Brotherhood. However, this new tactic proved to be equally disastrous. In 1990, at the moment when the Gulf crisis put

Iraq and Saudi Arabia in opposing camps, major sections of the Sunni fundamentalist movement, which Riyadh had supported, took Iraq's side in order not to cut themselves off from their social base. This was a stinging fiasco for the Saudi monarchy.

With the collapse of the USSR in 1991 leaving only a remnant of communism behind, Washington decreed that the West's public enemy number one was now to be Iranian-style radical Islam. We had thus moved in a brief period from the "end of history" to the "clash of civilizations." Needless to say, the same hypocrisy that made the Saudi monarchy an ally of Western civilization has continued unabated. Its most recent "success" has been in Afghanistan, where Washington and Riyadh's collusion with the Taliban has been widely reported.[6]

Thus the anti-Western Islamic fundamentalism that has become the main channel for popular resistance in the Arab world combined with the Saudi monarchy's own anti-democratic influence to ensure that from 1990 onward—unlike the processes of political evolution elsewhere in the world—the Arab variant of the "new world order" was still built on despotism. It was to preserve the stability of the Saudi kingdom as much as to avoid pro-Iranian forces seizing power in Baghdad that General Schwarzkopf's troops stopped a few kilometers short of the Iraqi capital and let Saddam Hussein's dictatorship, faced with uprisings in the country's Kurdish north and Shiite south, shore itself up. For similar reasons, after the Islamic Salvation Front (FIS) of Algeria had taken Iraq's side during the Gulf crisis, the West chose to endorse the suspension of the democratic experiment under way in Algeria. For the same reasons once again, the Tunisian dictatorship could tranquilly go about "eradicating" Tunisian emulators of the Algerian FIS, while the Egyptian regime considerably intensified its repression of the same current.

So there is no need to go back to the seventh century to understand this Arab exception. The second half of the twentieth century provides perfectly adequate explanations.[7] But having examined the exception, perhaps we are entitled to take another look at the rule. After a close study of realities in the Arab world, can one still believe in the elective affinities between neoliberal, Western-dominated economic globalization and the values of liberal democracy?

First published in English in *Le Monde Diplomatique*, English edition, June 1997.

# PART II

# Afghanistan:
# Quagmire of the Great Powers

## CHAPTER FOUR

# On the Soviet Intervention in Afghanistan

*This draft resolution, a reaction to the invasion of Afghanistan by Soviet troops in December 1979, was written for an international meeting held in January 1980. Tariq Ali, my friend and comrade for over thirty years—I am repeating here what he kindly wrote about me in the acknowledgments of his* Bush in Babylon *(London/New York: Verso, 2003)—and I were the only ones to defend it. The majority in the meeting, while condemning the bureaucratic policies that had led to the invasion, refused nevertheless to call for a withdrawal of Moscow's troops, which they saw as playing a progressive role despite everything. The Afghanistan war would facilitate Ronald Reagan's rise to power in Washington and contribute greatly to the process culminating in the collapse of the USSR.*

[...] There is no doubt that the Soviet intervention in Afghanistan is being carried out in gross violation of the right of peoples to self-determination. It is in fact well-known that the Soviet troops themselves overthrew Amin in order to replace him with Karmal, whom they brought in from exile. It is also well-known that there is no qualitative difference between the regimes of Taraki, Amin, and Karmal, each of which has been supported in turn by the Kremlin. The recent release of prisoners by the Karmal government does not constitute evidence to the contrary. It did not succeed in winning Karmal popular sympathy, since his having been imposed from the outside has alienated him from the Afghan people. On the other hand, the imperialist support for the Afghan "mujahedin" led by feudal and religious reactionaries has never reached proportions comparable to that of the Soviet support for Kabul, even before the direct intervention of the Kremlin's troops. Imperialist support for the Afghan rebels never reached the dimensions of an outside interference that would have justified the intervention of Soviet troops, despite the claims of the Kremlin leaders.

If, however, the Kabul regime were indeed threatened with being overthrown by the mujahedin, the only correct way to prevent such an outcome would have been to urge the regime to abandon its methods of military dictatorship and seek to base itself on a mobilization of the masses around their own interests while promoting their independent organization. [...] Such a policy would be, as we know, the opposite of that being followed by the Stalinist bureaucracy, whose aim is to generalize its own methods. To state that a seizure of power in Kabul by reactionaries would have constituted a serious threat to the security of the Soviet Union is, moreover, totally ridiculous.

Condemning the intervention of Soviet troops in Afghanistan does not resolve, however, the problem of what attitude to adopt toward these troops. It is possible to hold the position that in light of this "fait accompli," to demand the withdrawal of Soviet troops would now serve the interests of the reactionaries and of imperialism. We, for our part, maintain just the opposite.

A prolonged presence of Soviet troops in Afghanistan can only fuel the following tendencies:

a) *The tendency that the Afghan rebellion will increase in strength and popularity, profiting from the national Afghan resentment against Soviet intervention and from imperialist support using this intervention as a pretext.* The Kremlin is in the process of getting bogged down in a war that it will never be able to finish, inasmuch as it is completely illusory to try to wipe out guerrilla forces in a mountainous country when they have in addition two bases of support at their disposal—Pakistan and Iran. The logic of such a "counterinsurgency" operation is permanent enlargement of the combat zone and incursion into the territories serving as bases of support for the guerrillas.

b) *The reactionary, anti-communist tendency of the Islamic movement throughout the Muslim world.* Reactionaries in the Muslim countries have now seized upon the Soviet intervention in Afghanistan to orchestrate an uproar against "atheistic communism," which is presented as the kind of regime the Soviet Union wants to impose by force on the Muslim peoples. Washington and its allies are counting on the Afghanistan affair to reverse the dominant anti-Western orientation imprinted on the Islamic movement by the affair of the American hostages in Tehran. In addition, this campaign can have repercussions inside the Soviet

Union itself, where bureaucratic oppression of the nationalities creates ideal conditions for this.

c) *The imperialists' justification for their resumption of the arms race, under the pretext that the Soviet Union is demonstrating in Afghanistan that it intends to use force to impose regimes loyal to it.* The Afghanistan affair has already made a shambles of the efforts of the workers' movement in the imperialist countries against the step-up of the nuclear arsenal in Western Europe. It helps dissipate the paralyzing effects of the Vietnam War on the capacities of American imperialism to carry out foreign military intervention. It also contributes to disorienting the antibureaucratic opposition in the workers states.

In this context, it is imperative that the Soviet troops withdraw from Afghanistan immediately and that the Kremlin recognize the right of self-determination of the people of this country, thus repairing the damage caused by its intervention to the process of permanent revolution in Afghanistan and in the entire region. The possibility of the Muslim rebels taking power in Kabul—which is in no way inevitable—is, on the whole, much less harmful to world revolution than a prolonged war by the Soviet Union in Afghanistan. [...]

January 27, 1980; first published in English in *Intercontinental Press*, vol. 18, no. 8, (March 3, 1980).

## CHAPTER FIVE

# Afghanistan: Balance Sheet of a War

*This balance sheet of the war was written in 1987 as the process began that would lead to the withdrawal of Soviet troops from May 1988 onward. It is an analytical retrospective of the Afghan tragedy, confirming the hypotheses I had put forward seven years earlier. The following analysis is still relevant:* mutatis mutandis, *replacing the words* Soviet forces *with the words* U.S. and allied forces *many ingredients of the Afghan situation today are recognizable in this picture.*

The latest session of the "indirect" negotiations between the Afghan and Pakistani governments, held under the aegis of the United Nations, concluded on March 10, 1987, in Geneva without reaching an agreement. The first session was held in June 1982. These negotiations enabled the Kabul and Islamabad governments to come to an understanding in June 1985 on the principal conditions for settling their conflict over the Afghan question.

They were the following: reciprocal noninterference, guaranteed by the United States and the USSR; return of those refugees who wish to return; and phased withdrawal of the Soviet troops. Since then, the stumbling block in the negotiations has been the timetable for the Soviet withdrawal.

Under pressure from Washington, the Pakistani government has held firmly to the demand for a rapid withdrawal, not exceeding six months. The Soviet government has considerably softened its position, speaking through its Afghan allies. While Kabul initially proposed a withdrawal of the Soviet troops over four years, they are now proposing a timetable of only eighteen months. That is, the USSR considers that it still needs eighteen months to assure that the regime it set up in Kabul will not collapse on the departure of its troops. Today, it is eighty-seven months since the troops were sent in.

Massive intervention of Soviet troops in Afghanistan began on December 24, 1979. First of all, on December 27, some 5,000 men took care of overthrowing Hafizullah Amin. Then, a few days later, "on the request of the Afghan government" of Babrak Karmal, their stooge, the Kremlin leaders boosted the numbers of their intervention army to 80,000.

Today, over seven years later, the Soviet army is still there and includes more than 100,000 soldiers. While Gorbachev seems genuinely anxious to disengage from Afghanistan, this is far from the simplest of the problems that Leonid Brezhnev bequeathed to him. If Brezhnev's commitment to withdraw the Soviet forces from Afghanistan "as soon as the causes that brought them there have disappeared" is to be kept, then such a withdrawal is not right around the corner, nor even around the next bend in the road.

In fact, today, after seven years of Soviet intervention, the regime installed in Kabul and run by the People's Democratic Party of Afghanistan (PDPA) is as weak, if not weaker, than it was before the Soviet troops came in —from the military standpoint in particular. The rebel forces, on the other hand, are far stronger than they were in 1979 even if they seem to have marked time for two years. Moreover, the support of U.S. imperialism and its allies for the mujahedin is out of all proportion to what it was before, and there is no indication that it is going to be scaled down or ended.

Whatever gains may have been scored by the Kabul government and its Soviet protectors over recent months, the fact remains that for the seven years that have gone by since December 1979 the balance sheet of the intervention of Soviet troops shows an appalling bankruptcy. "The causes that brought them here" have been aggravated by their presence, so that Afghanistan has become a real quagmire for the USSR—to the great satisfaction of the American imperialists still traumatized by their Indochina experience.

## PUTSCH OR REVOLUTION?

[...] Afghanistan shares with North Yemen the peculiarity of having been the only Islamic country to enjoy a real measure of independence before World War II. It was an independence that bordered on autarky; and the concomitant of that was preserving an archaic society that stood out as a medieval island in a rapidly changing world. A visit to these two countries in the early 1960s was like a trip in a time machine.

The Bolshevik revolution found itself confronting similar societies in Central Asia and on the borders of the former czarist empire. There was a

great temptation to export the revolution, disregarding the extreme imma-
turity of the sociopolitical conditions. That was what Bukharin wanted to
do in his ultra-left period in 1919, inspired by the example of Bashkiria,
where the nationalists had done an about-face and gone over completely
from an alliance with the Whites to an alliance with the Reds. This success
contrasted with the difficulties encountered by the revolutionary troops
with the Uzbeks (the defeat of the Red Army at Bukhara in 1918) and in
the Muslim territories in the Caucasus. Ultra-leftists and Great Russian
chauvinists joined together on the Bolshevik side to call for forcible sovi-
etization of these territories, against the will of the majority of their inhabitants. Bukharin justified these designs by reserving the right of
self-determination to those nations struggling against imperialism. Lenin
rebelled against this cynicism:

> We cannot deny [recognition] to a single one of the peoples living within the
> boundaries of the former Russian Empire. Let us even assume that the Bashkirs
> have overthrown the exploiters and we have helped them to do so. This is possi-
> ble only when a revolution has fully matured, and it must be done cautiously, so
> as not to retard by one's interference the very process of the differentiation of the
> proletariat which we ought to expedite. What, then, can we do in relation to such
> peoples as the Kirghiz, the Uzbeks, the Tadjiks, the Turkmen, who to this day are
> under the influence of their mullahs?... Can we approach and tell them that we
> shall overthrow their exploiters? We cannot do this, because they are entirely sub-
> ordinated to their mullahs. In such cases we have to wait until the given nation
> develops, until the differentiation of the proletariat from the bourgeois elements,
> which is inevitable, has taken place.[1]

However, in the event, it was not Lenin's point of view that prevailed but
Bukharin's—mainly because of the momentum of the war against the
White armies and their imperialist allies. Thus, all the Muslim territories of
the former czarist empire were re-annexed by the Soviet state. Lenin's
warnings also proved correct: the Bashkirs soon rebelled against the new
representatives of the Great Russian state, and joined the *basmachis* (ban-
dits) and other mujahedin of the time, who made life difficult for the Soviet
Republic up until the advent of the Stalinist terror at the end of the 1920s.
Today, seventy years after the October Revolution, the Sufi mystical broth-
erhoods have more native members in the Muslim regions of the USSR
than the Communist Party.[2]

Lenin's concern not to violate the natural course of history was not limited to the problem of exporting the revolution. Any seizure of power carried out without the active support of a decisive section, if not the majority, of the toiling population can only be a putsch, whatever measures its organizers may later take. Such a regime would bear the marks of that until it was overthrown, either by an authentic revolution or by reaction. Logically, the more the ambitions of the putschists involve transformations of their society, for which it has not been prepared, the more their government is doomed to fail or to resort to external aid.

We already had the example of the palely republican and Nasserite putsch by Sallal in North Yemen in September 1962. This government could not maintain itself even for a few years against the tribal-monarchist reaction supported by neighboring Saudi Arabia without the massive intervention of the Egyptian army.

The history of Afghanistan itself offers an illustration of the inevitable failure of transformations "from above" in societies with little predisposition to change. King Amanullah, who succeeded his father to the throne in 1919, was an admirer of the Turkish dictator Mustafa Kemal and signatory of the first Soviet-Afghan friendship treaty. He was, as one historian put it, "to try to place his country at one stroke in the ranks of the civilized states." He was forced to abdicate, however, in 1929, after five years of warfare against a widespread Islamic, conservative tribal rebellion supported by the British.

The seizure of power in Kabul in April 1978 by the faction of the PDPA that is known by the name of its publication, *Khalq* (The People), and led by Taraki and Amin was even more certainly doomed to isolation. Equipped with a "socialist-oriented revolutionary program," the PDPA-Khalq had made its putschism into a theory. According to Taraki-Amin, "In developing nations, since the working class is not developed to the point of forming a government there is another source that can overthrow the oppressor feudal government, and it was constituted by the armed forces in Afghanistan."[3] In essence this amounted to a so-called revolution by means of the ruling class's own army, along the lines of what Ethiopia went through shortly before Afghanistan.

This sort of putschist government with radical social ambitions inevitably led to institute a regime of terror. Its putschist origins reveal themselves even in literacy campaigns and agrarian reform. In Afghanistan these campaigns were undertaken in the worst possible ways, those most apt to provoke the hostility of the broad masses, instead of arousing their enthusiasm.[4]

In this regard, it is instructive to compare the putschist methods of the PDPA-Khalq with the revolutionary democratic methods of the government that emerged from the revolution in South Yemen in 1969. Whereas in Afghanistan the agrarian reform —to cite only this example—was decreed from above and applied by military force, often against the will of those who were supposed to benefit from it, in South Yemen the leaders of the National Liberation Front were careful not to try to substitute themselves for the peasants and fishermen, and to arm them politically and materially to take control of their own means of production.

Whatever the later bureaucratic degeneration of the South Yemeni regime, the fact remains that it was able to overcome social and ideological resistance comparable to that existing in Afghanistan with infinitely more success and despite a much more hostile environment.

Only twenty months after the seizure of power by the PDPA-Khalq, the rebellion of reactionary Islamic tribal forces was becoming so widespread that the survival of the Kabul regime seemed doubtful. Accused of adventurism and ultra-leftism for trying to skip "the stage of the national democratic revolution," Amin did not bow to the Kremlin. Called on to put some (holy) water in his wine and broaden his government to include other forces, starting with the moderate, reformist wing of the PDPA, the *Parcham* (Flag) faction, which had been pushed out by the Khalq, Amin instead completed the concentration of power in his hands. In September 1979, he eliminated his old companion Taraki, who was inclined to follow Big Brother's advice. Two months later, Big Brother intervened massively, overthrowing Amin—who was killed—to replace him with the chief of the Parcham faction, Babrak Karmal.

## SOVIET INTERVENTION

"It was not easy for us to take the decision to send Soviet troops to Afghanistan," Brezhnev told *Pravda* in January 1980. There was no reason not to believe him, although some inveterate anti-Soviet commentators saw the intervention in Afghanistan as a striking demonstration of "Russian expansionism," which, according to them, only changed its flag in 1917. To take these people at their word, the Soviet operation was part of a vast expansionist offensive—marked by Angolan, Ethiopian, and other Soviet or Cuban military involvements—and in this case was heading for "warm water ports." According to these completely outmoded strategic criteria, the

Soviet invasion of Afghanistan was only a first step that was to be followed by an invasion of Iran or Pakistan.

In fact, as was well understood by those who do not look on the USSR as Ronald Reagan's "evil empire," the intervention in Afghanistan was essentially a conservative, defensive reaction on the part of the Soviet bureaucracy. To make this intervention understandable, it has to be placed in its real historic and political context.

Since 1919, Afghanistan had maintained good-neighbor relations with the USSR, which accorded a considerable importance to this. Had it chosen to act as a rear base for the Muslims fighting against the Soviet state, the Afghan kingdom—whose independence came from its position as a buffer state between British India and the USSR—could have caused the Soviet regime a lot of trouble.

Historical, religious, and ethnic factors predisposed it to play such a role. After his defeat at the hands of the Reds, the emir of Bukhara took refuge in Kabul in 1920. A number of his *basmachi* supporters and other anti-Bolsheviks had also crossed the long Soviet-Afghan border.

Amanullah's kingdom could have played the same sort of role toward the USSR that Zia ul-Haq's Pakistan is playing today toward Afghanistan. But it would also have been forced to give up its autonomy from the British, its ancestral enemies. It did not do that. It disarmed the *basmachis* on its territory, extracting a juicy quid pro quo from the USSR.

After World War II, Afghanistan became, in a way, the Middle Eastern equivalent of Finland in regard to its relationship with the USSR. The latter was by far its main source of economic, cultural, and also military foreign aid. The Afghan monarchy was equipped with Soviet arms, and the majority of its officers were trained in the USSR.

Afghanistan's dependence on its big neighbor was, of course, qualitatively increased after the PDPA came to power. This was owing to ideological affinities, naturally, but also to the fragility of the new government, which was going to avail itself of direct Soviet military support well before December 1979.The growing isolation of the Khalq regime involved the risk that for the first time in sixty years a government openly hostile to the USSR would be installed in Afghanistan—a government dominated by forces which included some that had accused King Zaher Shah, who was deposed in 1973 by his "republican" cousin, Prince Daud, and later Daud also, of infidelity to Islam and bowing the knee to Moscow.

If you add to this picture the victory of the "Islamic Revolution" in Iran in February 1979, it is understandable how great a fear gripped the Kremlin leaders at the time and impelled them to intervene in Afghanistan before, in their estimation, it was too late. The "Islamic Revolution" had proclaimed its profound hostility to "atheistic communism" and its determination to carry Islamic fundamentalist agitation to all areas, including the Soviet Muslim peoples, who total 50 million, or nearly 20 percent of the total population of the USSR. In their majority, the latter still identify with Islam, and in their conflict with the Great Russian chauvinism of the bureaucracy they do not even have the consolation of being Slavs.

In ordering intervention, Brezhnev and his cohorts were in no way moved by a desire to "structurally assimilate" Afghanistan (according to the term that some use to explain the social transformation of Eastern Europe after 1945). Still less could an analogy be made between their intervention and that of the Red Army in Outer Mongolia in 1921, which genuinely liberated the country from the domination of the Chinese and the debris of the Siberian White army, and established a revolutionary government that, from the start, demonstrated a certain political tact in directing the transformation of the country.

The idea that Moscow, through "structural assimilation," could go further than Amin had would imply that the Kremlin had an "ultra-left" interpretation of why Amin failed. But all the Soviet statements pointed in the other direction. Indeed, the Kremlin saw its intervention rather as an extension of the intervention by Hanoi's army against Pol Pot's regime in 1979. It expected that in overthrowing Amin its troops would be greeted by the Afghan population with at least the benevolent neutrality that greeted the Vietnamese troops in Kampuchea. Moscow intended to bring the Afghan regime to a moderate course of collaborating with the most retrograde social forces, so long as they were well disposed to the USSR. It thought that in this way it could cut the ground out from under the Islamic fundamentalists and other reactionary fanatics. To perfect this operation, the Kremlin took care at the beginning to use forces made up of soldiers from the Soviet Muslim republics that belonged to ethnic components of the Afghan mosaic, so as to facilitate fraternization with the local population.

How great then was the disillusion of the Kremlin bureaucrats when they saw, from the first weeks, that the massive intervention of their soldiers had produced a result contrary to what they were counting on. Not only were the Soviet troops not greeted as liberators, but Amin himself, who was liquidated in the course of the intervention, suddenly emerged as a martyr of national independence, while Karmal was more isolated than his predecessor had ever been. The institutions of the PDPA regime broke down, beginning with the army. The reactionary and Islamic fundamentalist forces experienced a massive influx of volunteers and a sudden growth of their popularity, so that while it had been doubtful that the Khalq regime could survive on its own, it was quite unthinkable from the outset that the Parcham regime could.

Moreover, the international commotion against the Soviet intervention was much greater than Moscow had expected, especially among Islamic and other nonaligned countries. This was reflected by majority disapproval in the UN. There was a similar outcry from many Communist parties.

As for the supreme objective of the intervention, that is, preserving the Muslim republics of the USSR against the danger of nationalist and Islamic contamination, the failure was glaring. Barely a month after the start of the intervention, Moscow withdrew soldiers coming from those republics, to replace them with Russians. Fraternization with the Afghan population was no longer an objective but a risk to be avoided, since the latter were almost unanimously hostile to the Russians. The Soviet troops had quickly to be put in quarantine, if only to protect them against the numerous terrorist attacks.

The Soviet-Afghan frontier became more permeable than ever to Islamic, anti-Communist, and anti-Russian propaganda. In recent years, several studies have been devoted to the expansion of Islamic fundamentalism and Islamic nationalism in the USSR. They all agree in recognizing the breadth of the phenomenon, which is reflected, moreover, by an accelerated development of government counter-propaganda and all sorts of measures aimed at holding back the development of Islamic nationalistic moods, such as mixing populations (in other words, still more Russification!). If there were still any skeptics left, the anti-Russian riots of December 1986 in Kazakhstan—despite its being the most Russified of the Soviet "Muslim" republics ethnically and culturally—provided a demonstration of the gravity of the situation.

On Afghan soil, Soviet troops were supposed to put an end to the tyranny of Amin and inaugurate an era of liberty. There is no reason to doubt the sincerity of this objective. The Karmal government's first measure was to declare a general amnesty and to release thousands of prisoners. But these troops were drawn by the same logic of a minority regime as described above to act like an army of occupation. The Parcham regime, still less legitimate in the eyes of the population than the Khalq government had been, could only put its "good intentions" into practice for a minority of the population concentrated in the cities and their immediate surroundings—

the "useful part of the country," which the Soviet army could control and where it sought to concentrate the largest possible number of inhabitants through forced settlement. For most of the rural areas coming outside the direct control of the Soviet and governmental forces, what the Soviet army sought to do was to neutralize them by patrolling the main arteries of communications and isolating them from the mujahedin's Pakistani and Iranian sanctuaries. Those regions constituting the mujahedin's main bastions, or their main transit zones, were deliberately depopulated by Soviet bombing and the massive destruction it caused. The result—besides the mass slaughter inherent in this sort of warfare—was that nearly a quarter of the Afghan population was forced to take refuge in Pakistan and Iran, creating an impressive reserve army for the mujahedin.[5]

"Mass slaughter" is an appropriate phrase.[6] To characterize the Afghan war as genocide, as has been done by certain press seeking to prove that Communism and Nazism are twins, amounts to belittling the term that was coined in 1944 to describe an operation of systematic extermination, which bears no comparison to what is happening in Afghanistan today. Despite its cruelty and its many and inevitable similarities with the U.S. war in Indochina—forced urbanization and desertification, for example—the Soviet intervention is still clearly less murderous and destructive than the latter was, even in relative terms. Pointing up these differences does not mean absolving the Soviet bureaucracy of its crimes. It means simply refusing to treat the crimes of Nazism and U.S. imperialism as something commonplace.

### THE PARCHAM REGIME AND GORBACHEV'S STRATEGY

The paradox of the Soviet intervention is that the cruelty of the military campaign it has waged is not associated with forced collectivization, combined with a ferocious campaign against religion, as was the case at the high point of the Stalin terror in the USSR. On the contrary, the Kremlin leaders and their Afghan stooges have remained faithful to their initial objective, which was to undo what Amin had set out to do in that respect. Hardly had Karmal been installed in government before he began stressing his government's determination to assure "a genuine respect for the holy religion, Islam, for the clergy, the noble national traditions and customs, the bases of family life and of personal property."[7]

In February 1980, the new regime freed the bazaar merchants from state control. And it has not ceased since then to shower boons on private entrepreneurs. Amin's cherished agrarian reform has been annulled since 1980, even in those rural areas controlled by Kabul (except, of course, for the lands of landowners liquidated by the Khalq or who have fled the country). Some big landlords, moreover, have rallied to the side of the new regime.

The status of women has returned virtually to what it was before Amin, except for a minority of urban women. The government boasts that it has built, with public money, more than one hundred mosques in six years. It is paying fat salaries to collaborationist clerics, and has reintroduced religious teaching into the schools (three hours a week) and established a daily religious program on the radio. Its attempts to outbid the Islamic fundamentalists in pious works sometimes border on the grotesque.[8]

Rather than committing itself to transforming Afghan society, the new regime, acting as a proxy for Moscow, is literally trying to buy it. It has been trying to do this not only by stepping up its spending on development in all areas, but also by the more unpretentious practice of bribing clan or tribal chiefs. The latter then, with their arms and their villages, leave the ranks of the mujahedin and pledge fealty to the central power, while maintaining their local autonomy. Thus, the so-called Guardians of the Revolution militias in Afghanistan have more in common with the armed tribes of the Arabian Peninsula than with the militias of Cuba or even South Yemen. Kabul is trying to beat the mujahedin on their own ground.

Finally, the Parcham regime has practiced an adept nationalities policy, promoting the specific cultures of the various Afghan ethnic groups. This has had the effect of counteracting the unifying role of Islam among the mujahedin. It has given special attention to the Pushtun, the main ethnical group in Afghanistan, and Baluchis. Since these two peoples also inhabit Pakistani regions bordering on Afghanistan, the objective is also to whip up their opposition to the Punjabi regime of Zia ul-Haq, in order to put pressure on him, and in order to divide these populations from the mujahedin who control the Afghan refugees massed on their territories.[9]

The Parcham regime's tribal policy and its nationalities policy, which are combined, have proven to be by far its most effective weapons. They include a good dose of "special" actions and are directed by the Afghan political police, the Khad, headed by none other than Najibullah, who succeeded Karmal at the helm of the party in May 1986. It was natural therefore for the Khad to be the spearhead of the new strategy that the Kremlin has adopted under Gorbachev, for whom the withdrawal from Afghanistan is a priority.

This strategy has two sides to it. One is "Afghanization" of the war, through broadening the Kabul government's social base and building up its own military force. The other side is the neutralization of Pakistan, in order to end that country's role as the main rear base for the mujahedin. Progress toward these two objectives is to be accompanied by proposals for a settlement formulated from the position of strength, but not failing to include important concessions, so as to keep the ball in the opponents' court and provoke some defections.

The implementation of Gorbachev's strategy started in 1985, and accelerated in the fall of the same year. In the best traditions of the Afghan monarchy, an assembly of notables (a *loya jirga*)—tribal chiefs, mullahs, and other "personalities"—was convoked. Then in September, 3,700 delegates attended an assembly of Pushtun tribal and clan chiefs. They included several hundred from Pushtun areas in Pakistan. This did not fail to prompt Islamabad immediately to order military deployments aimed at having a sobering effect on the tribes concerned and to offer enticing counterproposals. In November Karmal presented "ten theses" confirming this new course of political ecumenism. A system of local elections was instituted, in order to give posts to notables who were not members of the PDPA, including mullahs. The "Revolutionary Council" and Council of Ministers were broadened to include some notables and mullahs.

Najibullah's appointment in May 1986, which was clearly dictated by Moscow, inaugurated a new phase in this strategy. Karmal had been too discredited since December 1979. His "aristocratic" origins made him even more unpopular. As for the number two man in the regime, Kishtmand, he belonged to a Shiite ethnic minority of Mongol origin, the Hazaras, who are despised by the other Afghan ethnic groups (and even by the Persian Shiites). So Najibullah, the number three, was the man for the job. Along with the know-how he demonstrated as the head of the Khad, he had one of the best Pushtun genealogies for the new course.

Najibullah's first actions and declarations were devoted to reinforcing the regime's armed forces, the primordial element in Gorbachev's Afghan strategy. Then in December, from Moscow where he had met with the new Soviet party chief, Najibullah, whom the new ecumenism had made a preacher of "national reconciliation," proposed the "formation of a government of national unity into which can come forces that have been temporarily outside the frontiers of the country." This clearly meant mujahedin leaders and partisans of the ex-king (if not the king himself) who would agree to turn their coats.

In January 1987, the Soviet-Afghan offensive culminated in anticipation of a new round of negotiations between Kabul and Islamabad under the aegis of the United Nations, planned for February in Geneva. The proposals formulated in Moscow were confirmed in Kabul: the Revolutionary Council declared a renewable six-month unilateral ceasefire starting on January 15 and a general amnesty. Najibullah called on "all the belligerent parties to cease fire and begin a process of national renewal."

At the same time, the pressure on Pakistan reached its peak. Zia ul-Haq's government was already annoyed by Kabul's agitation aimed at the Pushtun and Baluchis on its territory. It should not be forgotten that Pakistan is a multinational state, separated from India solely on the basis of its inhabitants' adherence to Islam, and that it already experienced the breakaway of one national group in 1971, with the secession of Bangladesh. Now, it faces a veritable "Lebanonization" of the country.[10]

All the ingredients of the Lebanese situation have been assembled today in Pakistan. There are ethnic antagonisms (in Lebanon they are confessional) and a large mass of refugees (three million Afghans) under the control of autonomous armed organizations. These armed groups are well financed. And they support a gigantic black market in arms of all sorts, where the local ethnic groups do not fail to supply themselves. As in Lebanon, this situation of relative anarchy has opened the way for a spectacular growth of drug production and traffic. Moreover, as in south Lebanon, the areas where refugees are concentrated are more and more becoming targets for reprisals, in this case by the Soviet-Afghan forces against the mujahedin. All these problems are being aggravated by the actions of the Khad, in particular bombs planted at carefully selected spots, so that in the Peshawar region the resentment of the refugees on the part of the local people is beginning to assume Lebanese forms. In that area, clashes erupted not long ago between the two communities. In November, a *jirga* of the Pushtun tribes in the Pakistani provinces bordering on Afghanistan warned Islamabad and the mujahedin to reach a settlement with Kabul, or else these tribes would take it on themselves to make sure that no military actions were carried out from their territories.

Zia ul-Haq's regime for some time has been hard pressed by the opposition parties. They have been very active since the return in April 1986 of Benazir Bhutto, the daughter of the former Pakistani premier who was overthrown and executed by the present regime. On top of this, in December, Islamabad had to face bloody clashes in Karachi between Pushtun and

Muhajirs (Urdu-speaking Muslims who left India after the partition of 1947). These riots, the worst in forty years, are another aspect of the Lebanonization of Pakistan.

Thus, a regime in a precarious situation at home finds itself caught internationally between the Soviet-Afghan hammer and the Indian anvil, the latter far from being the least of its worries. In January, the Indian army, without bothering to give notice to Islamabad, opened up large-scale mechanized military maneuvers in the regions bordering Pakistan. This was followed by an explosive rise of tensions between the two states, which was reflected in the concentration of nearly a million soldiers on both sides of the border. It took five days of intensive negotiations between the two governments before an agreement was reached on February 4 providing for a limited disengagement "within 15 days." A broader agreement was put off, pending new discussions, which were to take place at the end of the month. Chance can account for many things. But in this case, it is evident that Moscow was not uninvolved in the behavior of its traditional ally, India, in particular since the Indian threat is hanging over Zia ul-Haq's head like the sword of Damocles at the very moment that the negotiations are going on in Geneva.

Thus, Islamabad faces a formidable combination of domestic and external pressures. In Moscow's eyes, they make Pakistan the weak link of the chain that has to be broken in order that it can cast off its Afghan ball. From this position of relative strength, the Soviet bureaucracy can afford to emit a stream of soothing statements, which were recently echoed by Henry Kissinger in person: "I had arrived in Moscow persuaded that the Soviet Union would never permit the overthrow of a regime established by Soviet power . . . I am no longer so sure." [11]

In reality, the former U.S. secretary of state is rushing to conclusions. Nothing indicates that Moscow is ready to accept a debacle involving its Afghan allies comparable to that which befell Kissinger's Vietnamese allies in 1975. The proximity of Afghanistan to the USSR and the potential source of contagion it could represent are out of all proportion to what Vietnam meant for the United States.

The minimum relationship that Moscow can accept with Afghanistan is one of the Finnish type. Within these well-defined limits, the Kremlin is ready to contemplate any sort of sociopolitical compromise, even a return of former king Zaher Shah from his exile in Rome, if he agrees to play the game. But Moscow could not accept an overthrow of the Kabul regime, since only the mujahedin, its sworn enemies, could accomplish that. It is only because they consider that they are on the brink of removing this danger that the Kremlin and its protégés are showing flexibility.

## THE MUJAHEDIN AND THEIR SPONSORS

If it depended only on him, Zia ul-Haq would probably give in without further delay. But it does not. He has to take account, first of all, of the U.S. attitude. Islamabad is Washington's protégé. As the kingpin, owing to its geopolitical position, in the imperialist strategic deployment in western Asia, Pakistan has seen its importance grow considerably in the eyes of the U.S. government since 1979.

Thus, Zia ul-Haq's regime unquestionably benefited from the Afghan crisis before it turned into a source of worry for him. It enabled him to overcome the tensions in his relations with the West created by his Islamic repressive excesses and his determination to equip himself with nuclear weapons—the celebrated "Islamic bomb," which has made news again recently—and to get a very large increase in U.S. economic and military aid. In seven years, U.S. aid came to nearly $4 billion. To this has to be added, moreover, another $4 billion in supplementary aid spread out over the next six years. And this does not count the U.S. army's enormous direct military investments (bases and equipment) in Pakistan, or the economic benefits derived indirectly or directly (in part, through diversion) from international aid to the mujahedin.

Islamabad, therefore, is dependent on Washington economically and militarily. For the Reagan administration, it is out of the question for its Pakistani ally to yield to Moscow. In response to the signs of weakness shown by Islamabad since 1985, Washington stepped up its pressure to make sure that Pakistan took a firm stance in the Geneva negotiations. At the same time, it increased its promises of support. Zia ul-Haq has made his attitude a bargaining card since 1979. On the other hand, the Reagan administration is also considerably stepping up its support, both quantitatively and qualitatively, to the mujahedin, especially to those factions opposed to any compromise with Kabul.

From a few tens of millions of dollars a year up to 1983–84, "covert aid" (provided by the CIA) to the "freedom fighters," as the U.S. establishment calls them, rose to $280 million in 1984–85, leaped to $470 million in 1985–86, and, according to the figures commonly cited in the U.S. press, will exceed $600 million in the present fiscal year. This U.S. financing is linked with that of the Saudi monarchy, which is recycling a part of its petrodollars into subsidies for the world anti-Communist jihad orchestrated by Washington. This has been revealed again recently by the Contragate affair in the United States. Along with this, there are all sorts of other aid, including from Iran, and the major profits that the mujahedin derives from all of the traffic in which they are involved.

Washington has, moreover, taken steps toward more official support for the Afghan rebels. The reception of their representatives in the White House in June 1986 was preceded by the decision of the U.S. administration in March to supply them with portable antiaircraft missiles of American and British makes (respectively, Stingers and Blowpipes).

Does this mean that the U.S. administration is hardly worried by the internal problems facing its Pakistani ally? By no means. What Washington is looking for in reality is not all-out war—although seeing the Soviets bogged down in Afghanistan could only please them, were it not for its own ally's precarious health. Rather, what it wants is a chance to trade a solution to the Afghan crisis acceptable to Moscow for a major Soviet concession in Central America. In other words, the U.S. administration wants to keep Zia ul-Haq from giving away the Afghan card, in which it has invested considerable sums of money. Facing the weakening of Pakistan and the recent military and political successes scored by the Soviet strategy in Afghanistan, it wants to shore up its allies in order to keep the stakes high.

In any case, for Washington the mujahedin cannot be more than "disposable" pawns. That is the reason for the ambiguity of its attitude. While it has called for firmness on the ground, and it has the means for that, it has given its approval to the negotiations in Geneva. And it has refused to close its embassy in Kabul and give the mujahedin the diplomatic recognition that they are demanding. In Washington's eyes the point of the mujahedin's struggle is not so much victory as better terms for its global negotiations with Moscow. The U.S. administration is accordingly refusing to tie its hands politically on Afghanistan.

The attitude of Iran, the mujahedin's other major supporter and base of operations, is more radical, but its motives are similar to that of the United States. Tehran too seeks to use the Afghan card in its own interests, which are focused today on its war with Iraq. Khomeini's regime would like to convince Moscow to reduce or even suspend its arms supplies to Baghdad, without which Saddam Hussein's regime could not keep going. To this end, Tehran is trying to outbid Islamabad and Washington. It rejected the Geneva negotiations, proposing instead a conference of the USSR, Pakistan, Iran, of course, and the mujahedin, without the participation of the Kabul government, which Tehran refuses to recognize even indirectly. Thus, the Khomeini regime is trying to get in place to succeed Pakistan as the Mujahedin's main handler, if Zia ul-Haq should choose to drop them.

This perspective is not very appealing for the organizations based in Peshawar, which represent the great majority of the forces waging armed struggle against the Kabul regime and the Soviet troops. These organizations (the major ones are in the Islamic Alliance of the Afghan Mujahedin) recruit their members from the Sunni ethnic groups that make up the majority (more than 80 percent) of the Afghan population. Nonetheless, it is not so much this religious difference that is the problem as it is political and financial considerations. The Khomeini regime has not hidden its ambition to dominate all or part of Afghanistan.[12] It already plays a dominant role in its relations with the Shiite organizations in the Hazarajat. It is trying unsuccessfully to establish similar relations with some of the groups in Peshawar, in particular the most fanatical of them, Hekmatyar's Hezb-i-Islami, demanding that they break with the Saudi monarchy, which after the United States is the mujahedin's biggest source of funds (and also of Saddam Hussein's Iraq!).

However, the Peshawar Alliance organizations are not only anxious to maintain the relative political autonomy that Pakistan has allowed up till now but above all are anxious to keep getting manna from Saudi Arabia. Some of them, especially the "moderates" (that is, the traditionalists) would prefer a compromise with Kabul and Moscow to domination from Tehran, which would mean being wiped out. In that respect, the "moderates" are the weak links in the Alliance, capable of yielding to Pakistani pressure in the event of an agreement between Islamabad and Kabul-Moscow. Najibullah's offers of reconciliation have been directed especially to them.

So the Islamic fundamentalists, the hawks in the Peshawar Alliance, had to react before it was too late. They opposed any suggestion of a move toward coexistence with the Kabul regime, no matter how democratic the suggestion might be. That includes the idea of having UN forces supervise free elections in the country. This idea was advanced by some of the Peshawar groups, but Hekmatyar explicitly rejected it in a statement released on January 14, 1987. The fundamentalists managed to impose their point of view, getting the Alliance to adopt counterproposals designed to block the Soviet-Afghan political offensive. These counterproposals were made public on January 17. They turn on two axes. One is programmatic, concerning the future of Afghanistan as the mujahedin see it. The other consists of transitional measures designed to prepare the Alliance to play the role to which it aspires.[13]

On the basis of rejecting any dialogue with the "puppet regime," the Alliance demands a "total, unconditional and immediate withdrawal of Russian forces." It calls for armed struggle not only to this end but also for "the establishment of an Islamic order." Thus, the Alliance confirmed that it is not simply waging a nationalist struggle, but also—inseparably—a struggle for an eminently reactionary and totalitarian sociopolitical objective. The model for that, depending on the groups, comes somewhere between the Iranian example and the Saudi or Pakistani one.

Reading the scenario projected by the Alliance is instructive in this regard: 1) "An interim government of the mujahedin takes power." 2) It supervises "free and honest [sic] elections, which will lead to an Islamic government and parliament." 3) A "constitution for the Islamic state" will be drawn up that will "guarantee the application of Islam in all individual actions and in the life of our nation."

The transitional measures concern the creation of two bodies: 1) "juridical delegations" (guided by Islamic law, the Sharia) "responsible for arbitrating between individuals and armed groups of mujahedin in order to smooth out their differences and issue *fatwas* [verdicts] based on the Sharia"; 2) a commission charged with drawing up rules and procedures for "establishing an interim government." This commission was to begin work on February 1, 1987, and complete it at the end of the same month. Since that time, nothing has transpired in this respect.

Clearly, the Alliance is closing the door to the offers from Kabul and Moscow and trying to acquire the political credibility that it has lacked up until now. First of all, it is seeking to accomplish this by trying to settle the innumerable differences that have led the mujahedin to fight one another almost as much as they have fought their common enemies. The attempt at a settlement relies on religious tribunals, since Islam is the only common denominator of a heterogeneous alliance. However, while such arbitration can be effective in disputes relating to petty theft and other divisions of the booty, it is highly dubious that it could end the struggle for dominance among the gangs, or the tribal wrangles, which are a tradition that antedates even Islam.

The Alliance proposed, subsequently, to set up a government in exile, which would be the only body empowered to represent the mujahedin. This is a means, especially for the Peshawar hawks, not only to achieve the unity advocated by their American and Saudi patrons, but also to put the latter on the spot by creating a political fact conceived of as irreversible. Diplomatic recognition of this government in exile would then be demanded from the allied governments.

In other words, while Washington demands that the mujahedin close ranks in order to be in the best position to go into negotiations, the Alliance today is proposing to close ranks around an intransigent attitude excluding all negotiations. Washington may find an advantage in this stiffening of the Alliance, inasmuch as it enables them to up the ante to Moscow. On the other hand, there is no doubt that the U.S. administration, as well as its Pakistani ally, would be annoyed if the "interim government" operation came off. Nonetheless, the heterogeneity of the Alliance is such that the risk remains very limited.

## TOWARD SOVIET DISENGAGEMENT

The big advantage that Moscow and its protégés in Kabul have in the Afghan conflict is that they are pursuing a single strategy, decided on in the Kremlin, against an enemy "camp" comprising forces with motives as disparate as those of the various groups of mujahedin and the U.S., Pakistani, and Iranian governments.

The Soviet bureaucracy is undeniably anxious to extricate itself from the quagmire that Afghanistan has become. But it is trying to accomplish this without making any accounting to Washington. Operating in its own traditional sphere of influence, Moscow wants to prevent the U.S. administration from playing the Afghan card. If Moscow's pressures on Pakistan, which are today at a peak, do not succeed in forcing the hand of Zia ul-Haq's government because of countervailing U.S. pressures, it is not out of the question that Moscow will try to pursue its strategy of disengagement all the way without an agreement.

Gorbachev's USSR could then manage with a tacit agreement with a Pakistani government at the end of its tether; or it could keep up the pressure on Pakistan until the country broke apart. It could then progressively withdraw the bulk of its infantry and tanks, which it is using less and less, and keep a military force in Afghanistan quantitatively closer to what was there before December 1979 (5,000 military "advisers") than to the massive military presence it has had in recent years. On the other hand, this reduced force would be composed of elite airborne units (paratroopers) that have proven their effectiveness against the mujahedin. These units have the advantage of being highly mobile and therefore can be used intensively.

The USSR would not even have to send in its air force. It has trained enough Afghan pilots to fly the planes it has given the Kabul air force, which are sufficient to carry out the sort of bombing missions that would be required. The shipments of portable antiaircraft missiles to the mujahedin are not such as to transform radically the operating conditions for an air force that up till now has functioned with total impunity. It was, moreover, the Afghan air force that carried out the raids in February against refugee camps in Pakistani territory in order to put pressure on the Islamabad government at the start of the last round of negotiations in Geneva.

The hypothesis presented here about Moscow's attitude seems confirmed as this article is being completed by a rumor circulating in Kabul about an imminent withdrawal of a strong contingent of Soviet troops. According to the rumor, this would involve 50,000 troops, or about half of all those engaged in Afghanistan![14]

In any case, the more the Soviet military presence in the country is reduced, the less capacity the reactionary forces have to mobilize. Their main argument has been, and continues to be, resistance to the *shoravis* ("Soviets," in the local language). The mujahedin will certainly find fewer recruits for a jihad for their Islamic state than they have found until now for the fight to liberate Afghanistan from foreign troops.

MARCH 15, 1987; first published in English in *International Viewpoint*, no. 117 (April 6, 1987).

## CHAPTER SIX

# The Agreement on Soviet Withdrawal

*At the time when Moscow began withdrawing its troops, the prevailing opinion was that the Kabul regime would fall quickly because it lacked any real social base. This was not the standpoint of the following article. Going against the current, it maintained that Moscow's decision to "Afghanize" the Afghanistan war would prove more viable than Washington's 1973 decision to "Vietnamize" the Vietnam War. In fact, the Kabul regime would fall only after the collapse of the Soviet Union. The forecast I made here in 1988 is based on an evaluation of the progressive characteristics of the pro-Soviet Afghan regime, in contrast with the wholly reactionary character of the anti-Soviet Alliance.*

The Soviet troops began their withdrawal from Afghanistan on May 15, 1988. Half of the 100,300 soldiers that Moscow has on Afghan soil, the figure recently divulged by the Soviet high command, should be withdrawn by August 15. The troops should complete their total evacuation within nine months—that is, before February 15, 1989.

These are the terms of the accords signed in Geneva on April 14 by the governments of Afghanistan, Pakistan, the USSR, and the United States. Indirect negotiations under the aegis of the United Nations between the representatives of Kabul and Islamabad began in 1982. For a long time, they focused on the question of the timetable for the withdrawal of Soviet troops. The initial Soviet/Afghan proposal was to spread out the withdrawal over four years. On the other hand, the Pakistan/U.S. side demanded a time limit of three months.

But the gap between these two positions was to narrow quickly after 1986. Then suddenly, on February 8, Mikhail Gorbachev announced that the USSR and the Republic of Afghanistan had agreed to reduce the withdrawal schedule to ten months beginning on May 15, expecting the accord to be signed in Geneva on March 15.

The agreement was finally signed a month late because of differences that arose among the parties. It was not the final reduction of a month in the timetable proposed by Gorbachev that was involved this time, but new demands formulated by Washington and Islamabad which seemed to be obstructive.

As a new condition for signing the accord Pakistan raised a prior understanding on a provisional government to replace the one in power in Kabul. The Reagan administration, under pressure from Congress, revised the meaning to be given to the mutual disengagement of the two big powers. In exchange for cutting off U.S. military aid to the Afghan rebel forces, Washington no longer demanded simply the withdrawal of Moscow's troops, but also the breaking off of Soviet military aid to the Kabul government.

Gorbachev had already given a peremptory answer to the Pakistani demand in his February 8 statement. "This is a purely internal Afghan problem. Only the Afghans can settle it.... When it is suggested that the Soviet Union must take part in negotiations over this, and still more with third states, we answer clearly: Spare us this, it is not our problem or yours."

Faced with Washington's new position, Moscow threatened after March 17 to conclude an agreement on the withdrawal of its troops with the Kabul government alone. This was a thinly veiled threat to Pakistan, inasmuch as the Geneva accords also involved an agreement that Kabul and Moscow would stop supporting subversive activities on its territory. Finally, a tacit agreement was concluded between the United States and the Soviets on a "positive symmetry" of aid from each of the two great powers to their respective protégés. In other words, Washington pledged to measure out the aid to the mujahedin in proportion to Moscow's aid to Kabul. Pakistan would continue to serve as a bridge for foreign aid to the Afghan rebellion, but the rebels were to shift their military equipment and the training of their troops into Afghan territory. The Geneva accords could finally be signed, although they were tacitly emptied of a good part of their substance.

## MOSCOW'S DETERMINATION

The determination shown by Moscow to begin the troop withdrawal confirms the assessment we made a year earlier that Gorbachev was "genuinely anxious to disengage" from the Afghan bog, and that, to this end, if the U.S. attitude stood in the way of an accord, "it is not out of the question that Moscow will try to pursue its strategy of disengagement all the way without an agreement."[1] This judgment was far from a unanimous one at the time it was expressed. Many commentators saw Gorbachev's attitude as only a "political maneuver" and heavily stressed the military value that they thought the "Afghan training field" represented for the Soviet army.[2] For those who accept the view of "Russian expansionism," Gorbachev's decision must seem totally extraordinary. On the other hand, as was noted recently by a CIA expert: "Only those who might have argued in 1979 that the Soviet Union never really wanted to go in the first place, that such an act was atypical of Soviet behavior, can now say that they are less than deeply impressed by the implications of the move."[3]

The discomforted advocates of the theory of Soviet expansionism are now trying to save face by saying that the Kremlin's decision was the result of a military defeat. But if there was a "defeat," it had been evident for a long time. As we pointed out a year ago, it had already been possible for several years to say that "the balance sheet of the intervention of Soviet troops shows an appalling bankruptcy."

The fact remains, however, that the strategy Gorbachev has followed in Afghanistan since 1985 has unquestionably borne fruit, even though it is far from decisively changing the relationship of forces. Besides, can anyone seriously believe that the USSR did not have the means to send more than 100,000 soldiers to control a territory of 650,000 square kilometers on its borders, when Israel dispatched as many soldiers in 1982 to occupy 6,000 square kilometers of Lebanese territory, and five times as many U.S. soldiers were deployed over the 170,000 square kilometers of South Vietnam before 1973? Moreover, the Soviet intervention in Afghanistan never aroused domestic and international opposition comparable in scope and intensity to that experienced by the United States and Israel in the cases cited.

It is the economic and not the military vulnerability of the USSR that explains the course followed by Mikhail Gorbachev. For the United States, Vietnam represented a major stake in its policy of dominating the world market and a windfall for its "military-industrial complex." However, for a Soviet bureaucracy frightened by the expansion of Islamic fundamentalism on its borders after Khomeini's victory in Iran in February 1979, the stakes in Afghanistan were essentially "defensive" and political. The objective was not to "Mongolianize" Afghanistan, or effect any "structural assimilation," but to prevent the development of an Islamic fundamentalist regime in

Kabul, which was considered certain in 1979. The limitations of the Soviet deployment in Afghanistan continued to be dictated by this objective. Even with these restrictions the Soviet intervention represented a serious drain for Moscow. It increased the overall burden of military spending in a faltering and uncompetitive economy, in which the military industries did not represent any special private interest.

Moreover, settling the Afghan conflict seemed to be one of the main prerequisites for a détente with the United States, an objective put back on the agenda by a Gorbachev anxious to improve the external conditions for his *perestroika*. A secondary but still important consideration was that, far from stopping the Islamic contagion in the Central Asian republics of the USSR, the Afghan intervention had given impetus to it.

That the Soviet decision to withdraw from Afghanistan is an inseparable part of Gorbachev's overall foreign policy is attested to by the way that it has been presented by the Kremlin leaders themselves, as well as by their Afghan protégé. Since the inauguration in 1986 of the "national reconciliation" policy in Afghanistan, "Dr. Najibullah," the new president of the republic, has not missed an opportunity in Ho-Chi-Minh City, Havana, or in the international publications sponsored by Moscow to note that this policy has "aroused interest among many people abroad, especially in Kampuchea and the five Central American countries. The idea of reconciliation has in itself an essentially universal human character."[4]

In January 1988, Shevardnadze, Gorbachev's minister of foreign affairs, told the Afghan press agency that this policy was "a reflection of great worldwide trends," and was leaving "a beneficial effect in the international climate." He went on to say quite clearly that "having been tested in Afghanistan, it is more and more frequently being adopted as a model for settling conflicts in other regions."[5] Finally, in his February 8 statement, Gorbachev was even more explicit, resorting intensively to the surgical metaphors that he seems to like:

If the arms race . . . is an insane rush of humanity into the abyss, regional conflicts are bloody wounds that can create gangrenous infections on the body of humanity. The earth is literally ulcerated by these dangerous points of infection, each of which causes not only suffering for the peoples directly involved but also for everyone else, whether in relation to Afghanistan, the Middle East, the Iran-Iraq war, South Africa, Kampuchea, or Central America.... Achieving a political settlement in Afghanistan would be a breakthrough in the chain of regional conflicts . . . and

would make it possible to raise the question: What will be the next conflict to be
overcome? Because it would necessarily lead to that.

This is the language of a future Nobel Prize winner, of which the Pope
himself could approve.[6] In the area of "peaceful coexistence," the late
Khrushchev has been put in the shade.

The universal policy of "national reconciliation" and disengagement of
foreign troops advocated by Gorbachev has already had the practical consequences that we have seen in the regions mentioned. What is generally forgotten is that it has taken its inspiration directly from a rather inglorious
precedent, that is, the U.S. disengagement from Vietnam, and that it harks
back to the foreign policy of the first decade of the Brezhnev era, before the
U.S. debacle in Indochina. The "interventionist" decade in Soviet policy
that followed has tended to make people forget what went before. From this
standpoint, Gorbachev's foreign policy is far less original than it might
seem at first glance, even if it is a good deal more spectacular.

The major features of Gorbachev's Afghan policy seem modeled in
every aspect on the U.S. precedent in Vietnam. The Afghanization of the
Soviet war is occurring after a Vietnamization of the U.S. war, against the
background of withdrawal of the interventionist troops in both cases.

### "NATIONAL RECONCILIATION"

The "national reconciliation" touted by Gorbachev and Najibullah echoes the
National Council of National Reconciliation and Concord provided for by the
U.S.– Vietnamese accord signed in Paris in 1973. There are even some similarities in the text of the accords, notably the peculiarity of not mentioning
directly one of the parties in the conflict—the Provisional Revolutionary Government in 1973 and the Islamic Alliance in 1988. "The accord that ended the
war in Vietnam," Henry Kissinger wrote in his memoirs of his White House
years, "to my knowledge is the only document in diplomatic history that does
not mention all the parties involved." It is no longer the only one.

A major difference between the two cases, however, is the attitude of the
native forces. In this regard, the dangers are the opposite. The U.S. strategy
of disengagement from Vietnam ran up against the recalcitrant attitude of
Thieu in Saigon, described at length by Kissinger in his memoirs while
their enemies showed a great tactical flexibility.[7] In Afghanistan, on the
other hand, the mujahedin are the intransigent ones, while Najibullah is

toeing the line of Gorbachev's strategy meticulously, even if he sometimes needs to be cajoled a little.

Since he came to power in Kabul with the Kremlin's blessing in May 1986, Najibullah has championed "national reconciliation." In line with this course, spectacular measures have been adopted. The main ones up to March 1987 were described in a previous article.[8] The subsequent steps have gone further in the same direction.

## MOVES TOWARD DEMOCRATIZATION

In the following months, the regime passed a new law on investment in the private sector. The tax exemptions and other facilities it includes make Afghanistan one of the countries that offer the best conditions for private enterprise, were it not for the uncertainties that hang over its political future.

A new agrarian law raised the maximum landholding from six to twenty hectares on the most fertile soil. At the same time, Najibullah confirmed that "the size of the land owned by those who have played a great role in the realization of the policy of national reconciliation"—that is, the collaborationist big landlords—"is not to be limited."[9] The Islamic rules of inheritance were restored and even legitimized by the new constitution, which accords Islam and traditional practices a much larger juridical and legislative role than the preceding one.

This new constitution was adopted at the end of November 1987 by an ad hoc meeting of the *loya jirga*, the regime's own version of the traditional assembly of notables which figured among the institutions of the Afghan monarchy. Even the official designation of the state was changed in a moderate direction, with the term "democratic" being eliminated. The emblem and the flag of the state have been Islamicized. More than a thousand mullahs and *ulemas* (theologians) have been "elected" to various positions in the institutions of the regime.

Some real political democratization measures have been adopted, alongside others that were more symbolic than real. In particular, several thousand political prisoners have been released. The regime's desire for a political opening is not pretense. Najibullah summed this up in the formula, "Anyone who is not against us is with us."[10] He offered a share of legal power to anyone willing to cooperate with his government.

The People's Democratic Party of Afghanistan (PDPA) no longer holds a monopoly of governmental posts. According to Najibullah, the only civilian posts that are still held exclusively by the party are the presidency of the republic and the ministries of defense, the interior, and finance—the key posts, that is to say. In fact, several ministries have been given to nonmembers of the PDPA who held responsible positions in the regimes that preceded the party's seizure of power in April 1978. The most spectacular measure in this respect was the appointment in May of Hassan Sharq as premier. He was Prince Daud's chief of staff when the latter served as premier under King Zaher Shah from 1953 to 1963. He then became deputy premier under the same Prince Daud when the prince seized power, ousting his cousin the king and declaring a republic in 1973, before being overthrown in his turn five years later by the PDPA. From 1980 to 1986, Sharq enjoyed the gilded exile that the job of ambassador often represents. He was recalled to the country in the context of the new policy of "national reconciliation."

Following the advice so readily offered by Moscow, after December 1986 Najibullah stepped up his appeals to all the tendencies in opposition to his regime, and especially to the monarchist components of the Peshawar-based Islamic Alliance, offering to share power with them in the framework of a coalition. Up until now, these appeals have received little response. No major personality or tendency in the opposition, in particular in the armed opposition, has grasped the hand offered by the regime. Doubtless, however, some have been tempted to do so and still are. Why don't they do so then?

## A HETEROGENEOUS OPPOSITION

The first reason is uncertainty about the regime's ability to survive the withdrawal of Soviet troops. If the regime collapsed, anyone who had accepted Kabul's offer would share its fate. The second reason has to do with the composition of the opposition itself, its heterogeneity. Whereas the homogeneous, if not monolithic, Vietnamese resistance could afford to maneuver politically, the Afghan Islamic Alliance is a conglomerate of rival organizations, held together by nothing but their fight against a common enemy. The most important components of the Islamic Alliance, the fundamentalist organizations, because of their fanatical ideological rigidity have little inclination to exhibit any tactical flexibility. The resulting atmosphere in Peshawar is of the various groups constantly trying to outbid one another, of great tension among the components of the Islamic Alliance, which is in continual danger of breaking up.

The heterogeneity of the opposition to the PDPA regime is a major consideration in Gorbachev's Afghan strategy. In fact, Moscow and Kabul are relying on divisions among their Afghan enemies to beef up their "national reconciliation" policy. They know that, aside from their role of channeling the hundreds of millions of dollars in aid of all sorts that they get from the United States and the reactionary Muslim regimes, the Peshawar organizations enjoy little popularity. These organizations are not even very well thought of among the three million Afghan refugees in Pakistan, who they are trying by every possible means to prevent from going home as the Kabul regime has invited them to do. After the signing of the Geneva accords, this invitation is more likely to be listened to.[11] The unpopularity of the leaders ensconced in Peshawar has been attested to by sources that can hardly be suspected of harboring sympathy for Kabul. For example, a Western diplomat stationed in Islamabad was quoted in the U.S. magazine *Newsweek* as saying: "The leaders are not popular with the refugees. There's grumbling in the camps that the leaders are getting rich and passing the war in comfort in Peshawar, far from the front and from the refugee hovels."[12]

A poll was recently carried out among the Afghan refugees in Pakistan and cited in the international press. The U.S. researcher Selig Harrison, a specialist on Afghanistan, summed up its results in this way:

> All the exile leaders have been discredited by persistent rumors of drug trafficking and diversion of U.S. aid to the black market. Out of 2,287 refugees questioned in 106 out of the 249 camps, 71.65 percent wanted the former king—who symbolizes a period of relative stability and good neighborly relations with the USSR—to preside over the future government. Barely one percent wanted this role to be given to a leader of the resistance.[13]

This poll confirmed what was said, a few months before his assassination in Peshawar, by one of the most eminent intellectuals in the Afghan opposition, Professor S. B. Majruh:

> The Soviets know that the leaders in Peshawar will never represent a real obstacle because of their political weakness, so the only danger could come in the person of the king. Their intention was to eliminate this possibility by presenting it as a solution coming from the Soviet side. They hoped that this maneuver would also have the effect of aggravating the divisions in the Alliance.[14]

Whatever the Soviets' intention, that has indeed been the effect. The cordiality of relations in the Islamic Alliance has been illustrated recently by the episode reported by Western correspondents stationed in Peshawar.[15] Accused at a meeting of the mujahedin by the leader of one of the three traditionalist (monarchist) components of the Alliance of having ordered Professor Majruh's assassination, Hekmatyar, chief of the most powerful and fanatic of the four fundamentalist organizations in the Alliance, pulled his gun and nearly shot down his accuser.

Disagreements have been increasing among the organizations in Peshawar since the signing of the Geneva accords: disagreements over what attitude to take toward the accords, disagreement about what to do about the Soviet troops while they are withdrawing, and so on.[16] But the fundamental difference among the seven groups in Peshawar, the one around which all the others turn, is what attitude to take toward former King Zaher Shah, who is in exile in Rome. What could be more natural when you consider that the three main organizations in the Alliance, all of them fundamentalist, were founded under the monarchy and in opposition to Zaher Shah, who was accused of being a puppet of Moscow and an anti-Islamic modernist? This fundamental difference is also reflected in the contrasting proposals about how to choose the political representatives of the Alliance. For example, Hekmatyar, who holds the advantage in Peshawar because he gets the most foreign aid and has the best structured organization, proposed general elections among the refugees in Pakistan (for men only, of course). The chief of another fundamentalist group that split from Hekmatyar's organization did not like the suggestion according to B. Delpuech, writing in a publication devoted to supporting the mujahedin:

> Since Yunos Khales expressed the opinion that democratic elections would be contrary to the principles of Islam, a theological-exegetical dispute developed over the way prescribed by the Koran. Assemblies of mullahs were even called together in Peshawar to come up with a solution acceptable to all.[17]

For their part, the royalists favor the idea of a *loya jirga*, an assembly of notables.. According to Delpuech, Mujaddedi proposed initially "to form an electoral college in which each of the organizations in the Alliance would appoint 15 representatives (10 theologians and five 'laymen')," on the model of the system of co-optation employed for the second and third caliphs of Islam.

Finally, the seven organizations in Peshawar decided for the time being simply to name the members of their government themselves. So far, they have only managed to agree on the "president" of this government, a certain Ahmed Shah, whose principal virtue is probably that he is a bland enough figure to be accepted by the seven organizations. This selection provoked a sour commentary from one of the royalist leaders in the Alliance: "Anyone who has not been chosen by all the Afghans will not be supported by the Afghan people."[18]

## SOCIOPOLITICAL COMPROMISES

So by opting to make public overtures to the ex-king in exile in Rome from 1986 on, Gorbachev—whose line was reproduced by Najibullah—was on target. Informed by their secret services, both know that Zaher Shah (like Sihanouk in Kampuchea) enjoys the widest popularity among Afghans, and especially among the Pushtun tribes who make up the great majority of the refugees in Pakistan. Is this only a "Machiavellian" maneuver by Moscow and Kabul? Nothing could be less certain, especially for Moscow, which has nothing to lose and everything to gain from collaboration with the ex-king. As we wrote in March 1987: "The minimum relationship that Moscow can accept with Afghanistan is one of the Finnish type. Within these well-defined limits, the Kremlin is ready to contemplate any sort of sociopolitical compromise, even a return of former King Zaher Shah from his exile in Rome, if he agreed to play the game."[19]

This last condition means, however, that for the moment what Moscow is offering the monarch does not go beyond an honorary role, perhaps even a presidency of the republic devoid of its present powers, in the framework of a regime where the real power will continue to be held by the PDPA. Inasmuch as today a big question mark hangs over this regime, Zaher Shah has nothing to gain by accepting the offer. He prefers to wait, relying on an erosion of the Kabul regime that would force the Soviets to turn to him as a "savior," thereby putting him in a strong position in relation to them. He has definitely not lost hope of reestablishing his throne.

Everything is going to depend, then, on what happens to the Kabul regime in the coming months. Will it fall or not?—that is the question everyone is asking today. Many in the Western media believe they can proclaim peremptorily that Kabul will inevitably, sooner rather than later, experience the same fate as Saigon. That is, of course, the view of the opposition forces.

Najibullah retorts that his detractors are trying to count their chickens before they are hatched.

One thing is certain: a large part of the Afghan countryside, and probably some cities as well, especially those closest to the Pakistani frontier, will slip entirely out of the PDPA's control. To a large extent, this has already happened. Even if these regions are put under a single political authority, this authority will remain purely theoretical. The tribal fragmentation of the country will be combined with a quasi-feudal mosaic of the territories of the local military chiefs, who are real warlords.

It seems probable, moreover, that the Uzbek and Tadzhik areas in the north of the country will remain firmly in Moscow's grip. What will happen to the territory controlled by Kabul? It claims to exercise authority over two-thirds of the country's provinces, where a million and a half people are said to have gone to the polls between April 5–15, 1988, to elect the 299 deputies in the two houses of the Afghan legislature. In fact, the cornerstone of all this is the capital itself, Greater Kabul, which today, according to converging estimates, includes about three million people—that is, about a third of the population living within the country's borders!

Numerically and technically, the PDPA's armed forces certainly have the means to resist the inevitable assault of the rebel forces. But everything will depend on their internal cohesion, which is far from certain. Having returned from Kabul, Alain Gresh summed up the situation well:

When questioned, an important cadre in the Central Committee of the PDPA responded unhesitatingly: "We have to prepare ourselves for the worst. First of all, we have to reinforce our armed forces, whose potential has increased considerably in recent years. We have nearly 130,000 men in the regular armed forces— the army and the *Tsarandoy* (militarized police), and 60 percent of the 200,000 members of the party are in the army or the militias."

Wages in the army have been raised seven to 25 times, and there have been a lot of promotions with the aim of guaranteeing the loyalty of the soldiers and cadres. Tens of thousands of them have undergone training in the USSR over the last ten years. It is on them to a large extent that the future depends. The mujahedin have neither the heavy arms nor the unity of command necessary to take Kabul. Only a swing in the army could offer them a decisive victory. If, on the contrary, the officers and soldiers remain loyal, the PDPA can fall back on its urban bastions and withstand assaults.[20]

If the PDPA can hold out, it is possible that there could be a break in the Islamic Alliance, with a faction—the traditionalists—opting for a favorable response to Kabul's offers. That could substantially alter the relationship of forces throughout the country. Another faction, the fundamentalists, would continue the struggle indefatigably. Their outlook makes them incapable of accepting any compromise whatever, and they can find a human base for their activity in the large numbers of men who have developed a taste for guerrilla warfare, especially among the generation that remembers nothing else. In other words, in all the possible scenarios, the Afghanistan war is not about to end.

## WHAT THE AFGHAN PEOPLE WANT

Two factors will have a considerable importance for the future of the Kabul regime, that is, for its internal cohesion. First and foremost is the attitude of Moscow. If the USSR gave the impression that it was abandoning the PDPA, that would certainly mean a debacle for the latter. But there is no sign today, any more than in the past, that this is Gorbachev's intention. As we wrote in March 1987, we continue to think that the USSR could "keep a military force in Afghanistan quantitatively closer to what was there before December 1979 (5,000 military 'advisers') than to the massive military presence it has had in recent years."[21]

The second factor is the feelings of the Afghan population. Again, we wrote in 1987 that "the mujahedin will certainly find less recruits for a jihad for their Islamic state than they have found until now for the fight to liberate Afghanistan from foreign troops." *Newsweek* expressed the same idea recently. Melinda Liu, the author of the article, mentioned the aversion to the mujahedin among a section of the urban population:

> That apprehension was particularly acute among educated women, who have gained a measure of liberation from the conservative Muslim practice of *purdah*. "Those people in the mountains, with their long hair and long beards, we are afraid that after ten years they will be wild," said one young Kabul resident whose fashionable Western-style dress contrasted dramatically with the head-to-ankle *chador* demanded by radical fundamentalists.[22]

This inhabitant of Kabul has indeed good reason to worry, to judge from the fate meted out to women in the Peshawar refugee camps, which was described as follows in a previous issue of *Newsweek*: "Conditions are especially hard on the women, who end up virtual prisoners. Forbidden by their menfolk to wander among the thousands of strangers in the camps, they must remain indoors, even when wearing the veil of devout Muslim females." [23]

The comparative fates of women in the two Afghan camps opposing each other since 1978 is one element among many others that confirms, if the sociopolitical evidence alone were not sufficient, that this is a confrontation between a progressive and a reactionary camp. [24] The origin of the Afghan rebellion, it should be remembered, was a classical Vendee-type rebellion against a regime that had features reminiscent of Jacobinism. The rebel forces represented, and still represent, a conglomerate of the traditional forces that the PDPA clumsily tried to shake up or dislodge after it came to power in April 1978, and which were joined by the fundamentalists. The PDPA proposed eradicating illiteracy and promoting secularization, the emancipation of women, detribalization, radical agrarian reform, and industrialization, trying to carry all this out using dictatorial and bureaucratic methods.At the same time, the rebel forces defended a continuation of the old medieval, obscurantist society, the role of the mullahs, the inferior status of women, tribalism, the domination of the big landlords, and the perpetuation of social and economic backwardness, or even fought for a totalitarian Islamic dictatorship.

The intervention by Kremlin troops after the end of December 1979 had to be condemned and their withdrawal demanded, not because it was counterrevolutionary, as was the case in Hungary in 1956 and in Czechoslovakia in 1968, nor because we oppose intervention by Moscow's troops in all circumstances. In fact, we called for them to intervene in defense of Vietnam, as we have approved the intervention of Cuban troops in Angola, which was done with Moscow's help. The problem was that the invasion of Afghanistan by Soviet troops as it unfolded could not have any effect other than to strongly reinforce the camp that Moscow thought it could crush.

## DEFEAT THE REACTIONARY FORCES

However, the civil war that has gone on in Afghanistan since 1978 has not changed in nature because of the Soviet intervention. Even if for eight years it has taken on the appearance of a national war against the Soviet invader, to the great benefit of the reactionary camp, the latter, even more than in 1980–82, is made up essentially of the same political and social forces that were fighting the PDPA before December 1979. Likewise, although the PDPA has watered down its program considerably since 1986 and is more than ever a hireling of Moscow, its social and political nature has remained fundamentally the same since 1978. It can be described as progressive, petit bourgeois and "democratic" in the social meaning of the term.

In this war, which the Soviet withdrawal is returning to the dimensions of a civil war, we cannot be neutral nor, even less, can we support the reactionary camp. We are firmly for the defeat of the reactionary forces, although this does not mean that we identify ourselves in the least with the Kabul regime. We want to see it overthrown by a genuine revolution. The conditions for that are a long way from having been assembled today in Afghanistan, unfortunately. However, we are convinced that the withdrawal of the Soviet troops will improve the chances for this in the long term. On the other hand, keeping these forces in the country can only further the putrefaction of Afghan society.

This is why we are for the withdrawal of Moscow's troops, even if this leads to a collapse of the Kabul regime. If it proves incapable of maintaining itself, with technical and financial aid from the USSR, against the motley gangs of the Afghan reaction, the past eight years have clearly shown that the attempt by Soviet troops to prop up the regime has drawn this army into an endless war. [...]

JUNE 15, 1988; first published in English in *International Viewpoint*, no. 145 (July 11, 1988).

## CHAPTER SEVEN

# The "Lebanonization" of Afghanistan

*The Soviet empire pulled down its Afghan client as it fell in 1991. The pro-Soviet regime in Kabul had survived the withdrawal of Moscow's troops, but the USSR's end sounded the regime's death knell. In this article I made a new prognosis: that the new "Islamic" government would not last very long. The Taliban would in fact overthrow it two years later, after internecine warfare among mujahedin and other onetime allies in the "anti-communist" jihad had caused tens of thousands of deaths. The Taliban won their gamble of stabilizing the country under their obscurantist, ultra-puritanical regime. Their overthrow as a result of the U.S. invasion launched on October 7, 2001, sent Afghanistan back to the same situation it was in when this article was written in 1992.*

The only possible cause for surprise at the fall of Najibullah — the head of the Kabul secret police (Khad) whom the KGB "modernists" put at the head of the "progressive" Afghan regime in May 1986, during their hour of glory under Gorbachev — is that it took so long. It is hardly likely that the new government that succeeded it, in a bloody mess that gives a foretaste of what the "Islamic" day after will be like, will last as long. Afghanistan seems to be sliding inexorably into the kind of fragmentation in warring political-military areas, resulting from all sorts of fractures, which is known in modern times as "Lebanonization."

Four years ago we highlighted the reasons why the Kabul regime would be able to survive the withdrawal of Soviet troops that took place in September 1989.[1] This view was based on the one hand on an assessment of the regime's policies and its real social base and on the other on the heterogeneity of the Afghan Islamic Alliance, the cartel of fundamentalist and traditionalist factions opposed to the Kabul regime and its Soviet mentors.

The Najibullah regime attempted to present itself as the promoter of "national reconciliation," echoing Gorbachev's policy for dealing with regional conflicts. Although spurned by the Alliance organizations based in the Pakistani city of Peshawar, the new regime in Kabul nevertheless succeeded in extending its social base. To this end it combined measures of political and economic liberalization and clever manipulation of fluid and venal ethnic/tribal allegiances, drawing on the long experience of the former leader of the Khad in this field.

## THE BEGINNING OF THE END

By such means Najibullah was able to survive quite "honorably" the departure of his Soviet protectors; indeed in this respect the Soviet-inspired "Afghanization" of the conflict was more of a success than the earlier U.S. Vietnamization in Indochina. He could probably have held on for a long time if the whole Soviet edifice had not collapsed at the center. Economic and military support from the Big Brother to the north was essential to the survival of the Kabul regime, which was as incapable as its adversaries of funding permanent war out of its own resources.

The growing paralysis of the central Soviet regime had already taken its military toll on the Afghan protégé with the fall of Khost in April 1991. But the final tragicomedy played out in Moscow between August and December 1991, resulting in the downfall of both Gorbachev and the KGB, meant the certain end of the Kabul government; its days were numbered since the start of the following year. Its struggle did not cease for lack of fighters, but for lack of any means of paying them. Its opponent, the Islamic Alliance has never lacked petrodollars from Saudi Arabia and Co. to cover any interruption in U.S. funding and, furthermore, has been able to draw succor from the return of the military-Islamic coalition to power in Pakistan after Benazir Bhutto's overthrow in August 1990.

Najibullah, in the tradition of the country's rulers, is a Pashtun, like the great majority of inhabitants of the southern half of Afghanistan and the northwest of Pakistan. However, he did not succeed in winning decisively on the ethnic/tribal level; the influence of Pakistan and the Muslim fundamentalists remained decisive among the Pashtun outside the capital. The weight of the USSR and its Tadzhik and Uzbek border republics had an influence on the corresponding ethnic groups in the north of Afghanistan, who were in direct contact with their brethren living under Soviet rule.

After the pathetic collapse of the empire to the north, the Uzbeks and Tadzhiks who had stayed faithful to Moscow and Kabul shifted massively over to the Islamic Alliance, while continuing to make alliances according to ethno-tribal allegiances. Thus the Tadzhiks have rallied to the famous commander Massud, the Afghan Rambo, who is based in the Tadzhik zone and who belongs to Rabbani's fundamentalist Jamiat-i-Islami, which has close links with Pakistan. At the same time the Uzbek chief Dostam, whose men are notorious for their terrible raids and which had supported the Kabul regime, now again changed sides to join the Alliance loyalists, supported by Massud.

This camp brings together the majority of the organizations in Peshawar, a hodgepodge of more or less strict fundamentalists and partisans of the restoration of the monarchy overthrown in 1973. Its motley complexion flows from the fact that it brings together the so-called minority (that is, non-Pashtun) peoples. They have reached agreement on an interim government council of fifty-one members that has to organize elections in two years. The least powerful of the Peshawar leaders, Mujaddedi, has been put at the head of this council, which says a lot about the nature of the compromise. Already disputes are raging over the division of offices in the new regime between the numerous and diverse factions, whether political, ethnic/tribal, or even ethnic/religious—such as the Shiite Hazaras, supported by Iran, who are demanding extra representation.

However, the most threatening competition comes from the Hezb-i-Islami of Hekmatyar. He is a hardcore fundamentalist and a Pashtun who has played this ethnic card for all it's worth and has thereby won the allegiance of some factions of the former Najibullah regime. The installation of the new government in Kabul was preceded by days of fierce fighting for the control of the capital between supporters of Massud and Hekmatyar— both belonging to the same Islamic Alliance and represented in the Interim Council. And the story is far from over yet.

APRIL 29, 1992; first published in English in *International Viewpoint*, no. 229 (May 25, 1992).

PART III

# Palestine: From One Intifada to the Next

## CHAPTER EIGHT

# The Palestinian Uprising

*Barely one month after the beginning, in December 1987, of what was not yet referred to internationally by the Arabic word* intifada, *the following analysis placed the problem of the "occupied territories" in historical perspective. It identified three different options that could be put forward within the Israeli establishment:* transfer *(this euphemism for expelling the Palestinians had just been revived), the choice of the radical fringe of the extreme Zionist right;* creeping expulsion, *the choice of the right and another section of the Zionist extreme right, which Ariel Sharon has put into practice since his arrival in power in February 2001; and the Allon Plan, the choice of the Labor Party, led at the time by Shimon Peres.[1] The Allon Plan meant that "Israel would maintain on the West Bank... a belt of strategic colonies and military bases," while "the Israeli army would withdraw from those parts of the territories densely populated by Arab, while keeping the right to oversee their demilitarization." This option became reality six years later in the form of the Oslo and Washington accords, with a new twist: King Hussein, the partner originally envisioned in the Allon Plan, was replaced by Yassir Arafat. At the moment when the intifada broke out, Arafat was still accusing this solution's advocates—rightly!—of wanting to create a "Bantustan."*

The year 1987 was a double anniversary in the Middle East. It marked the two chief stages of the Zionist seizure of Palestinian territory, 1947 and 1967. The Palestinians did not let the anniversary pass without commemorating it. Since December 9, 1987, the broadest and most protracted popular uprising ever seen in Palestine since the creation of the state of Israel has been in progress. It hardly matters what the straw was that broke the camel's back; its back has been bent to the breaking point for a long time.

Forty years have gone by since the United Nations adopted its iniquitous partition plan on November 29, 1947. That was the signal for Zionist
armed gangs to launch their war of annexation. In 1948 they seized, in
total, 80 percent of the lands of the former British mandated territory of
Palestine. (The UN plan granted them 55 percent.) In 1947 the Jews owned
only 6 percent of this territory and represented only a third of its total population: 630,000 inhabitants out of nearly two million. In December 1949,
in the wake of the war by which the Israeli state was founded, there were no
more than 160,000 Palestinian Arabs on the usurped 80 percent of this
territory, as against more than a million Jews. Massive expulsion of Arabs
and massive immigration of Jews in the name of "biblical rights": these
were the two pillars of the Zionist colonial enterprise.

## 1967: CREATION OF THE "OCCUPIED TERRITORIES"

In June 1967, the Israeli occupation of the West Bank and the Gaza Strip
completed the Zionist usurpation of Palestinian territory, with the addition
of Syria's Golan Heights and Egypt's Sinai Desert. Israel has withdrawn
from only one of these territories since then: the Sinai, in 1982. East
Jerusalem was officially annexed for "biblical" reasons right away in 1967,
and the Golan Heights, for "security" reasons, in 1981.

The rest of the West Bank, as well as the Gaza Strip, retain to this day
the official status of occupied territories, and for good reason. Unlike the
Golan Heights, where the great majority of the population (more than
150,000 before June 1967) had to flee during the Six-Day War without
being able to return, and where Jewish settlers now outnumber the
natives, these territories are still inhabited by Arabs numerous enough to
upset the ethnic and political makeup of Israeli society should they
become Israeli citizens—a corollary of formal annexation. That would be
contrary to the essence of Zionism. In the long term, the very nature of
the state of Israel as a "Jewish state" would be imperiled, given the difference between the growth rate of the Jewish population and the much
higher one of the Arab population. This, by the way, is the reason why the
Zionist movement attaches so much importance to Jewish emigration
from the USSR: it is the only source of massive potential immigration into
Israel that exists today and therefore the only available means of compensating for the relatively low birth rate of Israeli Jews. It is not labor power
that Israel lacks, but cannon fodder.

In the aftermath of the June 1967 war, the Zionist state already had almost 1,400,000 Arabs under its control, including more than a million on the West Bank and in Gaza, as against 2,400,000 Jews. This time the Palestinian exodus was not as large proportionally as in 1948, when the vast majority (80 percent) of Palestinian Arabs had fled the usurped territories. Even though since 1967 the majority of all Palestinians increasingly live outside the frontiers of the former British Mandate of Palestine—compared with only a quarter at the beginning of the 1950s, and nearly 35 percent after the June 1967 war—less than a third of the residents of the West Bank and Gaza fled these territories in 1967.

The reason for this was not that the 1967 invasion was any "gentler" than the preceding one, although it did not give rise to deliberate collective massacres, such as the one perpetrated by the Zionist terrorists of Irgun at Deir Yassin in 1948. The exodus in 1967 was proportionally smaller for a combination of several different reasons. In 1948, for two-thirds of those involved, the exodus was from one part of Palestinian territory to another. This was no longer possible in 1967, since the whole of Palestine was occupied. Second, the great majority of the 1948 refugees thought that they were leaving their homes only temporarily. By 1967, the lesson had sunk in. The fact that Arabs who remained under Israeli rule in 1948, while persecuted, were not massacred was also an important factor. Finally, the poverty in which the 1948 refugees were living could only encourage the people of West Bank and Gaza to hang on to their homes and their livelihoods. The bulk of the 1967 refugees consisted of people who had already fled in 1948 and had nothing particularly desirable to leave behind; they were moving on from one refugee status to another.

### A TIME BOMB

As a result, when the Zionist state took over the remaining 20 percent of Palestine territory, it brought under its control nearly 40 percent of the Palestinians, in addition to those already under its jurisdiction. This was the main flaw in the Zionist expansionist project—a veritable time bomb that successive governments of Israel have not succeeded in defusing, and whose explosive power grows with each day that passes. Today [in 1988], according to Israeli figures, 2,125,000 Arabs are living under Zionist jurisdiction (two-thirds of them on the West Bank and in Gaza), compared with 3,590,000 Jews. The ratio is thus 37 to 63. The Israelis' own projections are that, given the present rates of growth, this ratio will be 45 to 55 in the year 2000, that is, in twelve years!

This explains the worry of the "enlightened" Zionists (a more appropriate epithet than "moderate"). It was enough to hear their leader, the Laborite Shimon Peres, exclaim with chills going down his spine on December 30, 1987, that "in twelve years, there will be a million Arabs in Gaza and the demographic density will be greater there than in Hong Kong." At the same time, he lamented that today "out of every hundred children born between the Jordan and the Mediterranean, fifty are Arabs and fifty Jews, and nobody is going to stop this phenomenon."[2]

This is Zionism's fundamental dilemma—the contradiction between its expansionist territorial ambitions and its racist project of a "Jewish" state. The latter, of course, is the overriding principle. "To preserve Israel's Jewish character," as Peres says, is the chief concern of all Zionists.[3] How can this be reconciled, therefore, with the demographic data presented above? This is a debate that goes back twenty years in Israel. Among the Zionists, four different answers to this question can be discerned.

## DIFFICULTIES OF AN "APARTHEID" SOLUTION

First of all, there is the answer of the most lunatic or most outspoken extremists, such as the fascist rabbi Meir Kahane, the leader of the Kach party, who is fighting to make Israel *araberrein*—free from Arabs—just as the Nazis wanted Germany to be *judenrein*. Unable to expel the Arabs by military force, he is offering visas, airline tickets. and financial aid to any Arabs willing to leave. Another example is the general who a few months ago made the term "transfer" notorious in Israel by proposing massive deportation of the Palestinians from "Greater Israel."[4]

Then there are those who, while proclaiming their unfailing attachment to the same "Greater Israel," and in particular to Judea and Samaria (the biblical names of the West Bank territories), realize that "transfer" today is impracticable. They know that Israel's extreme dependence on the United States makes a massive expulsion of the Palestinians from their territories quite impossible in the present circumstances.[5] They prefer nonetheless to hold on to the territories in question, even at the price of maintaining indefinitely the apartheid that took shape several years ago under Zionist auspices. This is the view of the Zionist right and part of the extreme right that Tehiya Party leader Geula Cohen expressed recently in the U.S. magazine *Newsweek*: "I prefer to keep the million-plus Arabs here, where they are under our control, despite all the problems. At present, the idea of a mass population transfer seems to me impossible, although not immoral. It is the most moral idea in the world."[6]

However, this "realism" of the Zionist right in no way evacuates the dilemma described above. It cannot resort to the argument that in the country where apartheid originated five million whites control six times their number of Blacks. The magnitude of Israel's Arab environment and the small size of Palestinian territory are major factors making Israel's situation qualitatively different from South Africa's. This is why, in fact, the Zionist right envisions defusing the demographic threat by "creeping" expulsion of a large number of Palestinians, even if it does not always avow this openly. As early as the 30th Congress of the Zionist Movement in December 1982, Menachem Begin replied to Peres's demographic argument by saying that the statisticians were often wrong in their predictions because they did not take account of the growing emigration of Palestinians! The worsening in recent years of repression, persecution, and provocations against the Palestinians in the territories occupied in 1967 has been designed precisely to goad them into leaving "voluntarily."

Enlightened Zionists for their part consider that this option is both illusory and impossible, just as much as "transfer" pure and simple. It is illusory because there is nothing to indicate that emigration of Palestinians from their territories is compensating for their birth rate. On the contrary, a number of factors have increased Palestinians' attachment to their homeland: the closing of the traditional outlets for emigration—especially the oil states of the Arab-Persian Gulf, which have suffered an abrupt fall in their purchasing power; the strength of the Palestinians' political determination; and the spectacle of the misfortunes undergone by the refugees in Lebanon, the last country where they enjoyed a certain autonomy.

The Palestinians will leave en masse only if they are forcibly driven out, in such a way that no one would mistake their departure for something "voluntary." This makes "voluntary" departure as impossible as "transfer." When Peres, with his hypocritical air, says that Israel must not lose its "democratic" soul, he means that such a deterioration of its image could be fatal for the Zionist state, in view of its dependence on outside support from its U.S. tutor as well as the "diaspora."

## PERES'S PROPOSALS

Peres therefore proposes simply to maintain control of the territories, while leaving the Jordanians the job of controlling the population. According to the Laborite plan worked out by Yigal Allon after the June 1967 war, Israel would maintain on the West Bank—where so far 55,000 Israelis have settled—a belt of strategic colonies and military bases, especially along the Jordan Valley, which is considered Israel's intangible "security frontier." The Israeli army would withdraw from those parts of the territories densely populated by Arabs, while keeping the right to oversee their demilitarization. Civilian administration and police order would be entrusted to King Hussein, in the framework of a settlement coming out of an "international conference," which Peres sees as a sort of second Camp David, only this time with Jordan.

Given the reluctance of Israeli public opinion to accept his party's plan, and faced with Likud's Zionist demagogy about "Judea-Samaria," Peres has chosen recently to divide the problem by focusing his campaign on the fate of Gaza. It seems to him easier to get a majority on the question of Gaza for several reasons: there is not the same Zionist "biblical" attachment to it as there is to the West Bank; it is a small territory (360 square kilometers) with in addition a dense population (600,000 inhabitants) with a well-established reputation for rebelliousness; fewer than 2,000 Israelis have settled there. Finally and above all, on the other side of Gaza lies the immense buffer zone of the Sinai Desert, which was restored to Egypt on condition that it be demilitarized under U.S. supervision.

At the beginning of December 1987, even before the spread of the ongoing Palestinian uprising mainly based in Gaza, Peres opened his campaign about this territory's fate. He took the offensive again at the end of December, as soon as the Palestinian struggle seemed to have subsided. His proposals for Gaza are identical to those concerning the West Bank, except that in the first case no role is foreseen for the settlements, whose current numbers are negligible.

## THE DEAD END OF INTERNATIONAL CONFERENCES

"Peres proposes the creation of a Bantustan," ingenuously protested Yassir Arafat, leader of the PLO and of its dominant right-wing faction. As if anything else could be expected from an international conference for a negotiated "settlement" of the Palestinian question on the basis of a Jordanian-

Palestinian "confederation"—that is, in the framework of the program adopted officially by the PLO in 1983 and reconfirmed in 1987. As if it were not entirely clear that

> leaving aside the totally illusory independence of such a mini-state completely trapped in the Israeli vise, with its back to Jordan on the one side (the West Bank) and to the sea and desert on the other side (Gaza), with Israel stuck in between the two—it would be quite impossible to achieve this through a (negotiated) Israeli agreement to withdraw from the territories occupied in 1967. At best, the Zionist state would agree to a very partial withdrawal from the West Bank—where it has already "appropriated" almost half the land—and Gaza, involving draconian conditions which would render these territories little more than Bantustans, and this at the price of a total political capitulation, Sadat-style, by the Arab states.[7]

No partial self-determination of the Palestinians on the West Bank and in Gaza could be real unless Israel withdrew unconditionally from these territories. But in the present relationship of forces this will never come out of an international conference. Achieving it would require a combination of irresistible Palestinian pressure on the occupying forces, firm Arab support for their struggle, strong international pressure on the Zionist government, and a powerful movement for unconditional withdrawal inside Israel itself. Today, the supporters of such a withdrawal, both anti-Zionists and "Zionist doves," are in a small minority among Israeli Jews—only 2,000 demonstrators came out on December 26, 1987, in answer to a call issued by Peace Now. But the realization of the other three conditions cited above could only reinforce their arguments.

For this to happen, the determination shown by the Palestinian masses in revolt has to be matched by that of a no less determined leadership rejecting the various schemes for an international conference to decide the fate of the Palestinians, whether these schemes are U.S., Soviet, Arab, or Israeli. This leadership would have to demand unequivocally a total and unconditional withdrawal of the Zionist army from the territories occupied in 1967. For a partial self-determination of the Palestinians to be real, in particular on the West Bank, the Jordanian threat hanging over them would also have to be removed. This means not only that it is necessary to sweep away the proposals that would subject the Palestinians' fate to King Hussein's tutelage, including the notorious "confederation" idea. (Arafat's desire not to burn all his bridges to Hussein explains, by the way, his great reticence to proclaim a

"Palestinian government in exile," which has been much talked about late-ly.) It also means that the struggle of the Palestinians in Palestine has to be complemented by Palestinian struggle in Jordan, where they are in a large majority; a combined struggle with Jordanian progressive forces and working masses to overthrow the Hashemite monarchy, which has no less Palestinian blood on its hands than its Zionist cronies.

## GROWTH OF THE FUNDAMENTALIST CURRENT

The Palestinian uprising that is under way is creating the objective conditions for the emergence of a radical leadership, precisely to the same extent that, as everyone agrees, the movement is largely a spontaneous one. In fact, given the lasting blind alley into which the successive capitulations of the PLO leadership have led and the general political discredit of the other factions of the Palestinian resistance outside the country, the distinctive feature of the last few years has been the development of spontaneous expressions of the Palestinian struggle. They make up the great majority of the 3,150 "violent incidents" (from stone throwing to armed attacks), almost daily occurrences between April 1986 and May 1987, which Israeli sociologist Meron Benvenisti has counted.

Even if, for lack of any credible alternative, the majority of the Palestinian masses continue to support the PLO leadership, their new generation has already been radicalized by the experience of the current uprising. It is to be hoped that a left-wing leadership can emerge from this radicalization. If not, there is a great danger that the Islamic fundamentalist current will be the only one to profit. This current is already growing rapidly among Palestinians, in particular in Gaza. But such an eventuality would end in a new, yet more tragic and disastrous impasse than the one to which the PLO leadership's policies have led. [...]

JANUARY 7, 1988; first published in English in *International Viewpoint*, no. 133 (January 25, 1988).

## CHAPTER 9

# The Uprising's Fourth Month

*This 1988 article took a further look at the Allon Plan, which I saw as the most likely outcome of the situation created by the intifada and also as the outcome enjoying U.S. support. Two preconditions were still lacking: a "Labor election victory" and PLO recognition of "the 'right' of the state of Israel to exist—in other words a de jure and not merely de facto recognition of Israel. This would make possible the PLO's participation in the project. The Palestinian organization would fulfill the second condition in October 1988 (see the next article in this collection), opening the way (to begin with) for negotiations with Washington. The first condition, a Labor election victory, would be met only in 1992; it would lead to the Oslo accords.*

On the threshold of the fourth month of the Palestinians' heroic uprising in the West Bank and Gaza, U.S. Secretary of State George Shultz began a new tour of the Middle East. Shultz undertook his tour in desperation, seeing no prospect of a weakening of the Palestinian youth movement in the near future. Otherwise he would have had every reason to wait for the uprising to end before visiting the region, if only to avoid setting off a new wave of rebellion with his presence. But almost three months after it began on December 9, 1987, the uprising seems to have acquired the stamina of a marathon runner.

The uprising of the Arab youth in the territories occupied by Israel since 1967, including the Syrian Golan Heights, looks more and more like prolonged guerrilla warfare against the occupiers. It is a guerrilla war in which the fighters have no weapons but stones. Many Palestinian youth have developed a stone-throwing aim worthy of the biblical David.

## THE STRONGEST POSSIBLE CONDEMNATION

Nothing stops these young people—neither metal nor plastic bullets nor beatings. Every new victim of the murderous rage of Israeli soldiers and settlers, every addition to the already long list growing implacably day-by-day, adds new fuel to the undying fires of the rebellion. Every new Palestinian victim draws down more opprobrium on the colonist and racist enterprise that has long insulted the memory of Jewish victims of Nazi barbarism by perversely associating itself with them. The Zionists, in a narrow-minded, racist spirit, attribute "self-hatred" to any Jew who disapproves of their actions. But this is no explanation for the fact that there are many men and women today, among those who express the most deeply felt outrage at the repressive cruelty of the Israeli forces, who are much better qualified to represent the victims of the Holocaust than a Shamir or a Rabin.

What condemnation of the Zionists could be more powerful, more tragic, than this reaction, among others, which was reported from Jerusalem by *New York Times* correspondent John Kifner: "In a fashionable boutique Monday, a middle-aged sales women put down her sandwich as she read an article in the *Jerusalem Post* about a blood-spattered wall on a vacant lot in the West Bank town of Ramallah where Israeli soldiers had taken Palestinians to beat them. 'I can't eat my sandwich anymore,' she burst out. 'This is like what was done in the camps. I can't eat anymore.'"[1]

However, if a parallel is to be drawn between Israel and another situation, it is not with Nazi Germany (although there are inevitably common features in the repressive brutality of systems of national, racial or social oppression)—despite Yassir Arafat's verbal excesses at a recent UN session in which he said that the Israeli soldiers "exceed the cruelty of the Nazis."[2] Such overblown exaggeration serves the Palestinians of the interior, whose courageous struggle has won more sympathy for their cause in three months than the PLO had in twenty years, very poorly.

## THE SOUTH AFRICAN MIRROR

A real resemblance, which is being confirmed from year to year, is between Israel and South Africa. This is so clear that even the U.S. mass media, which are generally favorable to Israel, emphasize the analogy. The problem today is no longer the presence within an elitist Israeli democracy of a small minority of people condemned to second-class citizenship because of their religion, as was the case before 1967. Today, a real apartheid system is being imposed on a population that represents more than a third of all those living under Israeli administration.

Along with the various features of apartheid (such as segregation, denial of rights, restrictions on freedom of movement, super-exploitation and so on) that Israel has repeated against the Palestinians, there is now a further resemblance between the two states: the revolt of native youth has become an enduring factor in the situation. This has even prompted a person close to Shimon Peres, the academic Shlomo Avineri, to say recently that if Israel kept the territories occupied in 1967, "the next fifteen years will look more like the last weeks." And at this rate, in the year 2000, "we will look into the mirror and we will see South Africa."[3]

In *Newsweek*, the Israeli left-wing Zionist sociologist Meron Benvenisti also made the following analogy: "To understand the time frame of this civil war, one should recall that ... the Sharpeville massacre that started the black-white violent confrontation in South Africa occurred in 1960. The future is there."[4] The title of Benvenisti's article could not be more eloquent: "Israel's Apocalypse Now."

### THE MYTH THAT WON'T STAY ALOFT

The corollary of the prolonged Palestinian revolt is that the Zionist army, like the South African armed forces, turns increasingly toward the interior of the area it controls. In addition to its original nature as an army for colonial expansion and counter-revolutionary intervention, the so-called Israeli Defense Force is confirming its acquired character of an internal repressive body. In this respect, it is every bit as bad as the worst special forces of riot police, despite the fact that it is a conscript army. Already omnipresent in Israeli society and politics, the IDF's role will grow still further. The myth of Israel, the model democratic state, has already been dealt an irremediable blow.

Another aspect of Israel, a real aspect, that the Zionist leaders want to preserve is its character as a "Jewish" state. The enlightened Zionists, represented today by Peres, consider that the long-term survival of the Zionist state requires restoring its democratic reputation, which is important for the Western aid on which Israel is entirely dependent. The only way to do this, and at the same time preserve the "Jewish" character of the state, is to get rid of those parts of the territories occupied in 1967 with large Arab populations. To the Zionist right, which objects—not without arguments—that the security of Israel would be threatened if there were a substantial retreat from these territories, the Laborites have long given the following assurance: There is no question of letting the Palestinians in the West Bank and Gaza determine their own fate nor of abandoning control over these territories. What is in question is turning over the task of handling the populations concerned to the Jordanian police and keeping military control of the territories by maintaining a belt of settlements and military bases, especially along the Jordan River and the Dead Sea, which separate the West Bank from Jordan proper.

### AN OLD STRATAGEM

This Labor Zionist policy was worked out from 1967 on by its architect, Yigal Allon. But it was only after 1971, that is, after King Hussein of Jordan managed to crush the Palestinian resistance in his kingdom, that the conditions were assembled for it to become credible. Continually counterposed to this view of things has been the policy formulated by Moshe Dayan in the same period: "Coexistence between Israel and the Arabs is possible only under the aegis of the Israeli government and Defense Forces, under whose authority the Arabs can also lead a normal life (sic)."[5] Today the same policy is being defended by the Zionist right, in particular by the Likud, which is led by Shamir, prime minister of the current "National Unity Government." In Likud's view, there can be no future for the West Bank and Gaza that goes beyond maintaining Israeli occupation, with the granting of administrative "autonomy" to their Arab populations.

It is this principle of administrative autonomy, encompassed by an ambiguous suggestion of "transition," that prevailed in the Camp David Accords concluded in 1978 under U.S. auspices between Egypt and Israel. Likud had won the Israeli elections the year before, and was at the height of its power. Carter and Sadat could not risk a failure of the process initiated by the Egyptian president's visit to Israel in November 1977. Therefore they made a concession to Begin on the fate of the West Bank and Gaza. In 1982, on the occasion of the negotiated withdrawal of the Palestinian fighters from a Beirut besieged by the Israeli army, the Reagan Plan in fact revived the principles of the Allon Plan. "It is the firm view of the United States that self-government by the Palestinians of the West Bank and Gaza in association with Jordan offers the best chance for a durable, just and lasting peace."[6]

In order to put this "peace" into operation, the U.S. administration, its Israeli Laborite allies and their Jordanian cohort projected an "international conference" as the essential framework for negotiations between Israel and

Jordan. This was because the Jordan regime was too weak to be able to afford a Sadat-style process of open negotiations with the Zionist state.

The current Palestinian uprising has convinced the Labor Zionists and the Reagan administration more than ever that their common conception was well founded. Shultz's new Middle East tour fits into the framework of efforts to promote it. However, this policy today is running up against two main obstacles. One is the Likud's opposition, which Shultz and Peres hope eventually to get around through a Labor election victory. Since that possibility is not yet taking shape, however, the U.S. administration is trying to gain some time by re-launching, on a temporary basis, the idea of autonomy contained in the Camp David Accords, without abandoning the objective of an international conference. Shultz is bringing this suggestion in his baggage, hoping to be able to mollify both Shamir and the Palestinians with it.

## WHO SPEAKS FOR THE PALESTINIANS?

The other obstacle, of course, is the problem of who is going to represent the Palestinians. While it seems more and more impossible to "get around" the PLO in order to reach a "settlement" of the Palestinian question, it is no less true that this organization as such remains unacceptable as an intermediary for Washington and Peres, insofar as it fails to officially recognize the "right" of the state of Israel to exist. But in the present conditions such recognition would mean a new split in the PLO, already severely weakened by its successive capitulations since 1982. This is the last card the Arafat leadership has left. It is hesitant to play it without solid guarantees regarding the role reserved for it in the proposed "settlement." The PLO has already agreed to everything except this last concession. It has already officially adopted the principle of an "international conference," which Arafat has been playing up in recent weeks.

In other words, carried along by its substitutionist policy, the PLO is declaring its readiness to negotiate the fate of the West Bank and Gaza with Israel and the great powers, instead of holding firmly to the inalienable right of self-determination of the people of these territories. It goes without saying that nothing could come out of such an "international conference" but a diktat aimed at liquidating the Palestinian question and stifling the Palestinian people. [...]

FEBRUARY 25, 1988; first published in English in *International Viewpoint*, no. 136 (March 7, 1988).

## CHAPTER TEN

# Where Is the PLO Going?:
# The Long March ... Backwards

*The following three chapters, written in early 1989, draw up a balance sheet of the Palestinian struggle after 1988, a watershed year for the struggle in many respects. Not only was 1988 the peak year for the intifada—the most remarkable episode in the already long history of Palestinian resistance to the Zionist project; it was also the year of a decisive meeting of the Palestine National Council, which made the concessions necessary to establish official relations between the PLO and Washington. This first article in the series of three describes the developments that brought the Palestinian organization to take this paradoxical step.*

On November 15, 1988, Yassir Arafat proclaimed the "establishment of the state of Palestine." The chairperson of the Executive Committee of the Palestine Liberation Organization (PLO) made his announcement at the end of the nineteenth session of the Palestinian National Council (PNC), the PLO's broadest leading body. It came just three weeks before the first anniversary of the heroic and still uninterrupted uprising of the Palestinian masses in Gaza and the West Bank; and three-and-a-half months after the official renunciation by Jordan's King Hussein of any claim on the West Bank—a territory that his kingdom had annexed following the first Israeli-Arab war in 1948 and that Israel had occupied in 1967.[1]

The PNC's proclamation of the Palestinian state was doubly necessary.[2] This proclamation was needed to fill the juridical vacuum created by Hussein's abrupt decision. It was also necessary in order to respond to the expectations of the majority of inhabitants in the two territories where the uprising is taking place. Their immediate objective was to free themselves from the Zionist occupation and set up an independent state. But though the proclamation itself was indispensable, it was accompanied by other decisions that were absolutely not.

The most remarkable was the explicit acceptance of the United Nations Security Council Resolution 242 (1967). This, coupled with the acceptance of UN General Assembly's Resolution 181 (1947), amounted to recognizing the Zionist state within its pre-1967 war frontiers. This decision is contrary to the beliefs and sentiments of the vast majority of Palestinians in Palestine or in exile.

For the refugees—that is, the great majority of the Palestinian people, expelled from the 80 percent of their territory on which the Zionist state established itself in 1948—rejecting such recognition goes without saying. But the great majority of those living in the West Bank (of whom less than half are refugees from 1948) shares the same view. This was shown in a poll conducted among them on the eve of the PNC's last session: 98.6 percent of those questioned favored the creation of an independent Palestinian state, but 78 percent said they were against creating such a state if the precondition for it was recognizing the state of Israel.[3]

So though this decision did not respond to the Palestinians' aspirations, it nevertheless certainly met other expectations: those of the reactionary Arab regimes to begin with, notably Egypt, Jordan, and Saudi Arabia, which over the past few years have never let up the pressure for a move in this

---

UN SECURITY COUNCIL RESOLUTIONS 181, 242, AND 338

RESOLUTION 181: Adopted on November 29, 1947, by the UN General Assembly on the eve of the British withdrawal from Mandate Palestine, this resolution provided for partitioning the territory into two states. The Jews, most of whom had arrived during the preceding fifteen years, made up a third of the country's population at that point and owned only 6 percent of its surface area. Resolution 181 nonetheless granted the Jewish state more than 55 percent of Palestinian territory, on which half the population was Arab. The Palestinians, backed by the Arab countries, rejected the partition plan. With the completion of the British withdrawal in May 1948, the first Israeli-Arab war broke out. During the war the Zionists took control of almost 80 percent of Palestinian territory, the overwhelming majority of whose Arab inhabitants were forced to flee and never allowed to return. In June 1967, during another Israeli-Arab war, the Zionist state took control of the rest of Palestine (the West Bank and Gaza Strip) along with the Egyptian Sinai and Syrian Golan Heights.

direction. Second, the current head of the Soviet bureaucracy was keen on giving his advice to that effect publicly during his meeting with Arafat in Moscow in April 1988. Third, Europe, in particular the French government acting in concert with Mubarak's Egypt, was pushing in the same direction. Finally, and most important, the U.S. administration, after obliging the PLO leader to spell certain things out, considered itself satisfied, and decided on December 14 to start a direct dialogue with the Palestinian organization.

Without doubt, the PLO has just made a new and major political turn. In order to grasp fully its significance and consequences, it has to be located on the long trajectory that has brought the Palestinian organization, so far, to this spot.

### FOUNDING OF THE PLO

The PLO was created by the first summit of heads of the Arab states, meeting in Cairo in January 1964. In Jerusalem at the end of May that same year, the first session of the PNC, whose members were designated under the control of the Arab states, was opened by King Hussein. The PNC was then composed essentially of representatives of the Palestinian bourgeoisie and notables, including religious figures. An army (the PLA) was founded, linked to the armed forces of each of the states where its brigades were constituted.

---

RESOLUTION 242: Adopted by the Security Council on November 22, 1967, this resolution foresaw "termination of all claims and states of belligerency" and recognition of every state in the region and its "right to live in peace within secure and recognized boundaries free from threats or acts of force"—including through "the establishment of demilitarized zones"—in exchange for Israeli withdrawal from "territories occupied" (thus not from "all" territories occupied) in 1967. The resolution does not even mention the Palestinian people, but limits itself to calling for "a just settlement of the refugee problem."

RESOLUTION 338: Adopted by the Security Council on October 22, 1973, in order to halt the Israeli-Arab war launched sixteen days earlier. It reaffirms Resolution 242 and decides that "negotiations start between the parties concerned under appropriate auspices aimed at establishing a just and durable peace in the Middle East."

A National Charter was also adopted, reflecting the Palestinian and Arab nationalist consensus. It stipulated that "the partition of Palestine in 1947 and the creation of Israel have absolutely no validity, whatever time has elapsed since then, because they are contrary to the will of the Palestinian people and to its natural rights to its homeland." On the other hand, this Charter excluded the Palestinian territories not occupied by Israel—the West Bank and Gaza—from the PLO's sphere of sovereignty. In the Charter, the liberation of Palestine was envisaged as the responsibility of "the entire Arab nation, governments and peoples, the Arab Palestinian people being in the forefront." Lastly, vis-à-vis Jewish inhabitants in the Israeli state the Charter only proposed a distinction between Jews of Palestinian origin entitled to live in Palestine and the others—that is, the overwhelming majority, for whom it offered no perspective.

From 1964 on, however, diverse Palestinian factions and the left wing of the Ba'ath party challenged the PLO.[4] The criticisms they made, which were entirely correct, centered on two basic themes relating to the autonomy of the organization. First was the method by which the PNC was designated, to which they counterposed the demand for direct elections by Palestinians of their representatives. Second was the nature of the PLA, instead of which they put forward the project of an army independent of the Arab states.

## FATAH

A petit bourgeois group whose nationalism was strongly mixed with Islam, Fatah, concretized the idea of an autonomous and immediate Palestinian armed struggle. Launching its first commando raid against Israel on January 1, 1965, before all the other groups, it won a great deal of prestige. Thus when the Arab armies suffered their crushing defeat by the Zionist state in June 1967, Fatah was in the best position to take advantage of the extraordinary wave of radicalization that swept the Palestinian people, extending to the young people in the countries where they were concentrated as well as to the other Arab countries. It was under the pressure of this radicalization that, on September 1, 1967, the Arab summit in Khartoum adopted the famous three "no's" in relation to Israel: "No to peace, no to recognition, no to negotiations." Less than three months later, Egypt and Jordan betrayed this triple pledge by approving UN Resolution 242.

Unable to contain the Palestinian radicalization, much less confront it, the Arab states set to work to take it over. Faced with the emergence of a far left Palestinian current with the founding of the Popular Front for the Liberation of Palestine (PFLP) in November 1967 as well as a Ba'athist current, Egypt and Saudi Arabia chose to support Yassir Arafat's Fatah. Egypt offered Fatah control of the PLO, which was largely under Egyptian control. Saudi Arabia started showering petrodollars on the Palestinian movement, which very quickly had more money at its disposal than any liberation movement had ever dreamed of possessing.

The fourth session of the PNC, meeting in Cairo in July 1968, amended the National Charter according to the wishes of Fatah, so as to prepare the way for its integration into the PLO. The Charter was made more radical, but in terms of the ideological limitations of Fatah: "Armed struggle is the only way to liberate Palestine." Now it applied to the whole of Palestine, including the West Bank and Gaza, all the more because these territories had fallen under Zionist occupation in 1967. The accent was put on an "armed revolution" of the Palestinian people that the Arab states had a duty to support, notably by giving material aid.

### MAXIMALISM AND CONSERVATISM

The nationalist maximalism that characterized Fatah at the time shows up in the Charter's new Article 21, which rejects "all solutions which are substitutes for the total liberation of Palestine." It combined with an explicit rejection of any inter-Palestinian class struggle perspective or political struggle against the Arab regimes. This sociopolitical conservatism, a meeting ground between the bourgeois PLO and petit bourgeois Fatah, was the essential reason for the support given to Fatah by most of the Arab states. "The PLO shall cooperate with all Arab states," stipulates Article 27 of the Charter, it "shall not interfere in the internal affairs of any Arab state."

On the eve of the fifth session of the PNC, in January 1969, Fatah adopted a complementary platform that it got the PLO to ratify. It "categorically rejected" Resolution 242 and put forward, for the first time, the programmatic perspective of a democratic state "all of whose citizens, regardless of their religion, will enjoy equal rights." It was undoubtedly a step forward compared to the Charter, but its limitations were obvious: belief in the possibility of a "democratic" (bourgeois) solution to the Israeli-Palestinian question; a solution in the limited territorial framework of Palestine (which meant, in the most generous hypothesis, cohabitation of more or less equal numbers of Arabs and Jews in a Palestinian state); and finally, a solution that saw Israelis only as a religious community, ignoring the national character of the new society created in Palestine by Zionist colonization.

## THE LEFT AND THE PLO

When the fifth session of the PNC met a month later in Cairo, it sealed Fatah's integration into the PLO, as Arafat's movement took over the PLO leadership with the blessing of its Arab sponsors. It was the fusion of a petit bourgeois movement, in the process of bureaucratic and bourgeois degeneration under the impetus of corruption accelerated by Arab petrodollars, with a bourgeois institution where the Palestinian bourgeoisie was largely and directly represented.

For a while the PFLP, a left, petit bourgeois nationalist organization, refused to join the PLO, challenging its undemocratic makeup. Boycotting the PNC, where it had been offered some minor positions, the PFLP organized forty popular meetings among Palestinians in Jordan, presenting them as so many "national councils." However, it ended up joining the PLO, while demanding that it be transformed into a party front of Palestinian armed struggle organizations. Subsequently, and until this day, they demanded in vain that the PNC's composition be revised by taking into account what its members really represent.

Also in February 1969, a left group led by Nayef Hawatmeh split from George Habash's PFLP to form the Popular Democratic Front for the Liberation of Palestine (PDFLP, today the DFLP). During its first two years of existence, the DFLP was the Palestinian organization closest to revolutionary Marxism, not hesitating even to quote Trotsky, but not without eclecticism and theoretical confusion. It put forward the programmatic perspective of a revolutionary socialist solution to the Palestinian question: in the framework of a socialist, federal Arab state, a unitary Palestinian state where Jews would enjoy the right to "develop their national culture." Although stopping short of a consistent internationalist program such as the one adopted by Trotskyist groups in the region in 1974, the DFLP theses were far in advance of other tendencies in the Palestinian resistance.[5]

Starting from an approach inspired by the theory of permanent revolution, the DFLP criticized Fatah's Palestinian and Arab policies, notably its conception of "national unity" and its principle of "noninterference in the internal affairs of Arab states." It explained how harmful this principle was, even from a narrow Palestine-centrist point of view, since the Palestinian resistance was developing on the territories of Arab states that did not hesitate to "interfere" in its affairs.

As for Palestinian "national unity," the DFLP noted that this was established "under the leadership of feudal lords and millionaires ... up to and including the PNC, which brought together many representatives of Palestinian reaction led by a clique of millionaires, bankers, and big businessmen, to whom representatives of the fighting organizations were added after the fourth session."[6] This radical critique of the PNC did not prevent the DFLP, in its revolutionary phase, from using it and other PLO bodies as a propaganda platform.

Fatah's hegemony over the Palestinian movement and its political line of rightist self-limitation led to the crushing defeat of the movement in Jordan in 1970–71, in spite of the exceptionally favorable conditions at the outset. The Palestinian Left has explained at length the right wing's responsibility for this defeat, suffered under the double aegis of "noninterference" and "unity of Arab ranks against Zionism."

### A STATE APPARATUS WITHOUT A STATE

The scale of the catastrophe —a massacre of Palestinians and their vanguard and the loss of the main mass base of the Palestinian resistance — found expression in a rightward slide of the entire movement, which had retreated to Lebanon. Starting in 1972, Hawatmeh's DFLP turned progressively and definitively toward an alignment with the pro-Soviet Stalinist current. But this was a small degeneration compared with the qualitative completion of the double degeneration—bureaucratic and bourgeois—of Fatah, which became so fully integrated into the PLO that it became hard to tell the two apparatuses apart.

From this time on, we explained that the Fatah/PLO had become a "state apparatus without a state looking for a state at the least cost."[7] A report on the "PLO's structures," edited by "Yassir Arafat's office head," after describing at length the different legislative, executive, and judicial bodies of the Palestinian organization, including courts, prisons, and departments as various as those of any state administration, concluded, "The PLO differs in nature from other organizations who have represented, or who still represent, their respective peoples in their struggle for national liberation. The PLO is not a political party; it is bigger than a liberation front. It is an institution with a state-like nature."[8]

This transformation of the Fatah/PLO inevitably demanded a programmatic adaptation. The maximalism of the early years, suited to a social base of refugees in the camps—an impoverished and marginalized population—was no longer suitable to the enormous bureaucratic apparatus and its summit with its considerable privileges. A shortcut had to be found to provide the state apparatus with a territory, even at the price of an accommodation with imperialism and the Zionist state. The DFLP prepared the ground politically: aligning with Moscow—which had always recognized the "legitimacy" of Israel and therefore had until then considered the Palestinian organizations as dangerous ultra-leftists—it was the first to propose a Palestinian state in the West Bank and Gaza.

The rest of the Palestinian Left, the left wing of Fatah and the PFLP, fought back. These currents rightly denounced the implications of this project, that is, the perspective of a negotiated settlement and, in spite of the DFLP's denials, peaceful coexistence with the Zionist state: in short, a way of eliminating the Palestinian question, which definitely cannot be reduced to just 20 percent of Palestine occupied in 1967. But the maximalism of these same currents prevented them from formulating counterproposals with a transitional content, such as "the total and unconditional withdrawal of the Israeli army from the territories occupied in 1967." [9]

However, the Fatah/PLO remained dependent on a social base assembled in the Lebanese camps, without which it would have lost its usefulness in the eyes of its Arab sponsors. In order to adapt its official program it needed propitious political circumstances. They were furnished by the October 1973 war launched by Sadat's Egypt, described by the Arab and Palestinian revolutionary Left as a "war to open the way for a settlement." The so-called Arab victory in October gave Sadat the political means to embark on the course that would lead to Camp David five years later. The first initiative in this direction was the Geneva Conference under the auspices of the United States and the USSR, which opened up negotiations for a settlement of the Israeli-Arab conflict.

The Fatah/PLO had to put itself in a position to profit from a potential settlement. In expectation of an Israeli withdrawal from the West Bank, King Hussein, who laid claim to the same territory, was the PLO's direct competitor. So it was necessary to proclaim the demand for an independent Palestinian government in this territory. However, pressure from the mass base—the 1948 refugees—was still so great that the new program had to be formulated with extreme delicacy so as not to appear to be betraying the cause. The result was the "ten-point program" of the June 1974 PNC, a revolutionary program in comparison to the PLO's recent positions.

## THE 1974 PROGRAM

Reaffirming the "strategic objective" of a "democratic state" and the rejection of Resolution 242, the 1974 PNC program stipulated that the PLO would establish "a national, independent and fighting government in any liberated part of Palestinian territory." It added, "The PLO will fight against any project for a Palestinian entity whose price is recognition (of Israel), peace, secure borders, the renunciation of our national rights," and so on. In addition, against the Jordanian butcher of the Palestinian people, the 1974 program formulated the objective "of installing in Jordan a national democratic government, closely linked to the Palestinian entity that will be created thanks to our struggle."

However, beyond these good resolutions, the inter-Palestinian debate focused on the question of the Geneva Conference. The PFLP correctly denounced it as being incompatible with the inalienable right of the Palestinian people to self-determination. Nevertheless, the Fatah/PLO leadership openly looked for ways to participate in it, sealing an alliance with Moscow that the PLO's turn had made possible. Condemning this "historic deviation," the PFLP organized a "Rejection Front Against Capitulationist Solutions" and withdrew from the PLO's leading bodies.

Having become acceptable to Moscow and for the legitimacy defined by the United Nations, in October 1974 the PLO was recognized by the UN General Assembly as "the representative of the Palestinian people" by a big majority of member states that included France. A few days later the Rabat summit of Arab heads of state recognized the PLO as the "sole legitimate representative of the Palestinian people." The Arab states had chosen the PLO over King Hussein, whose narrow interests did not correspond to theirs; he thus had to give way temporarily. The Arab states needed the PLO, as George Habash explained well in a long interview/balance sheet given to the PFLP organ *Al-Hadaf* in December 1987:

> The rightist leadership hegemonic in the PLO has followed the policy of [negotiated] settlement for a long time, particularly after 1973, and it continues the same today.... This policy was a cover for the official Arab capitulation. The reactionary

Arab regimes, incapable of confronting the Zionist entity, waited until the PLO leadership gave them their chance by proclaiming the possibility of coexistence with this entity in order to commit themselves to a defeatist peace with it, as the Egyptian regime had done....

The alliance between the Palestinian right leading the PLO and the Arab right is an organic alliance. There are many reasons for this, of which the main one is of course the Arab right's need for a Palestinian cover for its capitulationist politics. This alliance meant of course that the Palestinian right got a great deal of support, both financial and in weapons, which contributed to tipping the balance in its favor. [10]

At the beginning of 1977—having missed the second historic opportunity for the Palestinian movement after Jordan, offered at the onset of the Lebanese civil war in 1975–76—the PLO leadership accelerated its rightist course. In February it made an official reconciliation with the Jordanian butcher and adopted a relatively watered-down program at the March PNC, which did not mention any task in Jordan. The 1977 program explicitly demanded that the PLO should "participate, independently and as an equal partner, in all conferences, meetings, and international attempts to discuss the Palestinian question and the Arab-Zionist conflict." However, it specified that the aim was to liberate the occupied territories "without peace with, or recognition of, Israel." The only positive consequence of the 1974 turn still reflected in the 1977 text was the greater attention given to mass mobilization in the West Bank and Gaza. The PLO leadership had understood that its project for a Palestinian state depended on this.

### CAMP DAVID

In November of the same year, 1977, Egyptian president Sadat began direct negotiations with the Zionist government with his famous visit to Israel. Under the patronage of the United States, they led to the signing of the Camp David accords in 1978 and later to the Egyptian-Israeli peace treaty in 1979. In reaction a "Steadfastness Front" was set up, in which the PLO found itself side by side with Algeria, Libya, Syria, and South Yemen. Under pressure from this front, the most reactionary Arab regimes reluctantly broke with Egypt.

Because of Jordan's scheming to get involved in the negotiated settlement discussions opened by Sadat, the "Steadfastness Front"—including the PLO—boycotted the Arab summit meeting in Amman in November 1980.

The influence of the 1979 Iranian revolution made itself felt. The "Rejection Front," led by the PFLP, returned to the PLO's leading bodies in 1981.

Israel's invasion of Lebanon in June 1982 was a fatal blow to the relative rectification of the PLO's policies during the previous five years. But while the leadership of the Fatah/PLO had needed more than two years to make its political turn after its evacuation from Jordan in 1971, it undertook its new right turn immediately after the evacuation of Beirut.

On September 1, 1982, while the last contingent of Palestinian fighters was leaving Beirut, Ronald Reagan threw out a line to the PLO leadership by proclaiming a peace plan that foresaw establishment of "self-government by the Palestinians of the West Bank and Gaza in association with Jordan" after an Israeli withdrawal from these territories. Calling on the Palestinians to recognize Israel and its "right to a secure future," and lauding the merits of Resolution 242 as a basis for negotiation, Reagan added: "I fervently hope that the Palestinians and Jordan ... would accept this opportunity."

The U.S. president's wish was soon granted. On September 20, while the blood of the Sabra and Shatila martyrs was still not dry, King Hussein called on the PLO to discuss with him the establishment of a future Jordanian-Palestinian "confederation." Arafat arrived in Amman on October 9, in response to an invitation from the king. A few months earlier, such a gesture would have been unthinkable. Nevertheless, a climate of defeat prevailed, while the dispersal of the combative Palestinian rank-and-file to the four corners of the Arab world left the PLO chief with a free hand. Nevertheless he wanted the PNC to ratify his new policy.

Meeting in Algiers in February 1983, the Council adopted a political resolution that marked a new slide to the right for the PLO, in spite of the efforts of the nationalist factions and the Left to tone down its formulations. By way of a compromise, the resolution stated that "future relations with Jordan must be established on a confederal basis between two independent states," at the same time explicitly rejecting the idea of a joint delegation with Jordan (meaning to reject negotiations for a settlement, though not making this explicit). Skillfully, the Arafat leadership won the PNC over to emphatically support the Brezhnev plan, published a few days after Reagan's. It knew perfectly well that the PLO Left—the DFLP, aligned with Moscow for a long time, or the PFLP, which had followed slowly but surely in the DFLP's footsteps since the beginning of the 1980s and picked up the pace after 1982— could not oppose it.

## BREZHNEV PLAN, REAGAN PLAN

The Brezhnev Plan already contained all the ingredients that would make such a sensation at the PNC in November 1988. It affirmed Israel's "right" to existence and security and called for peace between Israel and its neighbors, including a Palestinian state in the West Bank and Gaza. All this was to be brought about by an "international conference on the Middle East" under the aegis of the big powers, "the permanent members of the UN Security Council."

In fact, Arafat acted more in the framework of the Reagan Plan chosen by King Hussein. This demanded that Arafat adhere to the principle of a common delegation—including Palestinian delegates in a Jordanian delegation—to the peace negotiations. On this point—which the PNC had already rejected—the Fatah chief ran up against the veto of the Palestinian Left and Syria (whose Golan Heights had been occupied by Israel since 1967 but were not even explicitly mentioned in Reagan's statement) and with a section of his own movement. He decided to fight it out with all these opposing forces.

Evacuating the north of Lebanon after battles with his Syrian-backed opponents [the Fatah dissident wing], Arafat went directly to Egypt to meet President Hosni Mubarak, thereby breaking the official Arab boycott of the Egyptian regime that had begun after the signing of the Camp David peace treaty. George Habash demanded—vain hope!—that Arafat be deposed. Following on from this, the Fatah/PLO organized the seventeenth session of the PNC, again in Amman, in November 1984.

All the other Palestinian organizations boycotted this session, with the exception of two tiny pro-Iraqi groups. King Hussein, who had inaugurated the very first session of the PNC twenty years earlier, opened it. In the meantime he had massacred some tens of thousands of Palestinians.

The 1984 PNC ratified Arafat's policy: "joint action" with Jordan as well as relations with Egypt. In February 1985, the PLO chief concluded the Amman agreement with King Hussein. It involved a "common delegation" to the "peace negotiations" in the framework of an "international conference" on the basis of UN resolutions "including Security Council resolutions" (an allusion to Resolution 242). The accord also foresaw the establishment of an "Arab confederation between the Jordanian and Palestinian states."

This honeymoon did not last long. At the same time Hussein was finalizing a plan with his old Labor Zionist friends, who were back in business in Israel under the leadership of Shimon Peres, to "share out functions" in the West Bank. The Labor Party favors an agreement with Jordan and partial restitution of the territories occupied in 1967, but it did not want anything to do with the PLO. Judging that the PLO had become impotent, and using the pretext of its hesitation to recognize Resolution 242 openly and explicitly—an indispensable condition for any peace negotiations with Israel—Hussein suddenly sent the PLO packing in February 1986. He decided unilaterally to "suspend" the Amman agreement.

### "REUNIFICATION"

Following this total and lamentable failure of its policy, the Fatah/PLO leadership came under growing pressure—including from inside its own ranks—to backpedal and make up with the groups aligned with the Soviet Union. Nevertheless, for an entire year they tried to reestablish links with the Jordanian government through the intervention of their allies, the Saudi, Iraqi, and Egyptian regimes. When these initiatives failed, the PLO resigned itself to accepting the good offices of Moscow for the "reunification" of the PLO—that is, the reintegration of the PFLP and the DFLP into the unified organization.

The "reunification" was sealed by the PNC in Algiers, in April 1987. However, the nationalist factions linked to the Syrian regime kept their distance, including the dissident wing of Fatah. This meant that, despite the Palestinian Right's negative balance sheet, there was no pure and simple return to the positions previous to Arafat's Jordanian adventure. Rather, in the framework of a relationship of forces that was even more favorable to the Right than at the 1983 PNC, the outcome was a new compromise including new concessions by a left urged on by Moscow. The most radical faction of this left, the PFLP, is ending up progressively lining up with the "homeland of socialism." (According to George Habash's formulations, this is the final phase of his front's "transformation" from a "petit bourgeois" to a "proletarian" party.)

So on the two key disputed points in 1983–86—relations with Jordan and Egypt—the PNC's 1987 resolution virtually left the leadership of Fatah/PLO with a free hand, while noting the obsolescence of the Amman accord repudiated by King Hussein. On the other hand, the resolution reaffirmed "unrelenting rejection of Resolution 242," while reiterating support for an "International Conference for Peace in the Middle East ...

with the participation of the permanent members of the UN Security Council." In exchange for its good offices, Moscow obtained the following clarification: the PNC "stresses that the International Conference must be invested with full powers."

Under joint pressure from its Arab clients—Jordan, Egypt, and Saudi Arabia—Washington had since 1985 actually abandoned direct references to the Camp David accords as a framework for a settlement in order to take back onboard the principle of the International Conference. Shimon Peres had followed suit. Only the Likud continued to cling to the Camp David accords, which had been signed by Menachem Begin himself.

The 1985 Arafat-Hussein agreement, in the period of the rupture with the whole of the Palestinian Left and icy relations with Moscow, included the principle of the Conference. But the absence of any precision regarding procedure made this agreement entirely compatible with the Shultz/Peres interpretation of the Conference as a "fig leaf" (as *Newsweek* called it) for direct bilateral negotiations between Israel and a Jordanian/Palestinian delegation. Shultz and Peres aimed at keeping Syria and the USSR out of the real process. On this point, therefore, the PLO sided with Moscow in 1987.

## THE INTIFADA

But no sooner had the 1987 PNC ended than the Arafat leadership renewed its contacts with Egypt, to the great displeasure of the DFLP, PFLP, and Palestinian Communist Party. (The PCP, former West Bank section of the Jordanian CP, was brought into the PLO at the same PNC meeting to please Moscow. By way of compensation, a fundamentalist Islamic faction was also brought in, with twice the representation of the PCP.) The PLO seemed about to repeat the scenario that had led to the 1983 split. The Fatah/PLO leadership launched itself once again into deals with its reactionary friends in Baghdad, Cairo, and Riyadh, who were seeking to reconcile it with Amman. At the Arab summit that met in the latter capital in November 1987, Arafat, although treated as an underling, met with the Jordanian king in the presence of the Iraqi tyrant Saddam Hussein. A little later he declared that he had agreed with "His Majesty" to "begin where we had left off." [11]

The following month, understanding that from now on they had to count primarily on themselves and their own struggles, the Palestinian masses in the West Bank and Gaza began the intifada, without needing any signal from outside. Very quickly it proved to be the most formidable episode in the Palestinian anti-Zionist struggle since the uprising of 1936--39. Before the PNC meeting in 1988, the Unified Leadership of the Intifada never at any time expressed any inclination to recognize the Israeli state and Resolution 242. On the contrary, during the first few months of the intifada many of the leadership's communiqués explicitly rejected recognition of Israel and Resolution 242, and described the regime in Jordan as an "agent" (of imperialism). As for the state of mind of the population itself in the occupied territories, the poll cited at the beginning of this article—carried out on the eve of the last PNC—gives a good indication.

In view of the massive character and undeniable majority support for the intifada, its radical character in many respects and the outright hostile position to the Jordanian regime reflected in its communiqués, King Hussein could see how badly compromised the project was that he, along with his crony Shimon Peres, had cherished for two years.

## KING HUSSEIN'S DECISION

The breadth and the strength of the insurrectional fires blazing in the West Bank and Gaza—which the Israeli army could not extinguish in spite of its impressive deployment—put an end to any desire the Jordanian monarch had left to recover the territories. He had already demonstrated in his own kingdom that he was ready to crush a mass movement by methods far bloodier than those to which the Zionist government limited itself, thanks to the pressure of international public opinion and a section of the Israeli public. But taking everything into account, the two territories would now cost Jordan much more in repressive outlay than they would yield.

Moreover, King Hussein had to act quickly to contain the fire and prevent it from spreading to his own kingdom, where nearly 60 percent of the people are Palestinians. He had to prevent the insurrectional blaze from crossing the Jordan River. His repressive apparatuses had already greatly increased their activity to put out the first sparks of agitation in support of the intifada. On July 31, 1988, he announced his decision to "break the legal and administration links between the two banks of the Jordan"—in other words, to abandon his claim to the West Bank, which his kingdom had annexed in 1949. One week later he explained, "By opting for their own state, our Palestinian brothers have opted for independence vis-à-vis Jordan. If there is a split, therefore, it corresponds to their wishes."

These oily phrases could not hide his real attitude, visible even in the way the July 31 decision was taken—brutally, with no previous consultation with the PLO, so that it created a dangerous juridical vacuum and an economic problem. The Zionist government could have filled the legal vacuum, if it had been politically prepared to annex the territories concerned, as the Israeli extreme right had demanded. The economic problem—the wages of some 21,000 functionaries in the West Bank that Jordan had continued to pay—was partially resolved by Libya's promise to take them in hand. Of course, there was still the problem of the PLO being able to send in funds (five million dollars per month).

However, the most urgent problem was the legal vacuum. It became imperative for the PLO to proclaim a Palestinian state in the West Bank and Gaza. It could have done this without the least recognition of the state of Israel. (Jordan did not recognize Israel in 1949 and still had not formally recognized it in 1988.) The PLO could have combined the proclamation, so fervently desired by the vast majority of people in the two territories, with the political program outlined in September by the Unified Leadership of the Intifada in its communiqué no. 26.

This communiqué, expressing a broad consensus of Palestinians inside the territories and among the PLO's various factions, included a series of immediate demands as well as four more long-term objectives. The first three objectives, which repeat in a more radical way the elements of a platform adopted by the Arab summit in June 1988, are absolutely correct. The fourth objective includes an evident contradiction between the right of the Palestinian people to self-determination and the principle of an "International Conference with full powers" to decide their fate. This is evidence of the confusion that reigns in the minds of most Palestinians concerning this principle, which even the PLO left hotly defends, dear as it is to Moscow's heart.

On top of that, a revolutionary PLO acting from outside would have launched an appeal urging the Jordanian and Palestinian masses in Jordan to rise up alongside the intifada in the occupied territories to overthrow the hireling monarchy. This is indeed the sole, indispensable means to break the repressive vise encircling the West Bank, to say nothing of the tyrannical yoke around the necks of the masses in Jordan, among whom there are more Palestinians than in the West Bank and Gaza put together. The overthrow of the Amman monarchy is also a necessary step for the establishment of a Jordanian/Palestinian state free from imperialist and Zionist domination that would really be viable, unlike the project of a mini-state in the 1967 territories, which would consist of 5,812 square kilometers divided in two by the state of Israel.

## THE ROAD NOT TAKEN

But without asking too much from the PLO leadership, simply adopting the program in communiqué no. 26, in the continuity of the PNC's 1987 resolutions, would have represented a decision to fight, the decision of a leadership based exclusively on the mass struggle and understanding that a legitimate right is not something to be begged for. Sadly, this was not the PLO leaders' approach. They opted long ago for the strategy of a negotiated settlement with Israel, a strategy whose number one objective was to win recognition from U.S. imperialism.

However, the U.S. government's conditions for establishing a dialogue with the PLO were well-known: Henry Kissinger set them in 1975. George

---

**THE FOUR-POINT PROGRAM OF THE UNITED NATIONAL LEADERSHIP OF THE INTIFADA** (Communiqué no. 26, late September 1988)

1) Israeli withdrawal from Palestinian and Arab [Syrian and Lebanese] territory occupied since 1967, including Arab Jerusalem;

2) Abrogation of all measures of annexation and appropriation and elimination of the settlements established in the occupied territories;

3) Placement of the occupied Palestinian territories under UN authority in order to provide a guarantee to the Palestinian people, for a period not to exceed several months, to prepare for the free exercise by the Palestinian people of its right to self-determination; and

4) Convocation of the International Conference with full powers under the auspices of the UN, on the basis of its resolutions concerning the question of Palestine. [That is, the General Assembly resolutions that emphasize the Palestinian people's right to self-determination, not Resolution 242, which does not even mention the Palestinian people—G.A.]

*Source: Al-Raia* (Nazareth), 30 September 1988.

Bush [George Bush Sr. was then Ronald Reagan's vice president] cited them in an interview with the *Jerusalem Post*: "The PLO must not only clearly accept Security Council Resolutions 242 and 338, which recognize Israel's right to exist, but also renounce terrorism and the article in its founding charter advocating the destruction of Israel."[12]

In an article in *Le Monde*, then-Israeli Foreign Minister Shimon Peres added this clarification concerning his government, or at least his party: "The PLO must, in the final analysis, choose between two options: support from Syria ... or dialogue with Jordan.... It is only with Jordan that the PLO can work out a policy of negotiation with Israel."[13]

## ARAFAT'S CHOICE

Arafat had already received this message a long time before. But the radical pressure of the intifada during its first months, the communiqués from the interior and the PLO's left-wing partners—as well as the USSR and Libya—all pushed him in the direction of reestablishing an alliance with Damascus. The beginnings of negotiations with the Syrian government, following the assassination of Abu Jihad by the Israeli secret services in April 1988, delighted them all, but not for long.[14]

Indeed, Arafat was intensively exploring the Jordanian--U.S. option leading to negotiations with Israel. In March he had pushed two PNC members who have U.S. citizenship to meet with American Secretary of State George Shultz in spite of the Intifada Unified Leadership's explicit veto of any such meetings. Following the Reagan-Gorbachev summit in Moscow at the end of May—during which the Kremlin's chief bureaucrat synchronized his watch with Washington's on the Middle East question— Arafat, relieved, shifted into higher gear.

Boosted by encouragement from the leading lights of Arab reaction meeting in Algiers at the June 1988 summit, the PLO chief published a feeler article by Bassam Abu Sharif, a defector from the PFLP and now Arafat's official counselor. Everything was already there: acceptance of Resolution 242 and "bilateral peace talks with Israel" in the framework of an International Conference (in short, the "fig leaf"). The article provoked a general outcry from the PLO Left, but it was very well received by those to whom it was addressed in the United States and Israel.

Following the Jordanian measures on July 31, 1988, the PNC was convoked for September. The Right projected setting up a "provisional government" speaking in the name of the Palestinian people and composed of personalities acceptable to Washington. The Left opposed this loudly and forcefully. Moscow intervened to pour oil on the waters. The PLO's Executive Committee met in Tunis at the beginning of October. It decided to postpone the governmental question, to call a meeting of the PNC for the end of the month, and to proclaim a Palestinian state. The right wing and Moscow's followers, the DFLP and the PCP, proposed to do so on the basis of the 1947 Resolution 181. Arafat wanted to add Resolution 242, but he was ready to reconcile himself to this provisional compromise, which amounted to recognizing the state of Israel without making a decision about its frontiers. George Habash grumbled.

Moscow received a PLO delegation on October 10–11. The Soviets conveyed two messages. First, the PNC should be delayed so as not to proclaim the Palestinian state before the Israeli elections due on November 1—in this way Shimon Peres's "good Zionists" would not be upset. Second, the state of Israel should be recognized. On October 11, the Tass press agency reported that the discussions had underlined the necessity for "concrete steps that must be founded on balancing the interests of all the concerned parties," that is, the oppressors and the oppressed. Habash resigned himself to accepting Resolution 181 as a lesser evil, in a logic of permanent compromise that regulates the slide to the right of all the PLO factions via a sort of chain reaction.

With less and less to fear from his left, Arafat went to Aqaba in Jordan to meet with King Hussein and President Mubarak on October 22. *Le Monde* commented, "There is no doubt that, by thus displaying himself together with these two close allies of the United States who are favorable to a negotiated settlement, Mr. Arafat wanted to reinforce his image as a man searching for peace.... [He] has clearly shown the hard-liners in the PLO that the way forward must be that of negotiation and compromise."[15] From Aqaba, Arafat and Mubarak went to Baghdad, this time to display themselves with Saddam Hussein.

## THE STATE OF PALESTINE

The political choices made by the PLO leadership are clearer than ever, full steam ahead toward a Sadat-style capitulation. After all, Sadat, whom the PLO has called every name in the book, only did what the PLO is preparing to do. He recognized Israel in exchange for the recovery of Egyptian occupied territory, the Sinai, with a demilitarization clause guaranteeing the security of the Zionist state. Both capitulations have been based on moral victories, the October 1973 war in one case, the intifada in the other—unlike the PLO's previous shifts (in 1974, 1977, and 1983), which took place against a backdrop of defeat. Abdul-Sattar Qassem, one of the prisoners from the intifada, has emphasized this eloquently.

When it finally met November 12–15, the PNC proclaimed "the state of Palestine." This decision, in itself a challenge to the Israeli occupation, was impatiently awaited by the masses of the intifada. It galvanized them, reinforcing their hopes of seeing the day approach when the Zionist army would withdraw from their land. But while the proclamation of an independent state by the masses struggling under the occupation is an act of bravery, the same thing is certainly not true for the PNC meeting in

---

ABDUL-SATTAR QASSEM, professor of political science
at An-Najah University (Nablus) on the West Bank, held prisoner in the Ansar 3
camp in the Negev since February 1988

Anyone who tries to cut loose from the criteria set by the intifada is trying to do an end run around it and divert it from its objectives, which in the end would mean seriously undermining it.... There is every reason to fear that the intifada will be exploited in order to carry out political tactics that were not yet openly proclaimed and that were waiting for a chance to be implemented. The situation is quite similar to the use Sadat made of the limited military achievement of the Arab armies in 1973. Sadat exploited the considerable moral boost that the war gave to Arab public opinion so that he could say he was entering the political fray from a position of strength. The result was that Egypt left the path of confrontation and recognized Israel.... If what some people call for today is right, then we have certainly committed a crime against ourselves and against others. We could, for example, have spared ourselves tens of thousands of deaths over the years and avoided all kinds of humiliation and suffering if we had accepted King Hussein's conception of peace.... It turns out that some Palestinian leaders are proposing today, after all the suffering we have been through, practically the same thing that King Hussein had already proposed since the start of the occupation [in 1967].

Source: Excerpts from an article in the Beirut daily As-Safir, 29 October 1988.

Algiers. (They did not forget to salute "the fighting president, Chadli Bend-jedid" barely one month after he had bloodily crushed another intifada!)[16]

One could legitimately ask why it was necessary to wait until after the Israeli elections and let the "legal vacuum" caused by Jordan's July withdrawal decision go on for three and a half months. Moreover, why was the proclamation not made long before, at the beginning of the intifada? Or in 1976, when the mobilization in the 1967 territories was already intense and municipal elections there, though under Israeli control, resulted in victory for PLO supporters? Or in 1974, when the PNC adopted the transitional principle of a Palestinian state in one part of Palestine?

### THE SHOCKING DECISION

For an answer we can turn to Bilal El-Hassan, a close collaborator of Arafat's and editor-in- chief of the Fatah/PLO semi-official journal:

> Why was the state proclaimed at this particular time? The crucial point regarding this is Jordan's [July 31] decision ... which created a vacuum that someone had to fill. It was natural that the Palestinian leadership should take the initiative in this respect, given that this measure is a natural right as far as they are concerned. Jordan's decision helped the Palestinian side to take this step, given that it came at a time when it would not raise any conflict or problem with Jordan. The PLO has always pushed to the fore the idea of the state as a militant and political objective, without accompanying this with any practical measures in order to avoid any premature and pointless conflict with Jordan. Now that Jordan has disengaged, the practical Palestinian measure could be implemented without raising any problem among Arabs.[17]

In other words, as I wrote at the same time, this measure no longer had "the character of a challenge to the monarchy of Amman and its reactionary allies that it would have if it had been made earlier."[18]

This is why a newspaper like *Le Monde*, for example, was right a few hours after the end of the PNC to devote its headline not to the proclamation of the state but to the following point: "The PLO has implicitly recognized the existence of Israel." This was really the shocking decision by the PNC: the last-minute acceptance of Resolution 242, motivated as far as Arafat was concerned by Shimon Peres's circular to Israeli embassies just before the PNC meeting. This circular explained that only acceptance of

Resolutions 242 and 338—and not Resolution 181—would amount to recognition of Israel within secure and recognized boundaries.[19]

The text proclaiming the Palestinian state was itself based on Resolution 181, after forty-one years and hundreds of thousands of Palestinian and Arab deaths in the struggle against the state that this resolution had established in the most iniquitous way. This same text, read by Arafat himself, declared that the Palestinian state rejects "the use of force, of violence or of terrorism against its own territorial integrity ... or that of any other state."

## INTERNATIONAL CONFERENCE

The PNC's political resolution goes even further. It reiterates the principle of the International Conference, but this time the phrase "with full powers" is replaced by "effective," in spite of opposition from Habash and others to this far from innocent change. Above all, the resolution specifies that such an International Conference "will meet on the basis of Security Council Resolutions 242 and 338"—this after twenty-one years of stubborn rejection of Resolution 242 by the whole Palestinian movement at the cost of tens of thousands of deaths. Only 15 percent of PNC members voted against this part of the resolution, including the PFLP members and some independents and Islamic fundamentalists.

Following in the footsteps of the resolution of the June 1988 Arab summit in Algiers and communiqué no. 26 of the Unified Leadership of the Intifada partly inspired by it, the PNC's resolution demands that the occupied territories be put under the auspices of the UN for a limited period. But though the first two texts envisaged this as a transition toward the exercise of the Palestinian people's right to self-determination, the November 1988 PNC saw this simply as the means to "create a favorable climate for the success of the International Conference, the reaching of a political settlement and the realization of security and peace for all, by mutual agreement and consent, and to allow the Palestinian state to exercise real powers over its territories."

This just shows how little importance the PLO leadership attaches to the free, real, direct, and democratic exercise of the people's right to self-determination in these territories. Equally significant in this regard is the total absence from the PNC's resolution of the central political demand contained in the Unified Leadership's communiqués from the beginning of the uprising up to the eve of the PNC: holding free elections in the West Bank and Gaza.

It should be noted finally that, in spite of Jordan's July 31 decision and the sentiments expressed by the rebellious Palestinian masses, the PNC resolution reiterates the principle of a "confederation with Jordan."[20] This despite the fact that King Hussein himself told Arafat, at their Aqaba meeting, that he would prefer not to make any premature announcements on this question.

So it is understandable that the imperialist powers unanimously awarded top marks to the last PNC session, just as there was grandiloquent praise for the PLO's "flexibility" and "realism" by many who had described it not long before as "terrorist" and who still proclaimed their undying attachment to the state of Israel. The Fatah/ PLO leadership believed it had scrupulously adhered to the conditions laid down by Washington for sitting around the same table with its representatives. Arafat had just played his "last card" in return for the mess of potage represented by recognition from Israel's guardian.

But to general astonishment, Shultz refused even to give Arafat a visa for the UN General Assembly in New York. However, the U.S. secretary of state turned out to be much shrewder than those who accused him of lacking in judgment at the time appreciated—as if this old fox was as dull-witted as Shamir. Shultz knew perfectly well that he had Arafat mesmerized with his carrot of recognition, but he wanted to squeeze out of him an even clearer, sharper and more precise support for the U.S. conditions.

What happened next is well-known: the mediation of the Swedish Social Democrats, and Arafat's speech on December 13 to the UN General Assembly meeting held specially in Geneva. Here Arafat again confirmed PLO acceptance of Resolutions 242 and 338 as the basis for an international conference and for a settlement, and once again condemned terrorism. Nevertheless, Washington once again turned a deaf ear. Shultz demanded that the PLO chief declare explicitly, and with no ambiguity, that he recognized Israel de jure and renounced terrorism (a way of forcing him to admit that the PLO had been "terrorists").

### RENUNCIATION

Having decided to grovel to the enemies of the Palestinian people, Arafat went to the bitter end—the bitter end of humiliation. In a press conference on December 14 called to do just that, without beating around the bush Arafat pronounced himself in favor of the "right of all the parties to exist in peace and security, including the state of Palestine, Israel, and their

neighbors." He added: "We totally and absolutely renounce all forms of terrorism, whether it be by individuals, groups, or states."

Shultz was then able to consider himself satisfied and to declare that in
future the United States would be "ready for a substantial dialogue with
representatives of the PLO." Even the B'nai B'rith League, a U.S. Zionist
organization, said now that they understood "the PLO having accepted the
condition set by the United States, it was proper to respect the commitments that had been made."[21] A few days later a grateful Arafat offered
Washington the help of his intelligence services in the inquiry into the
Pan Am Boeing explosion.

If the U.S. decision to establish direct contacts with the PLO was a "victory" for the PLO, it would be interesting to know what a surrender would
look like! Arafat—a grand organizer of defeats and grand master in the art
of going through them making a V-for-victory sign—did not hesitate to
explain that the U.S. decision was obtained thanks to "the tenacity of the
militants of the intifada" (in sharp contrast to his own "flexibility"), and to
"their natural and principal allies, Iraqi soldiers who defended the eastern
door of the Arab nation."[22] Only fools could believe this.

Abu Iyad, the PLO's number two, is more forthright.[23] In October he
confessed to the Kuwaiti newspaper *Al-Qabas*, "We must recognize that the
Zionist movement has succeeded in convincing the world of what it calls
the basic principles for a political settlement, encapsulated in the recognition of Resolution 242.... Some people say: Why must we give in to this
blackmail? My opinion is that the Zionist movement is not so much blackmailing us as blackmailing Europe and the world."

### SURRENDER

Leaving aside the misplaced boasting, Abu Iyad acknowledges the capitulation. But he presents it as inevitable in the face of an all-powerful enemy,
"the Zionist movement," which "succeeded in convincing the world." This
is an old refrain of right-wing Arab nationalism and serves as an alibi for all
its surrenders. The Zionists (the phrase they use to avoid saying "the Jews")
"manipulate" the United States, not the other way around. This argument
is made now at a time when, precisely, the Zionist movement's power to
convince is at its lowest historical level ever, thanks to the intifada, and the
struggle of the Palestinian people against the Zionist state has reached its
highest level in half a century.

George Habash was quite right when, addressing the leaders of the Palestinian Right who are hegemonic in the PLO, he asked, "Is this the time to make new concessions? We're in a period when the International Conference hasn't even begun, and already they want us to take off our jacket.

That's not enough for them; they want us to take off our pants. And that doesn't satisfy them either—they want us to take off our underclothes. They want us to go to the International Conference totally naked!"[24]

The PLO's trajectory indeed resembles a political striptease.

JANUARY 16, 1989; first published in English in *International Viewpoint*, no. 156 (February 6, 1989).

## CHAPTER ELEVEN

# Where Is the PLO Going?:
# The State, the PLO, and the Palestinian Left

*This second article of the series, while drawing a critical balance sheet of the experience of the Palestinian Left, deals with several fundamental issues about the Palestinian struggle: in particular, the program of the struggle against the Israeli occupation of the West Bank and Gaza and how the Left should decide its attitude toward the PLO.*

November 5, 1988, will go down in history as the day when the state of Palestine was proclaimed in the territories occupied by Israel in 1967—that is, on nearly 20 percent of Palestinian land. But it was also the day when the Palestine Liberation Organization (PLO)—created in 1964 as its name suggests to liberate the 80 percent of Palestinian territory on which the Zionist state was established by force in 1948—officially accepted United Nations Resolutions 181 (1947) and 242 (1967). In other words, when the PLO recognized the Israeli state and its "right to live in peace within secure and recognized boundaries" on four-fifths of Palestine.

A few hours after the end of the last session of the Palestine National Council (PNC) on November 15, George Habash called a press conference. Habash is the head of the Popular Front for the Liberation of Palestine (PFLP), the main left faction in the PLO and the second-largest Palestinian organization after Yassir Arafat's Fatah. He explained to the press that his movement would stay in the PLO, in spite of its disagreement with the PNC's political resolution, in order "to preserve national unity." Conscious of the weakness of this argument, Habash added that he was convinced that the new policy of the Palestinian right would lead nowhere, in any case. "Frankly, we no longer fear an American or Israeli settlement, because the maximum that can be gotten out of such an agreement cannot be accepted by any Palestinian, right wing or left wing."

## AN OLD PRETEXT

The pretext is threadbare. Fifteen years ago, the Left of Fatah used the same argument to justify its spinelessness toward a leadership that had chosen in practice a negotiated settlement with the Zionist state.[1] At that time, George Habash's PFLP argued against this pretext, withdrawing from the PLO's leading bodies in order to wage a political fight against the dominant bloc. And here we are, so many years later, at the end of a sadly historic PNC that capitulated to U.S. demands for the PLO's participation in a negotiated settlement process, with Habash using the same arguments that he fought before when the pretext was much more credible than it is today. But things should be judged on the evidence. What is the "maximum that can be gotten" out of a settlement from the standpoint of the United States and Israel?

First we can look from Washington's viewpoint. Ronald Reagan emphasized in his statement/plan of September 1, 1982:

> I call on the Palestinian people to recognize that their own political aspirations are inextricably bound to recognition of Israel's right to a secure future.... self-government by the Palestinians of the West Bank and Gaza in association with Jordan offers the best chance for a durable, just and lasting peace .... the Arab-Israeli conflict should be resolved through the negotiations involving an exchange of territory for peace.... UN Resolution 242 remains wholly valid as the foundation-stone of America's Middle East peace effort.

At the end of 1988, the bare minimum for the PLO, which had never stopped being lowered, had already essentially met this maximum envisaged by Washington. Admittedly, some nuances remained: the Reagan plan foresaw Palestinian "self-government" linked to Jordan, while the last PNC political resolution spoke of a Palestinian state (the term "independent" no longer appeared, as if by accident) in confederation with Jordan. Jurists would appreciate the distinction. However, Jordan's King Hussein himself had already resolved the debate by officially detaching the West Bank from his kingdom on July 31, 1988.

Is there then a disagreement on the framework of the negotiations, beyond the agreement on the principle of holding them? This is no longer the case, according to Arafat. He recently explained to the semiofficial journal of his movement that an understanding had been reached between Moscow and Washington that the International Conference would meet in "ongoing" session and break up into bilateral commissions.[2] The PLO chief made it clearly understood that he no longer considered there to be a divergence with the United States on this subject.

What about the admittedly fundamental question of Israeli withdrawal? In the framework of Resolution 242, the U.S. government has always been for an exchange—peace against the territories occupied in 1967—without ever specifying that the Israeli retreat must be total. In fact, Washington deliberately left the matter vague so as to be able to arbitrate in any potential negotiations between Arabs and Israelis, as it did at Camp David. The 1982 Reagan Plan limited itself to affirming that when negotiations took place the United States would be able to assess "the extent to which Israel should be asked to give up territory," depending on what was proposed in exchange.

## THE ALLON PLAN

With Washington reserving the role of arbiter to itself on this question of withdrawal, the ball was in Israel's camp. Enlightened Zionists, led by Labor Party head Shimon Peres, have always put themselves in the framework of Resolution 242 and its basic principles as defended by the U.S. government. After the 1967 war one of the big guns of Zionist Labor, Yigal Allon (who has since died), worked out a plan for a settlement with Jordan calling for an Israeli withdrawal from most of the West Bank. Some settlements and military bases were to be maintained at strategic points, notably along the Jordan River, which was considered as an inviolable security frontier for the Zionist state (the notion of "secure boundaries" contained in Resolution 242 lent itself to this sort of interpretation).

Since then, Labor's adhesion to the principle of withdrawal (partial, of course) has been strengthened—not for "noble" reasons, but through fear of the Arab "demographic peril." This fear in turn has been considerably boosted by the intifada (uprising), in which Peres has been able to see an illustration of his party's theses. On December 30, 1987, three weeks after the beginning of the uprising, he sounded the alarm. He publicly asserted that, in the year 2000, "the entire population between the Mediterranean and the

Jordan River (including the West Bank and Gaza) would be 45 percent Arab and 55 percent Jewish," because the Arab birth rate is "double ours."[3] Two months later Yitzhak Rabin—the Labor Party's number two and as minister of defense the main person responsible for repressing the uprising—made this confession: "During the last two months I have learned ... that it is impossible to govern a million and a half Palestinians by force."[4]

## MORAL GANGRENE

Indeed, besides the heavy economic burden that this has meant for the Israeli state and the damage to its image in the world—two dangerous consequences for the Israeli "security" system—the intifada represents a direct and serious handicap for the Zionist army itself. It is mobilizing many thousands of soldiers to repress continually resurging mass demonstrations. The result is not only the "diversion" of a considerable part of Israel's military potential, but also—and above all—a moral gangrene spreading through the ranks of the Zionist army. Although going back much further than the occupation of Lebanon (which ended in a quasi-debacle), the occupation of the 1967 territories has in its turn become more and more burdensome to maintain since the intifada.

So it is not surprising to note that the most passionate champions of a withdrawal are today to be found at the top of the Israeli military hierarchy. In March 1988, a group of retired Israeli generals (as such, free to act politically) founded the Council for Peace and Security. They included Aharon Yariv, ex-head of Mossad (Israeli intelligence); Moshe Sneh, previously the administrator of the West Bank; and Ori Orr, onetime commander –in chief of the northern region and therefore of the Israeli troops occupying Lebanon. Very quickly, the Council brought together more than thirty major generals and over a hundred brigadier generals, altogether nearly half of Israel's retired general officers. "We are all agreed in our estimation that the occupation must be ended because its continuation represents a worse danger to our security than its end," Orr said—a statement that is as clear as it is succinct.[5] "Most senior officers, from [chief of staff Ben] Shomron on down, would prefer a partial withdrawal from a demilitarized West Bank to Shamir's 'Greater Israel,'" added Sneh.[6]

Demilitarization and partial withdrawal are two key elements of Israel's maximum offer for a settlement. Avigdor Ben Gal, another member of the generals' Council, said, "We want a demilitarized West Bank; we want to keep control of its airspace, have some electronic warning stations, a military presence on the eastern slope of the hills overlooking the river Jordan, which, in any situation, will remain the military frontier."[7] As far as Gaza is concerned, the problem is much simpler: the sector is completely trapped between Israel, the sea, and the Egyptian Sinai desert, itself demilitarized under the Camp David accords.

There is another major difference between the two territories. In Gaza, there are only around 2,000 Israeli settlers, compared to about 70,000 in the West Bank [in 1988] living in 124 settlements, and even the most "moderate" Zionists do not envisage dismantling all of them. These differences explain why Peres has come out several times in favor of a total evacuation of Gaza, while in the West Bank he only proposes a withdrawal from those parts "where Arabs are in a clear majority." Ben Gal is more precise: "We could give up 100 percent of Gaza and 85 percent of the West Bank."

Of course, there is a large proportion of the electorate and the political-military establishment in Israel who reject the very idea of withdrawal. The Likud, led by Yitzhak Shamir, is clinging obstinately to the Camp David accords, which it interprets as granting administrative "autonomy" to the Arab inhabitants of the 1967 territories while keeping them under Israeli occupation. This position is, however, less and less tenable, not simply because of the intifada but also because it is totally isolated internationally. If Peres agreed to renew his governmental pact with the Likud in December 1988, it was only as a stopgap measure while he waited for the completion of the transfer of power from Reagan to Bush, after which the U.S. administration would again be in a position to intervene actively. Then Shamir, who has already begun to water down his position, will be obliged to yield or resort to new elections.

## "A TOTAL JOKE"

Likud's argument—that if Israel "abandoned Judea and Samaria" (the biblical names for the West Bank), the result would place the security of the Zionist state in grave danger—took no account of the conditions laid out by Labor for a withdrawal. This is why it is totally meaningless. U.S. researcher Jerome Segal, Arafat's friend and counselor and a strong advocate of a Palestinian state, replied to this argument as follows: "It's a total joke. We're talking about a pint-sized, demilitarized zone that has no access to the outside world except through two hostile and suspicious states that completely surround it—Israel and Jordan."[8]

Former Israeli Foreign Minister Abba Eban (Labor) is in complete agreement in refuting the Likud theses. He compares Israel's resources with those of the PLO: on the one side, "3,800 tanks, 682 planes with an impressive bombing capacity, thousands of pieces of artillery and missiles, and a formidable electronic capacity"; on the other, "zero tanks or planes, a few guns and no missiles," with "an assortment of grenades, mortars, stones and bottles." Eban rightly concluded, "An entity run by Arabs in a large part of the West Bank and Gaza, or a separate state, or, preferably, in a confederation with Jordan, would be the weakest military entity on earth."[9]

Are the limits of Israel's maximum offer for a settlement—partial withdrawal and demilitarization of the evacuated zones—unacceptable for the leadership of the Fatah/PLO, as Habash said? Concerning the withdrawal, it is true that even the last PNC's political resolution talks about "all the Palestinian and Arab territories occupied since 1967." It is also true that when one gets ready to do a deal, one demands the maximum. This is the case for all the Arab states, including Jordan and Egypt, for whom a total withdrawal is officially an inviolable principle.

But to the question "Will there be new Palestinian concessions if the International Conference meets?" the Fatah/PLO's number two, Abu Iyad, who is usually more forthright than Arafat, replied as follows after the last PNC in the PLO's semiofficial journal:

> Any solution that does not include a state is unacceptable.... After this, things become less complicated. Any negotiations will discuss practical questions, such as the definition of frontiers, relations, and so on. Here I must remind you that all Palestinian land is occupied. So if our leadership manages to rescue a section of Palestinian territory and proclaim an Arab Palestinian identity there, that would be very good.[10]

### DEMILITARIZATION

The question of demilitarization is even less complicated. Resolution 242, now accepted by the PLO, already foresees "the establishment of demilitarized zones." Second, the PLO leadership was itself the first to break the official Arab boycott of Egypt and establish a close coordination with the Mubarak regime, without demanding that it repudiate the peace treaty concluded with Israel in 1979, which was founded on the principle of the demilitarization of Egyptian territory evacuated by the Zionist army. Given all this, the Arafat leadership will have no trouble when the time comes in agreeing to let Israel impose a strict limitation on the categories of arms permitted in the West Bank and Gaza.

This does not mean limiting Palestinian armaments to kitchen knives. Demilitarization does not mean banning all firearms, even in Egyptian Sinai. Quite on the contrary, the Zionist state wants a situation where the authority that takes over in the zones it evacuates can assume "normal police functions" (Egyptian/Israeli treaty) so as to guarantee that "no acts or threats of aggression, hostility or violence originate or are committed on its territory, or by forces under its control or stationed on its territory." The authority that will replace the Israeli army if ever it evacuates zones in the West Bank and Gaza will certainly be authorized to have a police force equipped with light arms, as in the Sinai.

So to pretend that the Palestinian right, after the last PNC, could not accept the Israeli–U.S. maximum offer for a settlement—to believe that after making their bed, they are not prepared to lie in it—is to wallow in illusions. But beyond the illusory character of this moral comfort that George Habash is trying to wrap himself in, the real question, the one that he is trying in some way to dodge, should be asked: What are unacceptable concessions? What would really constitute treason to the Palestinian national cause and capitulation to Zionism and imperialism?

The answer does not lie where the PFLP chief seems to situate it, either in the partial character of withdrawal or in demilitarization. Let us start with the latter. Is there anyone who is stupid or naive enough to believe that after withdrawal of its troops from the West Bank and Gaza, the Zionist state would allow the inhabitants of these territories on its flanks to possess missiles, planes, and tanks as they pleased? The geography of the area and the relationship of forces being what they are, only a decisive military defeat of the Zionist state—which is not on the agenda in the foreseeable future— could ensure the Palestinians unfettered sovereignty, even if only on a small part of their territory. So who could blame them for settling— provisionally, of course—for an Israeli army withdrawal from the territories occupied in 1967 while they do not have the means to replace it with a real Palestinian army? This would be to put off such a withdrawal indefinitely.

### MAXIMALISM AND REALISM

The same reasoning can be applied to the question of a partial retreat. As soon as the maximalist logic of "all or nothing" is challenged, as soon as the necessity for tactical mediations and transitional objectives is accepted, "all the West Bank or nothing" is no more valid than "all Palestine or nothing." It is evident that the masses of the intifada, whatever the scale and duration of their struggle, do not have the means to get more than a withdrawal of the Zionist army from the zones in which they are concentrated. To dislodge the Zionist settlements adjacent to or outside of these zones—not to speak of, the military bases—much more than an uprising is needed. What is needed is a war of movement, something that all the Arab armies put together are not in a position to win today, even supposing they had any intention of waging it.

It has therefore been perfectly correct and legitimate for the Unified Leadership of the Intifada, in many of its communiqués since the first ones, to put up-front what it itself calls "immediate" demands such as "army withdrawal from the towns, camps, and villages." This same immediate objective figures in communiqué 26 of the Unified Leadership alongside the transitional objective of a complete withdrawal from the territories occupied in 1967, in the following formulation: "army withdrawal from Palestinian population centers."[11]

Trying to obtain this objective through the struggle, in the knowledge that the evacuated zones will inevitably remain under close Israeli military surveillance, is not surrender but revolutionary realism—realism, because this objective can be achieved through the intifada. The best proof that it is attainable is the mere fact that a decisive faction in the Zionist military hierarchy—under the pressure of the uprising and without being offered anything in return—has concluded that it is necessary for security reasons to withdraw the Israeli army from the Arab-populated zones—that is, from Gaza and most of the West Bank.

### A PARTIAL GAIN

The incomplete liberation (limited sovereignty) of a small portion of Palestinian territory would of course be a partial gain. In a manner of speaking, it would mean the inhabitants in these areas passing from a prison regime to house arrest. Such a gain would nevertheless be worthwhile for those who are enduring the occupation. A revolutionary Palestinian leadership would be entirely justified in settling for this immediate objective, attainable through struggle, while continuing to fight under the banner of the transitional demand for a total and unconditional withdrawal of the Zionist army from the territories occupied in 1967. Such a leadership would aim to transform

Gaza and the inhabited regions of the West Bank in the short term into "lib-erated zones," administered by the "people's committees" born out of the intifada that are giving the uprising its direct organizational expression.

But a partial gain, or anything resembling a compromise, is only legiti-mate from a revolutionary point of view if it is not in contradiction with continuing the struggle for the final objective. That it is, as Lenin said, a "compromise which in no way minimizes the revolutionary devotion and readiness to carry on the struggle on the part of [those] who have agreed to such a compromise."[12] As a matter of fact, it is not enough to quote Lenin on the need for compromises, as the Stalinists in Nayef Hawatmeh's DFLP do. We must also take account of Lenin's warning against those who

> imagine that the permissibility of compromises in general is sufficient to obliterate any distinction between opportunism, against which we are waging, and must wage, an unremitting struggle, and revolutionary Marxism.... In the practical questions that arise in the politics of any particular or specific historical moment, it is important to single out those which display the principal type of intolerable and treacherous compromises, such as embody an opportunism that is fatal to the revolutionary class, and to exert all efforts to explain them and combat them.[13]

### WHEN COMPROMISE BECOMES BETRAYAL

In the "practical questions" that we are discussing here, the intolerable compromise, the "treacherous compromise," is not, as previously explained, the inevitably partial and limited gains available today to the Palestinians. The "treacherous compromise," the capitulation, consists in renouncing the "readiness to carry on the struggle" in exchange for this gain—and moreover without any reason, at a time when the Palestinian struggle is at its peak. "Readiness to carry on the struggle" means holding to the fundamental objective: real self-determination for the whole of the Palestinian people through dismantling the Zionist state, which is intrinsi-cally founded on the oppression of this people—a state that the preamble to the last PNC's political resolution still described as a "fascist, racist, colo-nial state, founded on the usurpation of Palestinian soil and the extermina-tion of the Palestinian people"!

But the text proclaiming the Palestinian state, which was adopted unan-imously by that same PNC, is based on UN Resolution 181—that is, on recognition of the legitimacy of the Zionist state—and "rejects the threat of force, violence, or terrorism, or their use against its own territorial integrity . . . or that of any other state." The political resolution, adopted by a majority of PNC votes against a small minority that included the PFLP, only dotted the *i*'s, given that the proclamation was also based on "the international legitimacy embodied in UN resolutions since 1947." These include not just Resolution 181 but also Resolution 242, which the political resolution explicitly accepted. This means, if anyone needs reminding, that the PLO is committed to cease "all claims or states of belligerency," to recognize the state of Israel and its "right to live in peace within secure and recognized boundaries, free from threats or acts of force," with "the establishment of demilitarized zones" in exchange for an Israeli withdrawal "from occupied territories" (without even specifying the extent of the withdrawal).

In short, the PLO leadership has begun to implement the action plan that its U.S. adviser Jerome Segal, mentioned earlier, advocated eight months before in the *Washington Post*.[14] The first steps in this plan are: 1) that the PLO proclaims the Palestinian state in the West Bank and Gaza—this has been done; 2) that it turns itself into a provisional government—a measure that has been postponed for the moment; 3) that it promulgates "law number one" proclaiming that "the Palestinian state declares itself at peace with the state of Israel" and "will not have an army"; as well as "law number two ... banning all terrorist acts and instituting sanctions in the event of violations."[15] The essence of these two "laws" is already contained in Resolution 242.

What makes the state that the PLO leadership is preparing to set up into a Bantustan is not its size, or even the fact that it will be under surveillance. It is the fact that it will be a state under tutelage, a state whose government's main task will be repressing any hint of the Palestinians' continuing the armed struggle against a state that has expelled the overwhelming majority of them from their lands at gunpoint.

The principal means for which the PLO has chosen—direct negotiations with Israel—is entirely and exclusively adapted to this end. Indeed, nothing else can emerge from direct negotiations in the framework of an International Conference under the auspices of the big powers, which can only have Resolution 242—worked out by these same powers—as its basis. It follows that, as far as the PLO leadership goes, the "treacherous compromise" is not an unlikely future hypothesis, as George Habash said in self-justification after the last PNC meeting, but rather a choice that this same PNC has already made explicitly and which had been implicit since the 1983 PNC.[16]

## DEMANDING RECOGNITION

Does this mean that we should refrain from demanding recognition of the Palestinian state by those governments that have not yet done so? Not at all, because the importance of recognition is its impact on the masses involved in the intifada. The majority of them only wanted to see the aspect of a "declaration of independence" in the PNC's proclamation. This is what they celebrated and what galvanized them.

Their demand for an independent Palestinian state in the West Bank and Gaza is just and has to be supported. Right now, one expression of that support is fighting for the recognition of this state by governments, immediately and without conditions of any kind, such as the "security" of Israel and so on. The more the masses of the intifada have the feeling that their hour of liberation is approaching, especially because of growing international pressure on Israel and the United States, the more they will be determined to continue their struggle without letup.

But unlike Moscow, which supported the proclamation of the state without recognizing it formally (for legalistic reasons), we must fight for the formal recognition of the Palestinian state, but without approving of the text of the proclamation adopted by the PNC. On the contrary, support for the struggle of the Palestinian people must remain, more than ever, centered on demands for a total and unconditional Zionist withdrawal from the territories occupied in 1967, and the right for Palestinian self-determination without any form of diktat. [...]

## SUPPORTING THE PALESTINIAN PEOPLE

By maintaining clear political autonomy on this basis with no equivocations, it is entirely possible and legitimate to participate in all activities giving objective support to the Palestinian masses in struggle, whether alongside the PLO and its unconditional supporters or even—especially in the imperialist countries and the Israeli state—with Zionists or pro-Zionists opposed to the occupation of the West Bank and Gaza. At the same time, we must refuse to subscribe to any positions containing elements that contradict the orientation defined above, such as the "rights" of Israel, peace with Israel, or the International Conference.

Likewise, today it is more harmful than ever to endorse the sacred formula "the PLO, sole legitimate representative of the Palestinian people."

Indeed, this formula is not just recording the result of an opinion poll (in the absence of any direct democratic mechanisms for representing the whole of the Palestinian people). In the minds of those who invented it and as commonly interpreted, it is clearly a carte blanche given to the PLO, and therefore to its leadership, to decide the Palestinian people's future in their name. At a time when the PLO has unambiguously embarked on the road of capitulation, the pernicious character of this formula can be fully appreciated.

The U.S. administration began having direct talks with the PLO in December 1988, while a growing section of the Zionist establishment—including the current Labor minister Ezer Weizman, a quarter of the MPs of the same party and its general secretary, who just resigned for this reason—are calling for a direct dialogue between the Israeli government and the PLO. Was all this to celebrate the first anniversary of the intifada? Or was it because, between mid-November and mid-December, the Arafat leadership took some decisive steps in submitting to U.S. and Israeli conditions?

It should not be forgotten that the majority of Palestinians live outside of all Palestinian lands, the West Bank and Gaza included. The right of the Palestinian people to self-determination also includes its right to choose its representatives freely and democratically, with nobody having the right to decree from the outside who is its "sole legitimate representative." Admittedly the PLO enjoys the support of the majority of Palestinians—for the time being—because in a democracy representation is not an eternal right. The majority of the people can be wrong. Revolutionaries have the right, and the responsibility, to tell them so and combat their illusions.

## WHAT KIND OF SUPPORT?

To support the struggle of an oppressed people against its oppressors unconditionally means to support this struggle independently of the nature of its leadership (even if it is feudal or religious). That does not in any way mean unconditional support for such leaderships, and still less when they belong to the propertied classes. In this respect, the attitude of revolutionaries must be based on the distinction between measures that should be supported and those that should be denounced.

For example, unconditional support for the struggle of the Indian people against British imperialism had to be combined with a critical attitude toward Gandhi and the Congress Party, in spite of their enormous popularity and the fact that they had led some struggles like the civil disobedience campaigns—similar to those of the intifada in Palestine today. Many examples like this could be borrowed from other countries (China, Ethiopia, Tunisia, Iran, the Philippines, and so on). But the history of Palestine itself is sufficiently eloquent. Up until the 1948 defeat, the only leadership followed by the large majority of Palestinians was that of the Mufti of Jerusalem, Haj Amin al-Husseini. He was the spokesperson of the great Palestinian intifada from 1936 to 1939, and the person responsible for junking it when he went looking for a compromise with the British mandatory authority at the Zionists' expense.

In all confrontations between Zionism, imperialist governments, or Arab reaction and the PLO, the PLO should be supported without a shadow of a doubt. On the ground, alliances should be made with the PLO against the common enemy. [...] But one must know how to act with this kind of ally: as Trotsky said in relation to the left faction of the Chinese Kuomintang (which was much more radical than today's PLO), "Not by prostrating [oneself] before the Kuomintang at every one of its vacillations, but only ... by supporting every forward step of the Kuomintang, by relentlessly unmasking every vacillation, every step backward."[17]

This latter task falls to the Palestinian revolutionaries and those in the Arab countries, whose most reactionary governments are the PLO leadership's main allies, fervently supporting every step backwards. Of course, the same does not hold true for the public activity of those active among the Jewish masses in the Israeli state or the imperialist countries that support it.

## AN APPARENT CONTRADICTION

That said, there remains an apparent contradiction between our analysis of the PLO leadership and the fact that it has enjoyed, up until now, widespread mass support. The contradiction does not come from the characterization of this leadership as bourgeois—a quantifiable and incontestable fact that the whole of the Palestinian Left is agreed upon, including the Stalinist faction of the PLO. After all, a bourgeois leadership can perfectly well embody the national aspirations of its people against a foreign yoke. The contradiction relates rather to our description of the PLO's trajectory in the last few years, if not since 1973, as a capitulationist course. George Habash, who shares the same analysis, gave three reasons, in chronological order, to explain this apparent contradiction in a long balance sheet in the form of an interview given to the PFLP's paper *Al Hadaf* in December 1987.[18]

First of all, he said, the Palestinian Right had taken the initiative of armed struggle in 1965, which had given it a great deal of prestige and allowed it initially to win a leading position. Second, "The Palestinian bourgeoisie, because of its class nature and its tendencies to compromise and accommodate, is closely linked to the reactionary and bourgeois Arab regimes. They have accordingly given it a large amount of political and material support, which has contributed to its dominance."

Finally, still according to Habash, "The national enemy responded to the political deviation that characterized the positions and practice of the Palestinian Right with even more firmness and intransigence; as a result the Right has appeared to follow acceptable tactics in the eyes of the masses."

### DIFFERENT ATTITUDES

Habash's three explanations are true, but insufficient. The last one, which is absolutely basic, could in the long term become outdated. But it throws light on two things that are often overlooked regarding the attitude of the Palestinian masses toward the PLO. The first is that this attitude varies, in degree if not in nature, not only with social status, but also to a large extent with origin and residence: Palestinians who hold Israeli citizenship, who remained in the territory taken over by the Zionists in 1948; Palestinians from the West Bank and Gaza who still live there; 1948 refugees living in various places (the 1967 territories, Jordan, Lebanon, Syria), and so on. It is natural that the tactics perceived as "acceptable" should be different for each category. Similarly, their direct oppressor's attitude toward the PLO is decisive for them.

So the inhabitants of the 1967 territories, where the Israeli occupiers have traditionally seen Arafat as the devil himself, naturally tend to have a lot more sympathy for him than Palestinian refugees in Jordan, who are at least as numerous. The refugees in Jordan have trouble swallowing the fact that this same Arafat has never missed a chance to tenderly embrace his "brother" King Hussein, who has as much Palestinian blood on his hands as the Zionist leaders and subjects Palestinians in his kingdom to such a repressive regime that it makes the Israeli occupation look humanitarian and democratic by comparison. So while the masses can see the PLO as an acceptable representative of their struggle against the Zionist occupation of the 1967 territories, they do not see it as the representative of their equally necessary fight against the Jordanian oppressor.

## WHERE THE LEFT FALLS SHORT

A second aspect that is often overlooked about the Palestinians' attitude toward the PLO, which is linked to the first, is that even the masses who identify with the PLO often mistrust its leadership. Nevertheless, these masses support the PLO because they see it as the only available and at all credible point at which their struggles against the "national enemy" can focus. Noting this leads us to the fourth, and perhaps most important, reason for the persistent dominance of the Palestinian Right: the deficiencies of the Left, and primarily the traditional PLO Left.

---

## TWO PALESTINIAN VIEWS ON THE PLO

WEST BANK—Young militants of the intifada talk to Alain Gresh, special correspondent of *Le Monde Diplomatique* (May 1988):

Not many people escape the lash of their sarcasm today, not even the PLO leadership. The PLO is their "sole representative," they say loud and clear, but in private they denounce its sloppiness, the corruption of some of its leading figures—the "five-star PLO" they call it, bursting into loud guffaws—and its meager accomplishments.... The Palestinians in the interior have won more in a few months than the PLO did in twenty years, Bassam says.... But their statements about the PLO leave no room for misunderstanding: "The PLO makes the decisions; the PLO has to negotiate; we refuse to form an alternative leadership."

JORDAN—Bakaa Palestinian refugee camp, one of the biggest, is visited by Veronique Maurus, special correspondent of *Le Monde* (17 February 1988):

The uprising ... is seen as the expression of an authentic, violent Palestinian self-determination, after decades of manipulation by Israel, the Arab states and even the PLO, which is openly accused of powerlessness and collusion with "the politicians."... One dream is repeated again and again: of a "new leadership" emerging from the revolution. Who? On that point people are more reserved. "There will be a revolution, here and everywhere where they're oppressing us," a middle-aged man says repeatedly. "We have to reject any compromise. If the revolution is sponsored by the Arab governments or the PLO, it will abort."

Knowing the analysis of the PLO leadership that George Habash, leader of the main fraction of this left, has made himself, one has to wonder how he can proclaim his attachment to the PLO in the same breath, even describing it as the "sole legitimate representative of the Palestinian people" and rejecting any idea of building an alternative framework for leading the Palestinian struggle. The reply that he gives to this inevitable question is not new; it is more than sixty years old: for the sake of the cause, it is necessary to pin the label "national" on the "bourgeoisie."

In "the first stage of national liberation," Habash said in the interview previously quoted, "the national bourgeoisie, petit bourgeoisie, workers, and peasants" are united. Thus, "the PLO, in addition to being the framework that embodies the independent Palestinian personality, is this front including all these classes ... although it is currently led by the bourgeoisie."

Here we see the well-known ingredients of the Stalinist theory forged around the debate on China in 1926–27. Everything is there: stages, the bloc of four classes and its organizational expression (in this case the PLO, in China the Kuomintang—which at the time certainly incarnated the independent Chinese "personality" much more than the PLO does for Palestinians today). The critique of these conceptions is also more than sixty years old, and it is just as relevant and judicious today.

> To consider the Kuomintang not as a *bourgeois party, but as a neutral arena of struggle for the masses*, to play with words about the nine-tenths of the Left rank and file in order to mask the question of who is the real master, meant to add to the strength and power of the summit, to assist the latter to convert ever broader masses into "cattle."... The bourgeois "summit" tolerates or tolerated "nine-tenths" of the Lefts (and Lefts *of this sort*), only in so far as they did not venture against the army, the bureaucracy, the press, and against capital. By these powerful means the bourgeois summit kept in subjection not only the so-called nine-tenths of "Left" party members, but also the masses as a whole.[19]

In the same way, to consider the PLO not as a bourgeois organization, but as a "neutral arena," a "front of four classes" whose leadership can pass from the hands of one class to another (this is the DFLP's and PFLP's thesis), advancing as an argument the social composition of its base and its influence over the masses, means to "add to the strength and power of the [bourgeois] summit" and "assist the latter to convert ever broader masses into 'cattle.'" This is even more applicable to the PLO than to the Kuomintang.

Indeed, the statutes that the Kuomintang adopted in 1924 (inspired by the Comintern's envoy!) in principle designated the national congress—with delegates elected by local congresses—as the supreme leading body, which in turn elected the Executive Committee. By contrast, the Arab states that founded the PLO in 1964 took great care to create it in their image, that is, as a bureaucratic institution essentially based on appointment and cooptation, and not on the basis of direct representation of the masses via elected delegates.

This undemocratic mechanism is the main way that the PNC has renewed itself since its members were appointed at its first session in 1964 under the control of the Arab states. Through this same mechanism, following a decision of the PLO's Arab sponsors, Fatah took the organization over in 1969, as Abu Iyad implicitly admits in his autobiography: "All the Arab countries... greeted the PLO's takeover by the Resistance with satisfaction. This was because Fatah, which most of them trust, made sure of getting the overriding influence both within the PNC and on the PLO Executive Committee." [20]

### FATAH'S HEGEMONY

Since then Fatah's dominance inside the PLO has been literally immovable, because the organization's functioning rests on a vicious circle between the Palestine National Council, the Executive Committee, and back again. These two bodies mutually assure the simple (and sometimes enlarged) reproduction of Fatah's dominance. Thus Fatah had no great difficulty in mustering the two-thirds quorum for the PNC at the Amman session in 1984, in spite of a boycott by all the other Palestinian political-military groups with the exception of two tiny pro-Iraqi organizations.

At this same session, in response to growing dissension in the Palestinian movement since 1983, the Fatah/PLO leadership decided to modify the composition of the PNC. According to a journal sponsored by the PLO, "the number of representatives of socio-professional associations favorable to Mr. Arafat has more than doubled (to 26 percent of the total), while representatives of the diaspora have increased by nearly a third (to 44.5 percent of the seats)." [21] Added to this are 10 percent of the seats reserved for representatives of the army (the Palestine Liberation Army), who are directly appointed by the "commander in chief"—Yassir Arafat in person—as well as 7.5 percent reserved for Fatah's delegates. The other organizations have to be content to share 11.5 percent of the seats among them.

A good illustration of both the bourgeois and manipulative character of the PNC's composition is provided by comparing the representation of the PFLP, the second largest Palestinian organization after Fatah, with other "delegations." The ratio of the PFLP and other delegations is 2:5 with delegations of the Palestinian diaspora from the Arab oil-producing countries (the Gulf Emirates and Saudi Arabia); 3:5 with delegations of the diaspora in North and South America; nearly 1:5 with the group of "independent personalities," who represent only themselves—and often their wallets; and 3:2 with the Arab Liberation Front, a grouplet totally controlled by Iraq, Arafat's big ally. Moreover, the last PNC session, where only 15 percent of those voting came out against accepting Resolution 242, is undeniable proof that this body in no way reflects the real divisions in Palestinian public opinion.

## A SWOLLEN BUREAUCRACY

These statutory methods of maintaining the dominance of the bourgeois PLO leadership are combined with the classic means mentioned by Trotsky, notably bureaucracy and finances. The PLO's bureaucratic apparatus is swollen: thousands of functionaries, whose highest layer lives in a luxurious style that is an insult to the living conditions of the vast majority of Palestinians. This apparatus has some branches, like the "political" or diplomatic department (with eighty-five offices around the world), that would make many Third World states green with envy. In addition the PLO subsidizes, either regularly or occasionally, tens of thousands of people who constitute a major social clientele. As for finances, the PLO's treasury is, of course, considerable: it has an immense capital in liquid assets and real estate, and a regular budget mainly sustained by Arab oil producers that can be counted in hundreds of millions of dollars a year.

These facts enable us to understand why the PLO Left, in spite of its leaders' protestations, only has a token role—that of a leftist alibi for the strikingly rightist policy of the bourgeois Fatah leadership. This is shown by the pathetic spectacle that this left has provided for the last two years. Barely a few days after the two last PNC meetings (1987 and 1988) in which it participated under the slogan of "national unity," it was obliged to publish communiqués denouncing Arafat & Co.'s positions as contrary to the PNC's decisions (in fact, to its particular interpretation of those decisions). This shows to what extent the national consensus on which the Left claims to base its participation in the PLO's structures is illusory.

As Habash candidly acknowledged in the interview already mentioned:

We were winning the battle in theory, on paper. But the hegemonic faction in the PLO leadership, owing to its bourgeois nature, would not respect this in its subsequent political practice. In fact, this political behavior explains this right-wing faction's opposition to carrying out democratic organizational reforms in the PLO bodies and institutions, because they would limit its political maneuvering room for knocking at the doors of surrender in the reactionary Arab capitals. [22]

### JOINING THE PLO

Does all this force us to the conclusion that the Palestinian Left should have refrained from joining the PLO on principle? Not necessarily. But its very conception of PLO membership should have been radically different. The Palestinian Left should have been able to stay in the PLO on a tactical basis, as it did during the early years of its participation, with its banner held high and without sparing the rightist leadership. It should have been able to use the PNC as a platform for political agitation, while denouncing loudly and forcefully its undemocratic makeup and demanding that its central leadership bodies be elected by the Palestinian masses, including in the form of delegates from the people's committees in the refugee camps.

In any case, under no circumstances should the Left have agreed to endorse the PLO's Executive Committee—at least not after 1974, the year in which the PFLP, then much more radical than today, correctly suspended its participation in that body (it asked to be let back in four years later). Moreover, even from the point of view of the PFLP's own political limitations, logically it should have withdrawn again from the Executive Committee after the last PNC, which accepted Resolution 242. In 1974 the PFLP withdrew for much less than that!

Such are the shortcomings of the PLO Left. What about the dissident opposition then? The main organizations in this category—Fatah-Provisional Command (a 1983 split from Fatah), led by Abu Musa, and Ahmad Jibril's PFLP–General Command (a 1968 split from the PFLP)—represent a predominantly nationalist opposition allied to the Syrian regime's Palestinian tool, As-Saiqa, in the framework of the Palestinian National Salvation Front (PNSF). After the last PNC, these organizations published denunciatory communiqués together with other groups, including the Palestinian Revolutionary Communist Party, a left splinter group from the

PCP. Today, they are calling for founding a new PLO. According to Abu Musa it should include the Islamic fundamentalist current, which is also violently opposed to the PLO's last turn for its own reasons.

However, the PNSF has little credibility in the eyes of the Palestinian masses. It appears as what it really is: a grouping under the tutelage of Damascus, which totally discredited itself when it claimed responsibility for bombing Palestinian camps in Lebanon as part of its struggle against Arafat's Fatah. In addition, the advances that Abu Musa is now making to the fundamentalist current have all the hallmarks of pathetic political shortsightedness and a pitiful bankruptcy.

## THE FUNDAMENTALIST DANGER

The fundamentalist current is profiting in the Palestinian milieu from the same combination that brought about its considerable growth in other countries in the region: an explosive situation, bankruptcy of the traditional bourgeoisie, and the shortcomings of the Left. In the Palestinian milieu as

---

### A SAMPLE OF PALESTINIAN ISLAMIC FUNDAMENTALIST RHETORIC

We will establish our fighting Islamic state on every inch of liberated land. But nobody can make us recognize the supposed entity on the rest of our holy land [the Israeli state], or make us recognize its borders. We don't ask anyone to recognize our borders, which will not be set until all of our stolen land has been cleansed....Those who imagine establishing a Palestinian state through peace negotiations are dreaming, and confusing their people by making them think that this state will solve the Palestinian people's problems.... This state or mini-state will have its wrists and ankles shackled, its eyes blindfolded and its will paralyzed by the constraints and guarantees that it will have to accept at the International Conference.... The Palestinian people, who are dying today and have risen up in this fighting, blessed revolution, haven't done it so that the PLO's offices can be promoted to embassies, or to set up an illusory state with a paralyzed will and sovereignty.

—SHEIKH KHALIL AL-KUKA, Muslim preacher expelled from Gaza by the occupation authorities in April 1988, speaking for the Islamic Resistance Movement (Hamas) to the Kuwait newspaper *Al-Qabas*, October 1988.

elsewhere, the bourgeoisie has played the role of sorcerer's apprentice. Initially the Fatah leadership deliberately encouraged the growth of a fundamentalist Palestinian current, in particular after 1979 and in some cases up until 1987. Today this current has profited from the intifada and grown, to the point where over the last few months the Zionist authorities have become seriously worried. Previously, for a long time they had taken a laissez-faire attitude, hoping in this way to better "divide and rule."

The fundamentalist current is in a good position to attract Palestinians disappointed in the PLO, who have been growing in number since the last PNC. Today the fundamentalists are projecting a radical tone that is likely to convince large sections of the masses and young people. Even Habash confirms this. In the December 1987 interview, he made what seemed to be a confession of his own weakness: "I think that the religious current could take over the leadership if the PLO stopped the armed struggle and went down the road of deviation and surrender."

It goes without saying that the growth of this current represents a real curse for the Palestinian mass movement. Its fanatical religious talk reinforces Zionist cohesion in Jewish/Israeli society on the one hand, and on the other it repels the Palestinian Christian minority, whose role is far from negligible. Finally, it represents an enormous regression for a population that was, and still is, in the forefront of the progressive struggle on a regional scale. [...]

JANUARY 28, 1989; first published in English in *International Viewpoint*, no. 157 (February 20, 1989).

CHAPTER TWELVE

# The Dynamic of the Intifada

*This article, the third and last in the series on the PLO, examines the intifada at its apogee in 1988—a great moment in the history of the Palestinian struggle, worthy of a prominent place among the outstanding episodes in the history of liberation struggles. Within the limits of the information available to an outside observer, the article assesses the intifada's social dynamic and forms of organization. It analyzes as well the way the PLO took charge of the intifada and thus contributed to breaking its initial impetus, which was founded on self-organization by the occupied territories' own inhabitants.*

*Intifada* an Arabic word meaning "uprising" or "insurrection," has become part of the international vocabulary as a result of the new episode in the heroic struggle of the Palestinian masses on the West Bank and in Gaza. After fourteen months of continuous harassment of the Zionist occupation forces, the intifada is still showing no sign of flagging.

Abroad it is too often seen only as a spectacle of demonstrators of both sexes throwing stones at Israeli soldiers. That is, of course, the most visible aspect of the Palestinian challenge to the occupation. But the intifada is a much richer experience than simple stone throwing. Its lessons, moreover, have implications that go far beyond the Palestinian framework.

The outbreak of the intifada on December 9, 1987, was not a bolt from the blue. It was the product of a long process of maturation—an explosion of resentment built up over twenty years of occupation and repression. The oppressor power was even more intolerable because it came into the world, with the creation of the state of Israel nineteen years before the occupation of 1967, already based on the usurpation of the bulk of Palestinian territory. From this historical standpoint, the intifada also represents a new generation going into action, the third since the Palestinian exodus of 1948, which is now taking over from the generation of 1967, symbolized by the *fedayeen*.

But while these are generations of the same people, they have not grown up on the same territory. The fight of the 1967 generation was waged essentially by Palestinians in exile, first in Jordan until 1971, and then in Lebanon. The struggle of the 1987 generation, the intifada generation, is now being fought only in the territories occupied in 1967—at least for the time being. In the aftermath of the occupation, the population of these territories remained stunned, overawed by an army that had gained a reputation of invincibility in six days of war.

The maximalism of the Palestinian resistance organizations in exile offered the inhabitants of the West Bank and Gaza no credible perspective for liberation in the foreseeable future. These organizations, moreover, were mainly occupied with setting up secret cells for an armed struggle that was supposed to liberate the whole of Palestine. Given the effectiveness of the Zionist repression, under the occupation this sort of activity could only involve very small numbers, even if the fighters enjoyed the sympathy of the population.

The people looked elsewhere for deliverance—to the Arab states, which through diplomatic activity and military pressure might get Israel to evacuate the territories occupied in 1967, including the Palestinian lands. As a matter of fact, the latter had been under the jurisdiction of Arab states: Egypt had administered Gaza after 1949, and Jordan had annexed the West Bank. Therefore, the primary responsibility for recovering these lands fell on them.

## A TRADITIONAL SOCIETY

This political view of things prevailed in particular because the society within the 1967 territories (which we will refer to from now on as "the Territories") remained traditional—a small proletariat scattered in workplaces on a cottage-industry scale; a large peasantry and petit bourgeoisie; the predominant role in the hands of the commercial bourgeoisie, landowners, and lay and religious personalities who had been local relays for the Jordanian government. Thus, in the climate of bitterness that prevailed after the crushing of the resistance in Jordan, the municipal elections held in 1972 on the West Bank were won by personalities linked to the Jordanian monarchy.

However, the political turn made by the PLO the following year upset this state of affairs.[1] By adopting the objective, described as transitional, of an independent state in "any part of the Palestinian territory that may be liberated," the PLO staked its claim to govern the Territories if they were evacuated by Israel. All at once political action, until then neglected, became fundamental. A Palestinian National Front was formed in 1973 in the Territories, under the aegis of the PLO. It included the currents sympathetic to the Palestinian organization, as well as the local branch of the Jordanian Communist Party (which subsequently became the Palestinian Communist Party, PCP). The CP program had always been limited to the liberation of the territories occupied in 1967, thanks to the Stalinist tradition on the question of Israel.

Revolted by the massacres perpetrated by King Hussein's army, the popular majority lined up behind the banner of the National Front. It strongly opposed a return to Jordanian sovereignty, and favored Palestinian sovereignty in the event of liberation.[2] A major section of the bourgeoisie followed suit, attracted by the perspective of freeing itself from Jordanian tutelage in the future. The result was an overwhelming victory for the PLO's supporters in the April 1976 municipal elections on the West Bank.

A year later the Zionist right-wing bloc Likud won the parliamentary elections in Israel for the first time. Despite Egyptian president Sadat's "peace initiative," Likud leader Menachem Begin proclaimed a plan for creeping annexation of the Territories—maintenance of the Israeli occupation with administrative "autonomy" for the Palestinians and stepped-up Zionist settlement. With Likud's encouragement, the number of settlers in the West Bank rose from 5,000 (34 settlements) in 1977 to 70,000 (124 settlements) in 1988. Parallel to this, repression of the Palestinian national movement increased considerably. Between 1980 and 1982, the main mayors who supported the PLO were deported or ousted. Likud tried to set up a network of collaborator "representatives" (the "Village Leagues"). In 1982, the Likud government tried to liquidate Palestinian nationalism by invading Lebanon.

The bitterness of defeat—the evacuation of Beirut by the PLO fighters and the massacres that followed—was aggravated from 1983 on by inter-Palestinian conflict. Fatah split. Battles raged between the factions in Lebanon. A de facto split opened up inside the PLO over the Seventeenth Palestinian National Council in Amman in 1984, from which all the nationalist opposition and left formations stayed away.

The main cause of the conflict was the "Jordanian option" chosen by the Arafat leadership, which culminated in February 1985 in the conclusion of the Amman accord between the PLO leader and King Hussein. In the meantime Shimon Peres's Zionist Labor Party returned to government in Israel in the framework of a ministerial coalition pact with Likud.

## "SHARING ROLES"

Also in his own way a supporter of the "Jordanian option," Peres chose to appoint replacements for the ousted nationalist mayors in concert with Amman. In November 1985, he appointed Zafer al-Masri to head the city government of Nablus, the West Bank's main city (after East Jerusalem, which has been annexed to Israel). Al-Masri was a figure with a distinct profile. He was chair of the local chamber of commerce, nephew of the vice president of the Jordanian Senate and an uncle of the kingdom's minister of foreign affairs. A few months after accepting the appointment with Arafat's blessing, Al-Masri was assassinated by the Popular Front for the Liberation of Palestine (PFLP), a left nationalist organization and the biggest Palestinian formation after Fatah.

However, after King Hussein had worked out an overall plan for "sharing roles" with Peres, he decided to break unilaterally with Arafat in February 1986 and close the Fatah offices in Jordan. The bankruptcy of the right-wing PLO leadership was evident. It resigned itself to accepting Moscow's mediation in order to achieve a reunification with the opposition factions aligned with the USSR in April 1987. This tactical accommodation enabled Arafat to absorb the shock of his Jordanian fiasco, so that the opposition could not take full advantage of it. But it did not prevent him from resuming his moves toward Amman. The Arab summit that met in the Jordanian capital in November 1987 was the most glaring expression of the PLO's bankruptcy. Despite being treated with contempt, Arafat abased himself before King Hussein, while the PLO Left protested in vain.

It was against this background of the PLO's bankruptcy outside Palestine that the intifada broke out a month later. The resentment piled up over twenty years of occupation and repression combined with exasperation at the lamentable spectacle offered by the organizations outside to produce a spontaneous explosion that developed into a general uprising. Beginning on December 9 with a protest by young people at the Jabaliya refugee camp in Gaza against the death of four Palestinians killed in a collision with an Israeli truck, the demonstrations spread like a prairie fire throughout the territory. The day after the Jabaliya demonstration, a new fire broke out in the Balata camp near Nablus, and the flames quickly spread to the rest of the West Bank.

Since 1986, there had been an atomized but quite distinct revival of activities against the occupation. A few months before the intifada erupted, a report by the West Bank Data Base headed by Israeli sociologist Meron Benvenisti, noted "a new and disturbing evolution for Israel: the violence [in the Territories] seems more and more frequently to be carried out by unorganized, spontaneous groups.... Between April 1986 and May 1987, 3,150 violent incidents have been registered, going from mere stone throwing to barricading roads, and including 100 attacks with explosives or firearms." [3]

The political conditioning of the intifada and its incubation on the ground affected a population that had been profoundly changed in comparison with preceding decades. During twenty years of occupation/annexation the social fabric of the Territories went through the classical effects of the linking of backward traditional societies to an advanced capitalist market—dispossession and proletarianization of traditional small producers, partially absorbed by the needs of the advanced market.

> Palestinian social structure under Israeli rule can be viewed as the outcome of a system of internal colonialism, resulting in a distorted class structure, a peasantry that is alienated from its land, and, in the cities, a pattern of development dependent upon and peripheral to the dominant Zionist society. [4]

## "SOUTH AFRICANIZATION"

In this sense, there has definitely been a "South Africanization" of Palestine—the establishment of a veritable apartheid regime with its "homelands"/reservoirs of labor power (and soon perhaps its Bantustans). According to official Israeli statistics, a third of the labor force of the Territories is working within the 1967 borders of Israel in South –African–style conditions (travel controls, harassment, and so on). In reality it is a lot more—120,000 workers according to current estimates, taking into account the number that get paid under the table. If you add to this the workers employed in the settler economy in the Territories themselves, it emerges that the majority of the proletariat in the Territories—which makes up the majority of the labor force—is directly exploited by the Zionist economy in underpaid jobs looked down on by Israeli workers (construction, agriculture, certain services and jobs in industry). In addition, there are the workers in the Palestinian subcontracting economy.

At the bottom of the social ladder and in the vanguard of the struggle are the proletarians/refugees from 1948, eloquently described by Meron

Benvenisti as follows: "The refugees—stateless, impoverished, landless—are Israel's helots. On their way to work as Israel's menial laborers they pass by their ruined villages and plundered lands. They have nothing to lose except their chains of misery."[5]

Against the background of a demographic explosion, the proletarianization of the population of the Territories has gone hand in hand with a net increase in the proportion of young people—75 percent are under twenty-five years of age; 50 percent are under fifteeen. The proportion of young people is just as considerable in the working class. In 1984, 20 percent of the Palestinian workers crossing the 1967 border were under seventeen.[6]

### THE ROLE OF WOMEN

To complete this sociodemographic picture of the intifada population, the growing role of women should be noted. Their proportion has increased as a result of the economic emigration to the Arab oil-producing countries, which has essentially involved men. Women's social status has improved relatively, among other things under the influence of the Israeli example, which is much more advanced in this respect. So today a third of university students in the Territories are women, a high proportion for an Arab or Muslim society. Selective repression, one of the rare cases where sexism "benefits" women, has favored the participation of women in the struggles—all the more so because the 10,000 or so people presently detained in the Territories (out of a population of a million and a half!) are men.

Women, moreover, are the only ones who sometimes carry out specific public activities within the framework of the intifada, as mothers of detainees or even on International Women's Day. But most of the time they melt into the other social and demographic categories that make up the base of the uprising, in a struggle that is essentially a national one. All social classes and categories join the strikes of the intifada. Its base units are not the workplaces or educational centers but territorial units, the camps and the popular neighborhoods in the cities and villages, as the Palestinian Marxist researcher Khaled Ayed points out (see insert pp. 182-3).

### THE INDIGENOUS BOURGEOISIE

Ayed's analysis of the social classes and strata in the Territories brings out an important difference between the Palestinian case and that of South

Africa, with which it is usually compared: the weight and role of the native bourgeoisie, which includes the landowners, as well as various categories of lay and religious notables. In their great majority, the members of these possessing classes today swear by the PLO, since the pro-Jordanians have taken note of King Hussein's official renunciation of the West Bank on July 31, 1988. They are exercising their influence over the society in the Territories through institutions that they control—the municipal governments elected in 1976 and not dismissed, chambers of commerce, the Islamic High Council, local and religious courts, self-employed professional associations (lawyers, doctors, engineers), the Council of Higher Education, and so on.

These institutions are called "national" in contrast with those that are appointed by the occupiers or are directly controlled by them, such as the appointed municipal governments or the Palestinian police. The attitude of the Labor Zionists toward the "national institutions" is clearly different from that of Likud. For the Zionist right, consistent with its program for the Territories, even the most "moderate" of the Palestinians have to be repressed when they reject the occupation. This is the attitude that has prevailed since 1977. It sharpened at the beginning of the intifada, to the great annoyance of the "enlightened" Zionists, who were shocked by such shortsightedness.

As early as January 1988, the pro-Labor Israeli daily *Haaretz* issued a warning: "If we continue in this way to harass and eliminate the most moderate Palestinian leadership, we are going to find ourselves face to face with the one emerging from the camps, the young people of Balata and Jabaliya." A few months later, the same *Haaretz* could note bitterly:

> The intifada has greatly modified the character of the activities of the institutions of Palestinian society. On the one hand, organized social work has become clandestine, in particular because of the government's harassment of the Palestinian "national institutions" (the shutting down of several of them and the arrest of many of their active members). But on the other hand, and parallel to this, this work has become more popular, penetrating more widely and more deeply into the society. It involves essentially the activity of the "people's committees," which have formed in almost every village, neighborhood, and refugee camp.[7]

## PEOPLE'S COMMITTEES

The intifada has acquired an original form of grassroots self-organization, the People's Committees (PCs), which have largely supplanted the traditional institutions in the organization of society in the Territories. Two factors have combined to render these traditional institutions inoperative: being legal, they are known and therefore kept under surveillance, and the intifada's revolutionary character. The uprising has set in motion a mass vanguard that, because of its youth and social composition, had nothing to do with the established institutions. The latter were completely ill adapted to the new forms of struggle. Their role, nonetheless, has not been eliminated. It has changed. From claiming the leadership of the masses, they have come to seek to play the role of a moderating intermediary between the uprising and Israel, as well as its U.S. godfather.

The PCs spread throughout the Territories from the first weeks of the

---

## THE SOCIAL FORCES IN THE TERRITORIES
### By Khaled Ayed

The main centers of the intifada are the camps, where almost a quarter of the total population of the West Bank and Gaza (almost half in Gaza) lives in very crowded conditions.[1] If we add the [1948] refugees living in the poorer urban neighborhoods, the refugees as a whole make up more than half of the total population.... The majority of them belong to the working class or poor petit bourgeoisie....

The poor neighborhoods of the big cities, whose inhabitants belong to the poorer classes (workers, low-level employees, and petit bourgeois), resemble the camps.... The third milieu where the intifada is taking place is the villages, most of whose residents are poor peasants. Here the Israeli occupiers have seized the land ... and transformed tens of thousands [of peasants] into exploited, humiliated workers, working in the settlements or inside the Zionist state.... Young people are at the center of these three milieus: particularly the revolutionary intelligentsia [students and graduates], sons of the camps, poorer neighborhoods, and poor villages, who are the intifada's spinal cord and its day-to-day leaders on the ground....

On the opposite side of the popular uprising, there is a minority belonging to social layers that are linked by economic interests to the Israeli occupation or who waver between the occupation and the intifada. They are, first, the real estate brokers... the labor brokers... and the owners of subcontracting industries [all economically linked to the settlements or Israeli economy]. There are also major traders who work by cornering the markets.... Of all these layers, the big traders are the biggest threat to the intifada's future ... because:

intifada. It is thanks to them that the intifada has assumed a durable character. Sometimes formed from preexisting structures (committees of students, women, sympathizers of political organizations, and so on), and in their majority composed of previously unorganized rank-and-file activists, the PCs bring together on a geographical basis—blocks in the camps, town districts or streets, villages—all those who are active and ready to take on the tasks of organization, mobilization and direct action linked to the intifada. In this sense the PCs are only potentially similar to soviets, given that the clandestine methods required under occupation make it impossible for the inhabitants to elect delegates directly. For the time being, they are more like action committees of the new mass vanguard that has been thrown up during the uprising.

1) They have a legal, organizational framework at their disposal: the various chambers of commerce, spared by the occupation authorities' attacks;

2) During the intifada this layer has formed "patriotic merchants' committees," endorsed by the United National Leadership inside and the PLO outside; and

3) (Most important) this comprador layer oscillates between two positions: … its own interest in the establishment of some sort of Palestinian entity, following from the intifada, on the one hand, and possible threats to its own immediate interests on the other…

This layer of commercial procurers has expressed and continues to express its inclination to "negotiate" the national cause and play the role of an "intermediary" between the popular uprising and its Zionist and imperialist enemies…. Like its ideological agents, it is concentrated in the Jerusalem area.[2] It has considerable influence, shared by the PLO, on a number of "legal" institutions: newspapers and journals, the Bir Zeit University administration, the Society of Arab Studies, the Palestinian Center for Non-Violence Studies, local press bureaus and research and information centers.[3]

1    Khaled Ayed is an independent Palestinian Marxist and researcher at the Institute of Palestinian Studies in Beirut. Excerpts are from his *Al-Intifada al-Thawriyya fi Filastin: al-Abaad al-Dakhiliyya* (Amman: Dar al-Shuruq, 1988), pp. 50–55.

2    Ayad gives as examples Hanna al-Siniora, Fayez Abu-Rahmeh, Feisal al-Husseini, and Sari Nusseibeh.

3    The director of the Society of Arab Studies, Feisal Al-Husseini, the son of a prominent family of notables, was freed in January 1989 after several months of "administrative detention." He had discussions with Israeli Defense Minister Yitzhak Rabin shortly before his release.

The PCs are not, however, substitutionist bodies but truly organic forms of leadership for the population involved in the intifada. Their extension is in direct relation to the repressive conditions. For example, in the villages where the daily repression is less of a day-to-day reality, the committees' meetings are much larger than in the zones strictly controlled by the occupying army, such as the towns. In the latter, the PCs are forced to adopt a pyramidal structure.

### "SPECIALIZED COMMITTEES" AND POPULAR CONTROL

The People's Committees divide up the various tasks among their members or link up with "specialized committees" (bringing together professional or experienced people). The PCs' functions vary considerably and cover all aspects of social life and struggle in the framework of the intifada: propaganda and mobilization; organizing production cooperatives; boycotting Israeli products; solidarity fund-raising for victims of the repression and the unemployed; legal and material aid for prisoners; medical aid; teaching (to compensate for the closing of schools and colleges); provisions; and so on.

The PCs have also taken on legislative and judicial functions, the most important being the control and limits exercised over the upper classes: controlling prices; fighting hoarding; controlling the fees of the liberal professions (private medicine, lawyers); reducing rents; imposing the payment of wages for intifada strike days; setting up popular courts to sort out certain disputes; applying pressure for the resignation of functionaries appointed by the Israeli administration (police, municipal employees); and so on.

In order to carry out all these functions efficiently, as well as paramilitary tasks—organizing marshals at demonstrations, harassing the occupying army and colonists with stones and Molotov cocktails, keeping up the shopkeeper strike, arranging for night guards in residential areas, punishing collaborators—the PCs are equipped with "shock committees," a veritable revolutionary guard with the peculiarity that, for obvious reasons given the balance of forces, they do not use firearms: These shock committees have even recently proclaimed themselves as a "people's army."[8]

So the intifada, thanks to the PCs and their allied bodies, has at its disposal a real structure of people's power, essentially proletarian and peasant, that gives it its original contribution to regional and international revolutionary experience.[9] In the Territories it has created de facto a real duality of powers—incomplete, true, in view of the vast inequality of the opposing forces. Moreover, many villages and districts have proclaimed themselves "liberated zones," which they certainly are between two interventions of the occupying army. Israeli Defense Minister Yitzhak Rabin was right on target when he went onto the offensive against the PCs in August 1988, accusing them of wanting to "institutionalize the uprising." Since then, participants are liable to get ten years' imprisonment, something that has in no way discouraged them from keeping up their action.

The autonomy of the People's Committees at camp, town, or village level is perfectly adapted to the specific form of struggle practiced by the intifada against the Zionist army: "guerilla"-type demonstrations and scattered actions. This sort of harassment, which is unpredictable because it is the result of a multitude of autonomous decisions, exhausts the occupying troops and forces them to deploy themselves in large numbers. Their large-scale deployments are not very successful, moreover, because short of drowning the uprising in blood—an option that the Zionist government is avoiding for the moment for reasons that are as much internal as international —ensuring a dissuasive presence in all the populated areas of the occupied territories would require declaring a general mobilization in Israel, and stripping other fronts of troops in addition.

## THE UNITED NATIONAL LEADERSHIP

Evidently the PCs' autonomous role in the harassment had to be complemented by centralizing the intifada' s political decision making, the designation of general strike days and directions on rules of action and social organization whenever united action makes for strength and efficacy. But just as the conditions of the occupation prevent the PCs from being "soviets" of delegates, they make it impossible to give them direct democratic coordination and centralization on the scale of the whole of the Territories, or even at the level of the West Bank (it is possible, at the most, in the 360 square kilometers of Gaza). So there was a role to fill that only the existing clandestine organizational networks could take on; the main ones—the extensions in the interior of the formations brought together in the framework of the exterior PLO—did so.

Less than a month after the beginning of the intifada, as soon as it was apparent that the uprising was going to last, central "appeals" in the form of communiqués began to appear and circulate in the Territories. At first they came from a United National Leadership for the Intensification of the intifada, which became, starting from communiqué no. 4, the United National Leadership of the intifada (UNL). This leadership was self-proclaimed, to be sure, but it nevertheless played an indispensable role and was followed and recognized by the large majority of the masses. The political content of the first communiqués revealed the decisive role played in setting up the UNL by the PLO's Left: the PFLP, the Democratic Front (DFLP), the Communist Party (PCP), and even the radical current of Fatah in the Territories.

Indeed, the real relationship of forces on the ground, in the clandestine struggle under the occupation, has nothing to do with the bourgeois, manipulative composition of the PLO's leading bodies in exile.[10] While these are totally under the hegemony of Fatah's right-wing historical leadership, the UNL was, and remains a parity coalition of PLO formations with a mass base—that is, the three left-wing formations and Fatah. This is what led the head of the PFLP, George Habash, to say the following in an interview given to the Kuwaiti journal *Al Qabas* in July 1988:

> The UNL in the occupied territories is the arm of the PLO…. That doesn't prevent me from pointing out that this arm, acting for the PLO in the interior, puts forward the PLO's Charter, adheres to its program for this stage and to the PNC's resolutions—much more so than certain opportunists and capitulators in the framework of the PLO…. These latter currents live in fear and dread of being overtaken by the UNL.[11]

The difference in nature between the UNL and the PLO's leadership inevitably led to falling out and friction between the two. The UNL's first communiqués in January 1988, while insistently calling on the masses to rally around the PLO, were not presented as coming from the PLO.

Communiqué 2 defined the intifada's initial program. The strategic objectives were: return (of the 1948 refugees), self-determination, and an independent Palestinian state. The immediate objectives were "army withdrawal from the towns, camps and villages," "democratic elections for local and village councils," as well as a whole series of demands directed against the repression and other aspects of the occupation. Communiqué no. 4 expresses an approach completely opposite to the PLO leadership's: "The intifada has definitively buried the plans of the rulers of Amman, Cairo and Tel Aviv, and those of their agents, to settle the Palestinian question in the framework of the American imperialist project."

It was at this point that the first intervention came from the exterior leadership. A circular from the "coordination," dated January 27, 1988, explained that in the intifada "no organization was more worthy than another," and that many of the participants did not belong to any tendency. The circular proposed to centralize and unify the publication of communiqués. At the same time communiqué no. 5 appeared, for the first time with the signature PLO/UNL, which remained the signature from then on. The UNL was subsequently presented and recognized as an authority of the PLO and under its control in the final analysis. Communiqué no. 5 is a politically watered-down version of no. 4 (without the phrase quoted above).

## A MORE RADICAL LINE

In any case, the UNL had not lost its specific character. It therefore remained clearly more radical than the exterior leadership, even more so given that the repressive and clandestine conditions meant that it was not always the same people who participated in writing the communiqués. Thus number 6 (February 2, 1988) declared: "We reject Mubarak's plot [Egyptian president, a great friend of Arafat's], and the attempts of the Jordanian regime and its collaborators . . . to bypass our legitimate leadership and dictate to it capitulationist conditions such as the recognition of [UN] Resolution 242." Communiqué no. 6 reiterated the program in no. 2, and in addition contained—as would be the rule from then on—indications and directives for action for the People's Committees, as well as a program of boycott of institutions of the occupation and a call to those employed by it to resign.

Communiqués 8 (February 20) and 10 (March 10) vigorously denounced Reagan's Secretary of State George Shultz, who began a series of visits to the region on February 25 to try to defuse the intifada. The UNL called for demonstrations and a boycott of Shultz's visits. This went against the advice of Arafat, who, according to George Habash, had already given the green light in January for a trip to Washington and a meeting with Shultz of two "moderate personalities" from the West Bank who are close to the PLO chief (Siniora and Abu-Rahmeh). In March the same Arafat again authorized two PNC members with U.S. citizenship, Edward Said and Ibrahim Abu-Lughod, to meet the U.S. secretary of state.

## COMMUNIQUÉ NO. 17

The dissensions inside the UNL broke out into broad daylight in May 1988: two different versions of communiqué no. 16 were produced, and—above all—were followed by two politically contradictory versions of communiqué no. 17. It was the eve of the Reagan-Gorbachev summit in Moscow. A first version of communiqué 17, dated May 21, reflected the line of the Fatah/PLO leadership: it contained many religious references; added "under the leadership of brother Yassir Arafat" to its reference to the PLO; showered emphatic praise on the Soviet position; and defined its objective as "a comprehensive and just peace."

The other version, dated May 24, reflects the line of the main left Palestinian group, the PFLP, and in particular its branch in the occupied territories, which is particularly radical. The intifada, it says, has shown the impossibility of coexistence with the Zionist entity; "there is no alternative to the choice of struggle and protracted people's war." It has a radical attitude concerning the Arab regimes (demanding democratic freedoms and opening up borders to the Palestinian armed struggle). "We maintain our people's rejection of all suspect projects, notably the Camp David accords, [UN] Resolutions 242 and 338, the Shultz initiative and the division of labor" (this last formula refers to Peres and King Hussein's common policy in 1985–87). It calls for a general strike at the time of the Moscow summit.

The affair of communiqué no. 17 provoked an energetic intervention from the exterior PLO leadership. Starting with no. 18, centralization of the communiqués was ensured in the framework of the PLO majority consensus. From then on, they had as a heading the expression from the Koran, "In the name of God, the merciful, the compassionate." By way of a compromise, communiqué 18 asserted the "rejection of all liquidationist solutions" without mentioning Resolution 242, but called for the International Conference. It repeated the immediate objectives outlined since communiqué no. 2.

However, the functioning of the UNL's majority consensus definitely took place at the PFLP's expense, even though the PFLP played a key role in its creation. Thus, communiqué 29, dated November 20, 1988, reporting the results of the PNC, argued in favor of an International Conference based on Resolutions 242 and 338 (without even mentioning the other UN resolutions), whereas the PFLP's opposition to these resolutions is well-known. [...]

FEBRUARY 11, 1989; first published in English in *International Viewpoint*, no. 158 (March 6, 1989).

## CHAPTER THIRTEEN

# The Washington Accords: A Retreat Under Pressure

*This analysis of the Oslo-Washington accords is the text of a report presented to an international meeting in December 1993. Its judgment and prognosis on the agreements are: "In short, the Arafat leadership's 'Palestinian self-government' will be an extreme case of indirect colonial administration, closer to a 'puppet' government than to the neocolonial governments emerging from decolonization. Either it will be this or it will not be.... If this apparatus proves itself incapable of fulfilling the task, the Washington accords will end up in the dustbin."*

The accords signed in Washington on September 13, 1993, by the Arafat leadership of the PLO and the Zionist government of Rabin and Peres, under the patronage of Bill Clinton, are the product of three developments, summarized here in chronological order.

1

The culmination of the long process of political retreat by the PLO leadership under the joint pressures of the Zionist state, U.S. imperialism, the reactionary Arab governments, and Moscow—as much under Brezhnev and then Gorbachev as under Yeltsin.

The Arafat leadership—the emanation of the deeply corrupted bourgeois bureaucracy of the PLO apparatus in exile as well as of Palestinian capitalism of the territories occupied in 1967 and the Palestinian diaspora—lost its last links with the armed movement of the Palestinian masses when it lost its last positions in Lebanon in 1982–83, under attack from Israel and subsequently Syria. It then resolutely opted for a negotiated settlement with the Zionist state under the aegis of the United States, as expressed in its praise for the Reagan Plan in 1982; reconciliation with King Hussein of Jordan and then the Egyptian regime of Hosni Mubarak in 1983; the accord with the Jordanian monarch and the break with the PLO Left in 1985 (the accord was unilaterally annulled by the King in 1986, which led the Arafat leadership to reconcile itself with the PLO left in 1987); official recognition of the state of Israel and its right to exist within secure borders, reconfirmation of the "Jordanian-Palestinian confederation" project, and "renunciation of terrorism" in 1988.

2

The radical change in the conditions of Palestinian national struggle due to the great leap forward brought by the intifada: since the uprising began in December 1987, it has placed the Palestinian people—more exactly the part of it living in the West Bank and Gaza, under Israeli occupation since 1967—back at the center of regional politics once more.

Whereas the successive defeats of the PLO in exile had considerably marginalized its role in Arab politics by 1987, the spontaneous outbreak of the intifada in the occupied Territories, sparked by accumulated frustrations, strengthened the Palestinian factor in the Middle Eastern political equation at a stroke, more than at any time since the massacres in Jordan in 1970. King Hussein drew the necessary conclusion and officially renounced his claim to recover the West Bank, which had been annexed to his kingdom after the 1948 Arab-Israeli war. The plans to settle the regional conflict that sought to bypass the Palestinian people by negotiating directly with Jordan—in particular the Allon Plan, which inspired the policy of the Israeli Labor Party from the time of the massacres in Jordan in 1970, and was reactivated by Shimon Peres in 1986 following his return to office in the Zionist coalition government—became impossible to pursue without replacing the Jordanian negotiating partner with Arafat's PLO leadership. The Arafat leadership was the only Palestinian interlocutor credible both in terms of political representation and disposition to participate in a regional Pax Americana.

The Reagan administration reacted accordingly, demanding new political concessions from the Arafat leadership in 1988 before beginning an official dialogue with it. Nonetheless, this first official attempt came up against an impasse: its conditions of progress foundered as much on the Israeli side—very quickly, when from November 1988 the Zionist Right once again governed alone, under the leadership of Shamir—as on the Arab-Palestinian side. Faced with Likud's rejectionism, Arafat decided to gamble on Saddam Hussein's Iraq, which had emerged militarily strengthened from its war with Iran. Henceforth Baghdad became the principal base of political-military support for the PLO leadership, compensating for Gorbachev's abdication of any pretense of providing a counterweight to U.S. pressure.

### 3

The radical change in the balance of forces in the Middle East brought by the 1991 Gulf war, and the confirmation of Moscow's alignment with Washington's policy in this region of the world.

The destruction of Iraq was seen by the Palestinian people as a defeat for their cause, and not without reason: not because it was correct to gamble on Saddam Hussein's ferocious bourgeois dictatorship, but in the sense that the crushing of Iraq radically altered the balance of regional military strength to the benefit of Israel. This radical change was not, however, the work of the Zionist army—which this time did not have the means to do the job on its own, as in 1948, 1967, and 1973—but the army of the United States itself. For Washington, it was imperative to seal the confirmation of its military supremacy in the Middle East by the establishment of a "new regional order," a vital element in the "new world order" proclaimed by Bush.

For the first time in history, conditions seemed propitious to the establishment of a global Pax Americana in this region of the world. U.S. hegemony was stronger and less contested than ever, the traditional Soviet rival having become complicit; of the two bastions of Arab nationalism after the defection of Egypt, one, Iraq, had been crushed, and the other, Syria, had been "turned" and had joined the camp of Washington's allies; Arafat was weaker and more isolated than at any time, and hence ready for all kinds of compromises. Paradoxically, the principal obstacle to the Pax Americana had become the Zionist Right itself, in power under Shamir.

In the hope of obtaining the $10 billion loan that he said was necessary to absorb the flood of Jewish refugees from the USSR, Shamir agreed to take part in the negotiations inaugurated with great pomp by Bush in Madrid in October 1991. For the first time, all the official parties to the Israeli-Arab conflict were represented including the Arafat PLO leadership, which, as everybody knew, directed the Palestinian delegation—even if the purely formal humiliating conditions (no representatives from exile or from East

Jerusalem) imposed by Shamir were respected. Nonetheless, the negotiations became bogged down very quickly because of the obstinacy of the Zionist right. The result was the most spectacular trial of strength in the history of Israeli-US relations, with open discontent between the godfather and his godchild, and a refusal to agree to the loan request without a political counterpart.

## THE IMMEDIATE PRELIMINARIES TO THE ACCORDS

The U.S. pressure, the perspective of a break between the world's greatest power and its Zionist protégé at a time when the Israeli socioeconomic situation was ceaselessly deteriorating, was a determinant factor in the narrow victory obtained by the party of Rabin and Peres in the Israeli general elections of June 1992. The return of this team to power opened the road to the Pax Americana blocked by Shamir. In 1987–88, Rabin and Peres—supported by the upper crust of the Zionist military establishment—had already placed the question of "territorial compromise" at the center of their political campaign. For these two Laborite leaders, faithful to the Allon Plan, Israel was obliged to choose between "land" on the one hand and the "Jewishness" of the "democratic" state (sic) on the other.

Two other options seemed to them impossible to maintain in the long term, inasmuch as they risked damaging irretrievably the support of the imperialist countries and their Jewish communities for the Zionist state—support on which this state is structurally dependent. The Zionists' problem is that the Palestinians had learned the lesson of 1948 by 1967 and had stayed put on their land. Violent expulsion of the Palestinians without any credible pretext was unthinkable, except for the crackpots of the quasi-fascist Zionist far right represented in Shamir's government. Annexation of the West Bank and Gaza Strip was impossible too, because granting Israeli citizenship to the inhabitants of these territories, which annexation would involve according to international law, would radically transform the ethnic composition of the state of Israel, putting its nature as a "Jewish state" in peril.

Moreover, Likud's option, creeping annexation without granting citizenship, would perpetuate a situation of apartheid that—besides tarnishing the "democratic" image of the Zionist state—became increasingly perilous with the radicalization of the occupied Palestinians' struggle and their much higher rate of population growth in comparison to the Israelis (immigration excepted). Under the Camp David accords between Begin and Sadat under Carter's patronage, Likud has been committed since 1979 to the perspective of Palestinian administrative autonomy in the territories occupied in 1967, though without accepting the principle of "territorial compromise." For Begin and even more Shamir, Israel should keep these territories, rebaptized "Judea and Samaria," while conceding a sort of status of extraterritoriality to their Palestinian inhabitants: a kind of symbolic, juridical expulsion.

For Rabin/Peres and the enlightened Zionists in general, Israel had every interest in "exchanging land for peace." Of course, for them this did not amount to total return of the 1967 territories. Still less did it mean the only historic compromise capable of leading to a genuine peace between the Israeli people and the Palestinian people as a whole: returning part of the 1948 territories (including the Triangle and Galilee where Arabs are still a majority) and abolishing the racist laws that prevent the Palestinians from coming back to live where they want to on the land they have been expelled from and enjoying full equality of rights with all inhabitants, without any discrimination.

What is at stake for the enlightened Zionists, in the context of the Allon Plan, is only *partial* withdrawal from the territories occupied in 1967. This means withdrawing from the zones of Palestinian population—except for East Jerusalem, annexed by Labor in 1967—while maintaining the Zionist settlements in all the strategic parts of the territories, notably along the Jordan River (most of the settlements in the West Bank were established under Labor) and deploying the army to ensure control of these territories and filter human and material exchanges between the Palestinian zones and the Arab environment. In exchange for this caricature of "territorial compromise" the Zionist-racist state demanded recognition of its legitimacy by its Arab neighbors, their commitment to preserve the security of its frontiers and "normalization" of their relations with it, meaning essentially—beyond the diplomatic forms, which are certainly not unimportant — opening Arab markets to Israeli goods and capital (and even an influx of Arab capital into Israeli banks).

The historic developments described above have both given an urgency to this plan that it never had before and imposed an amendment to the initial version put forward by Yigal Allon, supported by Rabin and Peres: *The intifada has considerably increased the urgency of an Israeli withdrawal from the Palestinian-populated areas of the West Bank and Gaza.* By forcing the Zionist army to continually repress street demonstrations in which many women and children participate, the intifada has brought about a veritable "moral gangrene" in the ranks of an army for which ideological mobilization—

the conviction of fighting for "the survival of Israel"—has always been a key factor in its efficiency.

In this sense, the intifada has been inspired by the lessons of the Lebanese resistance to Israeli occupation, the first case in the history of the Zionist state where it had to withdraw from an Arab territory without having realized its objectives or imposed its conditions. The Israeli population and army had lost any motivation to stay in Lebanon in face of a growing mass movement and a military guerilla force sufficiently effective to fuel growing political pressure for withdrawal from Lebanese soil. From 1988 on, the elite of the Zionist military establishment was arguing for withdrawal from Gaza and the Palestinian-populated areas of the West Bank, even under the form of a unilateral, non-negotiated withdrawal, since in any case the army would keep these territories in its vise so as to prevent any threat to the security of Israel and the Zionist settlements while freeing itself of the exhausting task of controlling the civilian population.

Admittedly, as all observers have noticed, the intifada had experienced an overall decline and showed signs of exhaustion from 1989 on and following the Gulf war, though without ceasing and without ever returning to the pre-1987 situation. Nothing, however, gave anyone in Israel grounds to claim that the situation was on the way to becoming "normalized." Indeed, the intifada added a new dimension to its struggle, namely the obvious increase since the Gulf war of renewed violent actions, individual or organized, carried out by Palestinians against the Zionist settlers, against the army of occupation, and even on the official territory of the state of Israel. It goes without saying that these violent actions (many carried out without firearms) are not of a nature or extent to threaten the "security of the state of Israel," just as the Lebanese guerrillas could not *militarily* defeat the Zionist army. But these actions were and still are of a high enough level to create a feeling of insecurity among the Israeli population, in particular in the sectors in contact with Palestinians, including the settlers and the army, but also Israelis in contact with Palestinian laborers exploited in the South African manner.

This hardening of the intifada's forms of struggle, completely predictable precisely because of the relative exhaustion of the street demonstrations and the increasing Israeli practice of responding to stone throwing by shooting to kill, has been principally the work of a current that has been ceaselessly growing since the beginning of the intifada among the Palestinians of the 1967 territories: the Muslim fundamentalist current whose major expression is the Movement of Islamic Resistance, Hamas.

In Palestine, as in most other cases of Islamic fundamentalist resurgence, this current feeds on the frustration of the masses—young people in particular—faced with an increasingly intolerable oppression, at a time when the historic bankruptcy of bourgeois nationalism has become manifest (in Palestine, the Arafat leadership's successive retreats) and the Left is either negligible (in most cases) or politically incapable of constituting an alternative leadership to the bourgeois leadership on a historic scale (the Palestinian case). The growth of the fundamentalist current, in many if not most cases, is thus not *first and foremost* the expression of a shift to the right in society. It differs in this respect from the rise of fascism in Europe, which many cite to make false analogies and justify their support for the dictatorships of bourgeois nationalist origin.

This growth—and this is clear in the Palestinian case—can primarily express the radicalization of the national and democratic struggle, *disorientated and deformed* for the aforesaid historical reasons, in the same way as the struggle of the Iranian masses was against the Shah. It is still the case that fundamentalist hegemony on a mass movement born in these conditions tends to send it backwards toward reactionary forms of consciousness, combined with obscurantist and sexist repression inside the movement itself.

The resurgence of violent actions advocated and claimed by the Palestinian fundamentalists and the growth of their current among the population made them the favorite bogeymen of Yitzhak Rabin's government. Rabin thought he had struck a great blow by expelling 415 of them to South Lebanon in December 1992. In fact he committed a great blunder, handing a considerable political and media coup to their movement. Rabin had counted isolating the Islamic fundamentalists, who vehemently rejected the "peace negotiations" organized by Washington and violently criticized the Arafat PLO leadership. He learned the natural and predictable lesson that Israeli repression of this current, aimed at weakening it organizationally, strengthened it politically. The lesson of Jordan was again underlined: the intervention of the Zionist army on the other side of the Jordan in April 1968 in the battle of Karameh had galvanized those who it sought to dissuade from continuing their combat; only the action of the Jordanian army itself brought to an end the armed movement of the Palestinian masses. This same lesson was repeated in Lebanon where an Arab army (Syria's) was more effective in strangling the Palestinian mass movement than the many Israeli interventions.

In a sense, the Jordanian lesson of 1970 was at the source of the adoption of the Allon Plan, as indicated above. This plan sought to turn repressive control of the Palestinian populated zones of the West Bank over to the Hashemite monarchy. But since the intifada, this "Jordanian option," as it was called, had become obsolete. Given that the Likud itself had accepted to negotiate in a quasi-direct manner with the PLO leadership, Rabin and Peres could envisage this new "option," the Arafat option, without too many political risks. They ensured that Israeli law was in conformity with their action by decriminalizing contacts with the PLO. Then they went ahead with first indirect, then direct, but always secret negotiations with the Arafat leadership, which led to the Washington accords.

The only new element in the Oslo-Washington process compared with the historic project of the Rabin-Peres leadership is that it was carried out directly with the PLO leadership rather than with King Hussein or representatives of Palestinians in the 1967 occupied territories. To believe that the accords represent a break with the "Zionist consensus" on Israeli sovereignty over these territories is to misunderstand the nature of that consensus, which never rested on the "Greater Israel" of the Zionist ultras or even the "Judea and Samaria" of Likud and the mystics. The debate provoked by Rabin and Peres in 1988 on "territorial compromise" in continuity with the Allon Plan proves this. There was, on the other hand, an undeniable "Zionist consensus" on the question of direct negotiations with the PLO—though Shimon Peres in particular took care more recently—above all since the beginning of direct negotiations between Washington and the PLO leadership in 1988—to replace the absolute refusal of dialogue with a refusal conditional on concessions demanded of the PLO. These concessions were tantamount to a total renunciation of the PLO's whole historic identity and everything that allowed it to be perceived as the incarnation of Palestinian national struggle.

Rabin-Peres chose to break the Zionist consensus against direct negotiations with the PLO, instead of contenting themselves with dealing with the delegation of Palestinians from the occupied territories in the negotiations organized by the United States. To assess the historic meaning of this decision, leading to recognition of the PLO as "the representative of the Palestinian people"—without succumbing to the formidable media intoxication arising from the accords about a "peace" that strongly resembles the "new world order"—one must look at the thinking that used to lie behind the Israeli rejection. The problem was no longer the fundamental program of the PLO seeking the destruction of the Zionist state; this had been discarded for a long time and without any possible ambiguity since the end of 1988.

The PLO leadership had progressively abandoned the Palestinian National Charter of 1968 in order to apply for a negotiated settlement with the state of Israel, offering it recognition and peaceful coexistence in exchange for Israeli withdrawal from the territories occupied in 1967 leading to the creation of an "independent and sovereign Palestinian state," a state of all the Palestinians including the refugees. There has been a Palestinian national consensus on this last demand for several years now. It is the sole objective common to all the territorial components and all the political tendencies of the Palestinian people—a much more realistic transitional program than the maximalist objective of the "liberation of Palestine."

This consensus had nonetheless been recently broken *in practice* by the Arafat PLO leadership when it accepted negotiations in the framework of the "Madrid conference" on "Palestinian autonomy" envisaged in the Israeli-Egyptian Camp David accords, which the PLO had violently denounced at the time they were adopted. The objective of an independent and sovereign Palestinian state was, however, maintained in official discourse. If the Israeli Shamir government still refused to negotiate *directly* with the Arafat leadership, it is because it thought this would amount to recognizing the rights of Palestinians in the diaspora. The refusal to recognize *these* rights has, since the PLO's programmatic adaptation, became the fundamental reason for the Zionist consensus on nonrecognition.

Under the Camp David accords signed by Begin himself, the Israeli government has for the last fifteen years already recognized not only the "existence" of the Palestinians in the territories occupied in 1967 but also their right to administrative autonomy, followed, after a transitory period of five years, by the right to be consulted on their future. However, what the Zionist establishment has always refused to recognize, above all tendencies, is the rights of the Palestinian refugees—the *majority* of the Palestinian people, forced into exile by Zionism —whose very existence is a permanent reminder of the historic injustice that was at the root of the state of Israel and of the "Palestinian problem" well before 1967.

Rabin's recognition of the PLO as "the representative of the Palestinian people" would have been an event of major historic significance if it had this meaning, if it meant recognition of the *rights of the Palestinian people as a whole*. But the truth is that Rabin has not recognized the PLO as it was and as the Zionist establishment has always refused to recognize it. *What Rabin has recognized is a PLO reshaped to fit his and Peres's requirements*, to an extent beyond their fondest hopes.

They now have a PLO leadership that recognizes in advance the legitimacy of the state of Israel, a racist Zionist state founded on the expulsion and the bloody oppression of the Palestinian people, not to mention the neighboring peoples—this, if it requires repeating yet again, has already officially been the case since 1988. But they also have, above all, a PLO leadership that agreed to sign *"peace" accords that rank among the most unjust and humiliating in the history of capitulations. Not only do these accords sanction the partition of the occupied territory between the occupier (army and settlements) and the indigenous population. They also deny the right of the territories to be evacuated to dispose of the attributes of sovereignty, beginning with a national army, or even to be called a state (what they are to be granted is to be called only "self-government"). The accords recognize no rights at all of the 1948 refugees, the great majority of Palestinians—not even the right to live in the "self-governing" territory in the West Bank and Gaza.* Even in the case of the 1967 refugees (those who left the West Bank in 1967 fleeing the Zionist invasion), only some of them will be allowed to return, on the basis of lists agreed on by the occupation authorities.

One could certainly prolong this inventory of infamous conditions set down by the Washington accords: the "structure, powers, and responsibilities of the Palestinian Authority" and even "the system of elections" are subject to prior approval by the Zionist government; water resources are to be shared; prisoners are not mentioned, and so on. Nonetheless, what has already been cited is sufficient to amply characterize them for what they are, as has been done already by a broad spectrum of Palestinian forces from the Islamic fundamentalists to the far left (including some of the most moderate bourgeois nationalists who, up until the accords, were still part of the PLO establishment, indeed among its highest leadership).

This undeniable fact is a striking demonstration that *the most serious "rupture of consensus" occasioned by these accords is the rupture of the Palestinian national consensus*—very much more serious, massive, and profound than any division inside Israeli society. On the Israeli side, the debate is among Zionists equally attached to the "Jewishness" of the state and its security, who disagree on the best way of ensuring their long-term preservation. On the Palestinian side, the debate is between the partisans of an essentially collaborationist capitulation and those who reject this capitulation, sharing the sentiment of an injured national dignity and of elementary rights trampled underfoot.

This explains the well-known fact that the negotiations have been led on the Palestinian side by Arafat's faction, working behind the back of its own partners in the official PLO leadership—of which only a minority (eight out of eighteen) finally approved the accords—and of the delegation of Palestinians from the interior to the public negotiations (though all were chosen by Arafat). The official delegation, feeling short-circuited, had threatened to resign shortly before the accords were reached.

In exchange for this revamped Allon Plan, the PLO leadership has committed itself to halting the intifada and renouncing "the use of terrorism and other acts of violence." (Given the day-to-day Zionist violence, which is a thousand times more serious, this one-sided commitment is unspeakable). It commits itself to keep "public order" in the territories that will be ceded to it, through a "strong police force" which the accords envisage for this purpose. In the military and political context created by the accords, this order will be imposed mainly on the agreement's opponents—those who will seek to go beyond its infamous limits and continue the fight for dismantling the Zionist settlements and total withdrawal of the Israeli army from the territories occupied in 1967, as well as for the inalienable rights of the Palestinian people and its majority in forced exile. In other words, *in accordance with Zionist objectives since the Allon plan, a repressive Arab force— Palestinian this time, not Jordanian—will be charged with suppressing the Palestinians of the territories, as a proxy of the Israeli army and under its strict control.* (The Israeli army has even stipulated that it retains a right of "engagement" within the territory of the Palestinian Authority if need be.)

## "SELF-GOVERNMENT"

When Yassir Arafat boasts publicly of having proved his ability to maintain order in Lebanon, he puts his finger on the main consideration that led the Zionist government to negotiate directly with him. Since the revamped Allon Plan would be realized with the participation of a Palestinian authority rather than with the Jordanian monarchy, the Rabin-Peres government quickly understood that it would obtain much more from the Arafat PLO leadership, installed in Tunis and confronted with the problem of how to maintain its enormous bureaucratic apparatus, than it would ever get from the representatives from the interior, subject as they are to the daily pressure of a mass movement in struggle. This simple calculation has proved itself well founded.

Moreover, the Rabin-Peres government knows quite well that the Arafat leadership has "proved itself in Lebanon." It knows that no internal leadership had the bureaucratic repressive qualifications, the human and material resources, the necessary prestige, and the disposition to carry out the task of repressing by proxy any inclination to pursue the Palestinian national struggle—the main task devolved to the apparatus of Palestinian "self-government" agreed to by the Zionist occupation—that the Arafat leadership has.

This mistrust of the Palestinians of the interior and this confidence in the Arafat apparatus, publicly proclaimed by the heads of the Israeli repressive services, are perfectly illustrated by the only exception that they have allowed to the principle of non-return of Palestinian refugees. Namely, Arafat and the men of his apparatus (excluding all opponents of the accords) will be admitted to the territories handed over by the Israeli army. So will soldiers of Egyptian and Jordanian units of the Palestine Liberation Army (PLA), attached to the regular armies of these two countries since the Arab League created the PLO and PLA in 1964. (The agreement even specifies that these soldiers must be holders of Egyptian documents or Jordanian passports and "trained as police"!) The very designation of these units, to the exclusion of other PLA formations (Syrian and Iraqi), speaks volumes.

Already, this hard core of the future Palestinian police has undergone an intensive training under the Egyptian and Jordanian armed forces so as to be ready to assume the task assigned to it. It is also significant that a priority form of aid from the imperialist powers to the Palestinian "authority" is to endow it with means of repression. [Then president of the European Commission Jacques] Delors, for, example declared following his meeting with Arafat at the beginning of November 1993 that the European Union was going to make emergency deliveries of arms, vehicles, and helicopters to the Palestinian police.

Moreover, the Jordanian option of the Allon Plan has not been abandoned, but only replaced by the *Jordanian-Palestinian option* laid out in the 1982 Reagan Plan. The PLO has for a long time situated itself in the framework of this plan by adopting the principle of a Jordanian-Palestinian confederation. This project is at the heart of the Washington accords. The choice of Gaza as first stage is easily explained by the great difficulties of the Israeli occupation in controlling this heavily populated area (inhabited largely by 1948 refugees), but the choice of the backwater of Jericho can only be explained by the proximity of the Jordanian frontier (the Allenby Bridge). The headquarters of "Palestinian self-government" will thus be in direct contact with the Jordanian state.

For Rabin and Peres, the Israeli-Jordanian-Palestinian "regional structure," conceived as a common market, will be the Trojan horse of the economic penetration of the Arab hinterland by Israeli sub-imperialism. According to this schema, the Palestinian and Jordanian-Palestinian comprador bourgeoisies will become active agents of this penetration. A reserve of cheap labor could also be exploited on the spot by Israeli capital, without the security risks inherent in importing Arab labor into Israeli-populated territories.

In short, the Arafat leadership's "Palestinian self-government: will be an extreme case of indirect colonial administration, closer to a "puppet" government than to the neocolonial governments emerging from decolonization. Either it will be this or it will not be. The Zionist government has decided to proceed by stages, beginning with Gaza and Jericho, to test the efficiency of the Arafat apparatus in the repressive task that has been allocated to it. If this apparatus proves itself incapable of fulfilling the task, the Washington accords will end up in the dustbin. This Israeli sword of Damocles will be a permanent goad, and certainly the major pretext for Palestinian police repression. This is the infernal logic of any collaborationist regime with an occupying power.

This is by far the worst aspect of the Arafat leadership's participation in the Washington accords. It is necessary to avoid the sophisms of the "lesser evil" and the balance of forces, invoked as a justification for all surrenders (above all when those who actually suffer the occupation are being bypassed by bureaucrats in gilded exile in Tunis). In the framework of the relationship of forces existing since 1967 between the state of Israel and the fragmented Palestinian people, in the absence of any Arab and international support capable of changing this relationship, it was clearly not possible to obtain a complete and unconditional withdrawal of the Zionist army from the territories occupied in 1967. It was not possible, in other words, to realize the legitimate transitional objective, however illusory, of an independent and sovereign Palestinian state—in the true sense of these words, not in the caricatured, demagogic interpretation that Arafat has given them today.

The only realistic immediate objective was that of unconditional withdrawal by the Israeli army from the Palestinian population centers: the demand formulated by the leadership of the intifada during its first months. The pressure of the Palestinian struggle in its different forms could have reasonably culminated in this result, on the condition that the struggle was not sabotaged by sowing illusions about winning Palestinian objectives through diplomacy, thanks to Washington. If the intifada has been in decline, this is not only for objective reasons but also, above all, for reasons of leadership.

The Tunis leadership had done everything to reestablish its hegemony over a movement that had freed itself from it in its first months.

Admittedly, the Palestinian self-administration thus created would not have been entirely sovereign and would have been limited to the very territories that the Israeli army now envisages withdrawing from. But it would not have had to recognize the legitimacy of the Zionist state, and still less the legitimacy of its settlements and its army in the territories occupied in 1967. It would not have had to sign a proxy contract to strangle the Palestinian national struggle against the ongoing occupation. The refugees would no more have been authorized to return to the territories than they are by the Washington accords; but this would have concerned all the Palestinians in exile, without any exception being made for the bureaucratic and military repressive apparatuses.

It would be hard to deny that self-administration by the Palestinians of the interior, with the experience of the forms of self-organization from below born from the early days of the intifada, would have corresponded much better to the Palestinian masses' own true interests than a "self-government" whose spinal cord is the repressive bourgeois apparatus in exile. This apparatus is much more corrupt and repressive than the Algerian "army of the frontiers" led by Boumedienne, which was entrusted with aborting the revolutionary potential arising inside Algeria at the time it won independence.

The Israeli army is going to withdraw from the Palestinian population centers of the West Bank and Gaza, and this is good news for the masses that have directly suffered from the occupation for over a quarter of a century. But any continuation of the Palestinian national struggle, and any social radicalization of this struggle, will henceforth come up against a Palestinian police that has yet to demonstrate that it will be less repressive than the Israeli army, in the long if not the short term—all the more so that the Palestinian police will have to act in close coordination with the Jordanian and Israeli repressive apparatuses.

## WHAT NOW?

The problem that faces the Palestinian masses of the West Bank and Gaza today is not how to struggle against the Washington accords, in the sense of struggling against their application. In the absence of an immediate alternative, it would be absurd to define the tasks in these terms. What is at stake is *to go beyond the constrictive framework of these accords*. First and foremost, *the struggle must continue in all its legitimate forms* (ruling out any violence against unarmed civilians) *against the ongoing occupation*: against the presence of the army and the Zionist settlements in the territories occupied in 1967, against the Israeli stranglehold on the resources of these territories, against the penetration of Israeli goods and capital—*in the perspective of an independent Palestinian state*. The struggle should be above all for the revolutionary replacement of the Palestinian repressive bourgeois apparatus by *self-organization of the Palestinian masses*, reestablishing the tradition of the first year of the intifada.

For Palestinians in exile, in particular Palestinian refugees in Jordan, Lebanon, and Syria, the dream of liberation and a return to Palestine must not serve as a pretext for a passive attitude toward the existing regimes, which oppress the Palestinian people as much as their own peoples. The strategic interests of the Palestinian people require the revolutionary overthrow of the oppressor Arab regimes, in joint struggle with all those men and women who suffer from them. In particular, the immediate interests of the great majority of Palestinian people who live on the two banks of the Jordan—and who are in the majority in Jordan itself—are to break the chain that is choking them at its weakest point: the Jordanian monarchy. Jordan must be transformed once more into the regional epicenter of the anti-Zionist and anti-imperialist struggle that it was between 1967 and 1970. In other words, it is necessary to replace the confederation envisaged by Arafat and King Hussein with *a revolutionary reunification of the two banks of the Jordan*.

This orientation in struggle requires the emergence of a proletarian leadership of the Palestinian struggle, an autonomous movement of the Palestinian laboring masses in close symbiosis with the struggles of the exploited classes and the oppressed masses in the countries of exile. The balance sheet of the leaderships of the Palestinian left in exile must be drawn and their choices judged from this point of view. Their incapacity to put themselves forward as an alternative leadership to Arafat for the Palestinian mass movement is certainly due to the following features: they have never been able to formulate a class program combining the social, democratic, and national dimensions; they have been incapable of thwarting the successive recuperations of the mass movement by the Arafat leadership, and act resolutely to bring about a democratic reorganization of the representative institutions of the Palestinian struggle; they have constantly compromised themselves with regimes, the Syrian regime in particular, justly hated by the Palestinian masses. In short, they have acted within the narrow

limits of petit bourgeois nationalism, radically anti-Zionist and anti-imperialist admittedly, but not anti-capitalist.

The choice now made by these leaderships to form a "National, Democratic and Islamic Front" with organizations under the thumb of Damascus
as well as with the Islamic fundamentalist movement can only hamper the
objective they assign themselves: leading the Palestinian mass struggle.
First, allying with the organizations controlled by Damascus, which are
totally discredited in the eyes of the masses and subject to the good will of a
regime that is itself negotiating an accord with the Zionist state under U.S.
guidance, shows a great political shortsightedness. Second, accepting ideological compromises with the fundamentalists, including the very name of
the united front, is playing the fundamentalists' game. It means abdicating
the pressing task of an implacable ideological struggle against their eminently reactionary social program.

Alliances on the ground in Palestine against the Zionist occupation and
every other form of future repression with the Islamic fundamentalist movement, which has become an unavoidable component of this struggle, can certainly not be ruled out. But while it is necessary to "strike together" on precise
objectives with this movement, it is no less necessary to "march separately,"
that is, not to mix banners and not to put a damper on the ideological struggle
against the fundamentalists' religious fanaticism, obscurantism and sexism.

The current choices of the leaderships of the Palestinian Left in exile are
not helping with the indispensable construction of an Israeli movement of
struggle for complete withdrawal of the Zionist army from the territories
occupied in 1967 and dismantling the settlements that they protect. They
are still less likely to facilitate building an Israeli anti-Zionist radical left, an
absolute precondition to winning the Israeli working class away from Zionism, without which dismantling the Zionist state and de-Zionizing Israeli
society are unthinkable. This is all the more regrettable when one could
reasonably hope that the psychological shock of the Washington accords
might favor the development of critical thinking about Zionism among
Israeli workers and young people. [...]

DECEMBER 1993; first published in English in *International Viewpoint*,
no. 252 (January 1994).

## CHAPTER FOURTEEN

# Zionism and Peace: From the Allon Plan to the Washington Accords

*This article was published in an academic journal in 1994, about a year after the signature of the Oslo-Washington accords. It has circulated widely and been trans- lated into several languages. It puts the 1993 accords into historical perspective, showing their direct continuity with the strategic vision of the Zionist movement's labor wing—their continuity in particular with the Allon Plan, which modified the labor Zionist vision in response to the situation created by the June 1967 war.*

## PROLOGUE: ON THE "JEWISH AND DEMOCRATIC STATE"

Contrary to the dominant perception today and the most current ideology, democracy and discrimination—religious, racial, ethnic, or sexual—are not antithetical notions.[1] The recognition of so-called democratic rights—civil and political—does not predetermine their extension; even the principle of equality of rights does not imply their real universality.[2] Thus the demo- cratic form of the government is independent of the particular selection of the *demos*. And without going back to the slave-owning democracy of Athenian antiquity, one is aware that in the matter of human rights explicit universalism ruled out tacit particularisms[3] only a long time after the solemn declarations of the eighteenth century.[4]

The anteriority of the discriminatory particularisms and, perhaps, the difficulty of justifying them with regard to the democratic spirit that suppos- edly inspired the drafters of these declarations have meant that they have most often remained tacit, as parts of a hidden statement. Their abolition is generally explicit, in the manner of the Fifteenth (1870) and Nineteenth (1920) amendments to the United States Constitution, which suppressed racial and sexual discriminations so far as the right to vote was concerned, although these discriminations were nowhere mentioned in the original document. In fact, an explicit universalism of democratic rights was imposed on a worldwide scale, in the texts and the dominant ideology, only after the Second World War—in part as a result of the confrontation with its fascist antitheses. It was consecrated by the International Declaration of Human Rights adopted by the General Assembly of the United Nations in 1948, of which Article 2, in particular, proclaimed equality of rights—with a most extensive definition of rights—"without distinction of any kind, such as race, color, sex, language, religion, political or other opinion, national or social origin, property, birth or other status."

Egalitarian universalism carried the day on the level of declared principles, but not always, far from it, in the actualities of state and social practices. The hypocrisy then became manifest, the texts having lost any ambiguity. If the USSR and its satellites as well as Saudi Arabia and South Africa abstained during the vote in 1948, the three great Western democracies seated on the Security Council, although official sponsors of the declaration, would themselves infringe the proclaimed egalitarianism, not only from the point of view of gender relations, but also through racial and ethnic discrimination in the colonies, if not in the metropolis.

David Ben-Gurion was, then, in good company when he proclaimed, in the Israeli Declaration of Independence of May 14, 1948, that the new state "will ensure complete equality of social and political rights to all its inhabitants irrespective of religion, race, or sex." Nonetheless, the contradiction in this precise case figures in the very text, the falseness of the proclaimed egalitarianism being only more patent. The entire Declaration of Independence was placed under the sign of the "Jewish State," the central objective of the world Zionist movement. It was not simply the State of Israel that was proclaimed, but "a Jewish State in Eretz Israel [the land of Israel], to be known as the State of Israel," and which "will be open for Jewish immigration and for the Ingathering of the [Jewish] Exiles."

The contradiction between proclaimed egalitarianism and implicit discrimination had become inherent in the Zionist project of colonization when it targeted a territory already inhabited by a non-Jewish population.[5] It was necessary from that point that the "colonists" of the "Jewish Company" conceived by Theodor Herzl[6] establish their state through the expulsion of the indigenous inhabitants, before being able to show themselves generous toward their eventual hosts: "And if it should occur that men of other creeds and different nationalities come to live amongst us, we should accord them honorable protection and equality before the law. We have learned toleration in Europe."[7] This tension between the profession of democratic faith and the real colonialist project would characterize the thought of Ben-Gurion, disciple of Herzl and realizer of his project. The founder of the state of Israel could thus affirm, in 1937, that "the Arab inhabitants of Palestine should enjoy all civic and political rights, not only as individuals, but as a national group, just like the Jews"; then shortly afterward make this statement: "Were I an Arab... I would rebel even more vigorously, bitterly, and desperately against the immigration that will one day turn Palestine and all its Arab residents over to Jewish rule."[8]

It is well-known that even under the frontiers proposed by the partition plan adopted by the UN in 1947, the "Jewish" state was demographically only 55 percent Jewish.[9] It would have been much less so within the frontiers established by the 1948 war (650,000 Jews to 877,000 Arabs), were it not for the massive exodus of Palestinians (710,000) fleeing the terror and the fighting. The reasons for this exodus have been much discussed.[10] Jean-Paul Chagnollaud was completely right, however, when he affirmed that "in a certain sense, the question hardly has any interest today, for in essence the problem is no longer why they left when one knows perfectly well why they could not return."[11]

By an implacable "ratchet effect," the Palestinian refugees were prevented by the new state from recovering their lands and their homes (which were massively destroyed with entire villages being razed), prevented from returning (the notion of *return* is, in their case, unchallengeable) to their age old territory, now "open to Jewish immigration." On the other hand, the "Law of Return" of 1950 accorded Israeli citizenship automatically to all new immigrants, on condition that they were "Jewish," according to a definition which would be inexorably reduced to the most obtuse religious criteria.[12] Thus, by a cruel irony of history, the Zionist movement—fleeing a hideous European anti-Semitism that erected religious descent as a criterion of "racial" discrimination—had come to establish a state founded on discrimination based on the same religious criterion, with a more restrictive religious interpretation. And it was by the same inexorable logic that the Zionist "socialists" of Ben-Gurion's party came to make religious instruction compulsory in the schools.[13]

This outcome was entirely prefigured in the very idea of *The State of the Jews* (*Der Judenstaat*), the original title of Herzl's book, which became *The*

*Jewish State* in the principal European translations.[14] As many have observed, harking back to the original debate between the nationalist and secular state project of Herzl's "political Zionism" on the one hand, and on the other hand, Ahad Ha'Am's "cultural Zionism"—concerned with establishing in Palestine a Jewish spiritual homeland incarnating the highest spiritual values of Judaism, without sullying and degrading it through the recourse to arms rendered inevitable by the state project—the mistranslation comes close to the opposite sense. It is justified, however, by *the doctrinal logic of political Zionism, whose nationalism, from the point that it embraced not only the Yiddish nation, but all the Jews of the planet, became inseparable from the religious reference, the sole common denominator*—not as a system of spiritual values, but in its narrowest discriminatory conception, matched with the traditional obligations and restrictions.[15]

Much irony has been poured on the striking contrast between the reality of the state of Israel and Herzl's determination, proclaimed in his Zionist manifesto, that the clergy (and the army!) should not "interfere in the administration of the state."[16] But the same Herzl, in the same work, betrayed quite clearly the confessional logic of his approach, when he described the organization of the immigration: "Each group will have its rabbi, traveling with his congregation.... Local groups will afterward form voluntarily about their rabbi, and each locality will have its spiritual leader.... They will not need to address special meetings for the purpose; an appeal such as this may be uttered in the synagogue. And thus it must be done. *For we feel our historic affinity only through the faith of our fathers, as we have long ago absorbed the languages of different nations to an ineradicable degree.*"[17]

To the convergence between political Zionism and the most traditionalists religious Zionism was added another equally ineluctable convergence.[18] Rereading Herzl's work in 1946, Hannah Arendt stressed the point to which the "state of mind" of the founder of the Zionist movement was close to that of his anti-Semitic environment and inspired by the tradition of German nationalism.[19] This common state of mind in the dominant currents of political Zionism would lead to a convergence on the terrain of armed expansionism, between the "socialist" Zionism of a Ben-Gurion and the "revisionism" of a Jabotinsky, although the former had not hesitated, at the beginning of the 1930s, to compare the latter to fascism and Hitlerism.[20] The politics of power, the *Machtpolitik*, was built into the very logic of the "Jewish State" project ever since it was decided to establish it in Palestine: it could only be achieved by force, as advocated by the Revisionists.[21]

In 1946, Judah Magnes, a partisan with Martin Buber of peaceful coexistence between Arabs and Jews in a binational Palestine, noted bitterly that the Zionist movement had adopted de facto Jabotinsky's point of view.[22] Forty years later, Simha Flapan, former leader of Mapam, party of the Zionist far left, attacking the legend woven by the Labor Party around the historic figure of Ben-Gurion, wrote about him in his posthumous work: "Where the Arabs were concerned, he espoused the basic principles of Revisionism: the expansion of the borders, the conquest of Arab areas, and the evacuation of the Arab population."[23]

On the *Zionist* state, a qualification much more rigorous than that of the "Jewish" state, one of the most severe verdicts was that expressed, in 1959, by a prominent figure of the American Jewish community, James P. Warburg:

> Nothing could be more understandable than the desire of the European Jews, generated by centuries of persecution and fired by the inhuman Nazi atrocities, to escape forever from minority status.... But nothing could be more tragic than to witness the creation of a Jewish state in which the non-Jewish minorities are treated as second-class citizens—in which neither a Jew's Christian wife nor their children could be buried in the same cemetery as their father.[24]
>
> It is one thing to create a much-needed refuge for the persecuted and oppressed. It is quite another thing to create a new chauvinistic nationalism and a state based in part upon medieval theocratic bigotry and in part upon the Nazi-exploited myth of the existence of a Jewish race.[25]

And yet! This semireligious Zionist state, founded on a religious discrimination, is undoubtedly democratic for its inhabitants of Jewish descent. Moreover, the Palestinian Arabs who hold Israeli citizenship, although second-class citizens in many respects, also undoubtedly enjoy more political rights than the inhabitants of the Arab states. We return here to our point of departure: there is not at all an antinomy between formal political democracy and the existence of a constitutive discrimination of the *demos*. From whence the *possibility* of a Zionist ideology of the "Jewish and democratic state" as developed by Ben-Gurion in opposition to the Revisionists.

As to the *plausibility* of this ideology with regard to the egalitarian universalism proclaimed in 1948, it is precisely conditioned by the existence of an assured Jewish majority inside the *demos*—concealing the fact that it has been constituted by the discriminatory denial to the indigenous inhabitants of an elementary right of return. The maintenance of a minority of non-Jewish citizens inside the Israeli *demos* appears, therefore, as the indispensable token, not to say alibi, of Zionist democracy and its proclaimed universalism—on the express condition that this minority remains very much a minority and cannot put in question the "Jewishness" of the state.

Such is the rationale of the opposition of Ben-Gurion and his disciples to the program of the Zionist Right, advocating the extension of the frontiers of the "Jewish" state by the pure and simple annexation of the entire territory of mandatory Palestine, if not the two banks of the Jordan—prepared thus to include a great mass of Arabs and to accommodate itself to political discrimination inside its boundaries, making a nonsense of the myth of the democratic state.[26] "Labor," wrote Simha Flapan, "presents Ben-Gurion's ideas and strategies as the other alternative to Likud's concept of a Greater Israel, pointing out that he totally rejected rule over another people and was unconditionally committed to the preservation of the Jewish and democratic character of the state."[27]

The Mapam leader added this commentary: "Indeed, the concept of a democratic Jewish society might conceivably provide such an alternative were it free from the impulse toward territorial expansionism—for whatever reason: historical, religious, political, or strategic. But the fact is that Ben-Gurion built his political philosophy precisely on these two contradictory elements: a democratic *Jewish* society in the *whole*, or in most, of Palestine."[28]

Ben-Gurion did not hide indeed the fact that he only accepted partition out of tactical concerns, on a provisional basis, and that his objective was "Palestine as a whole."[29] The motivation for his expansionism was the necessary space for the original Zionist project of gathering in Palestine the majority of the world's Jews, a project he always placed above any other consideration. Thus, the disagreement between Jabotinsky's heirs and those of Ben-Gurion was never about the desirable position of the eastern frontier of the Zionist state: all are agreed that it should pass along the Jordan River and the Dead Sea, if only for "security" reasons.[30]

The disagreement rather concerned the way of settling the demographic problem in this framework, so as to preserve the "Jewishness" of the state—the concern of the Labor Party being to preserve at the same time its democratic reputation, a vital question for a state so dependent on foreign aid. It is then highly significant that the first coalition government grouping together the Revisionists (represented by Menachem Begin) and the socialists was formed on the eve of the war of June 1967 and in preparation for it. Then, when the state of Israel was reunited with the rest of the

British Mandate Palestine, the divergences between the two Zionist factions recovered all their sharpness.

## ISRAEL'S POST-1967 DILEMMA AND THE ALLON PLAN

Contrary to what happened nineteen years earlier and for several reasons, among them undoubtedly the desire not to share the unenviable fate of the 1948 refugees, the great majority of the Palestinian population of the West Bank and Gaza remained in their territory in 1967. The Zionist leaders found themselves confronted with a real dilemma. Having attained their objective of shifting the eastern frontier of their state to the Jordan River, they found themselves with a sizable Palestinian Arab population under their control. In these conditions, pure and simple annexation of the whole of the newly occupied Palestinian territories became impracticable; by granting Israeli citizenship to their inhabitants, it would imperil the *Jewish* character of the Zionist state; in refusing this citizenship, it would put in question its *democratic* character.[31]

By any logic, the only solution that would permit both remaining along the bank of the Jordan River and preserving the "Jewish state" as well as its democratic reputation, was to grant to the *areas of Palestinian high-population density* (with the exception of East Jerusalem, annexed from the beginning for ideological reasons) the status of *enclaves* within the new frontiers of the state of Israel.[32] It was Yigal Allon, a prominent figure of the Israeli political-military establishment and of the Labor left, who elaborated this concept for a settlement, which became known as the Allon Plan.[33] He presented it to the government of Levi Eshkol, in which he was deputy prime minister, at the beginning of July 1967. It is useful to cite the author of the plan to clarify the key factors:

> The territorial solution must respond to three fundamental imperatives:
>
> a)  the historic rights of the people of Israel on the land of Israel;
> b)  a state with a preponderant Jewish majority on the national level,
>     which is democratic on the political, social. and cultural levels;
> c)  defensible frontiers.[34]
>
> Consequently, if it is necessary to choose between a de facto binational
> state with more territory and a Jewish state with less territory, I opt
> for the second eventuality, on condition that it has defensible frontiers.

The alternatives are pitilessly clear.
If we held within Israel all the territories of strong Arab density by granting
their inhabitants all civic rights, we would no longer have a Jewish state.
If we annexed them in refusing these rights to the inhabitants, we would
cease to be a democratic society. But we want at the same time a Jewish state—
with an Arab minority enjoying equality of rights—and a democratic society
in the full sense of the term.[35]

In the light of these imperatives, Allon advocated the definitive acquisition
by Israel of a border strip of roughly 15 kilometers width along the Jordan
River, stretching to the west of the Dead Sea to the outskirts of Hebron, as
well as the acquisition, in addition to the old city of Jerusalem, of its eastern
flank up to the River—so as to reduce the Palestinian territories of the West
Bank to two separate enclaves to the north and the south of the "holy city"
linked by a narrow corridor.[36]

This formula, according to Allon, "allows an Arab solution for the population of the West Bank and leaves a sovereign corridor at its disposition
between Ramallah, Jericho and the Allenby Bridge.

This defense configuration could resist a modern army. It is meant to protect the
country, not only from its direct neighbors, but also from the entire region to the
east, which extends as far as the Persian Gulf and the Indian Ocean, *a fortiori* since
the countries that compose it are equipping themselves massively with ultramod-
ern offensive weapons. It creates also a *hinterland* destined to protect Jerusalem
and its environs from the dangers of guerilla warfare, and gives us the possibility
of settlement in the semi-deserted areas. I add that the territories that we would
return will be demilitarized, and that in installing ourselves on the flank of the population of the West Bank, we will in any case neutralize its offensive potential.[37]

As to Gaza, Allon advocated that it should not be returned to Egypt, but
rather attached to the West Bank enclaves, as access to the sea "with rights
of circulation, but without creating a corridor," while keeping control of the
south of the sector so as to control access to the Egyptian Sinai.

Yigal Allon was in no way motivated by some internationalist or pacifist
generosity; his entire past as a nationalist combatant attests to it, as does his
own line of argument, faithful to the Zionist tradition of Ben-Gurion.[38] At
the time when he formulated his plan, that is, immediately after the 1967
war, the territories concerned had only just been conquered. The Israeli

pacifists, the true "doves," proposed that they should be returned in their quasi-totality in exchange for peace treaties with the Arab states.[39] The Allon Plan envisaged, on the contrary, a prolonged occupation and a process of annexation by the requisition of lands and the implantation of settlements, so as to physically occupy the territory that it sought to acquire definitively.

Fundamentally, *the Allon Plan was thus a plan of colonization and partial annexation*, in the name of "territorial compromise," unlike the complete annexation advocated by the Zionist Right. In the debate between the Right and Labor partisans of the Allon Plan, it was not a matter of hawks and doves but "rather of hawks and vultures," in the words of the radical internationalist Eli Lobel.[40] The Allon Plan was, however, much more coherent and realistic than the aims of Likud. Having come to power in 1977, Likud did not dare anyway to carry out its program to the end, but got bogged down with the subtleties of a project of extra-territorial Palestinian autonomy that never convinced anybody. The Labor Party plan thus ended up de facto as the fundamental line of conduct of the Zionist state in the 1967 territories—even under the Likud, which, despite having amended it in its fashion, strengthened nevertheless its essential tendencies.[41]

Allon hardly said anything about the ultimate fate of the Palestinian enclaves, for reasons of elementary tactical prudence. To the extent that his plan was precisely a long-term one, it was necessary to allow some time for its implementation and for the ultimate emergence of an Arab interlocutor disposed to collaborate with the settlement dictated by Israel, but nonetheless armed with the authority needed to be credible.[42] Since the creation of a Palestinian state, that is, an entity enjoying the attributes of political and military sovereignty, had always been categorically rejected by the entire Zionist establishment, the three possibilities envisaged for the enclaves were to reunite them with King Hussein's Jordan, or to federate them with Jordan, or again to constitute them as an "autonomous entity."

> I will not enter into a debate here on what is known as the "Palestinian entity." I am among those who think that historic circumstances entail its constitution even if it does not have roots plunged deep into the past....Do not forget above all that it was in the name of the Palestinian problem that the Arab states unleashed war against us in 1948... and that, without its solution, one cannot hope for a real peace....
>
> The king's idea of [Jordanian-Palestinian] federation does not in principle obstruct the road of direct negotiations with the population of these territories.... From our point of view, there is room for negotiations with both. [43]

This well-perceived importance of the Palestinian factor in any credible settlement would lead successive Israeli governments to search for Palestinian negotiating partners.[44] In 1977, Allon excluded no hypothesis in this regard, including that of dealing with the PLO if it were to mend its ways. His words have today acquired a premonitory value:

> Certainly, if the PLO ceased to be the PLO, we could cease to consider it as such. Or if the tiger transformed itself into a horse, we could mount it. At that moment, we would get front-page headlines in our favor.[45]

### THE WASHINGTON ACCORDS

The front-page headlines were certainly there on September 13, 1993. The media affected total surprise, as if a new miracle had just come to pass in relation to a land that, to be sure, had witnessed many others. Only the discordant voices of some critics of the accords who were well acquainted with the situation, like Edward Said, Noam Chomsky, and Meron Benvenisti, pointed out that the accords signed on the White House lawn amounted to an updated version of the Allon Plan.[46]

What then, did the accords actually say?

It is undeniable that the texts made public, that is, the letters, the Declaration of Principles and its four Annexes, as well as its Agreed Minutes, fit in perfectly with the broad outline of the plan formulated in 1967. None of the measures in the Washington accords contradict in any way whatsoever the program set in motion by the Israeli Labor Party in relation to the West Bank and Gaza more than a quarter of a century before. This can easily be seen through examining some key points of these documents (without entering into every aspect of the question, notably the economic ones).[47]

Let us begin by what has been perceived as the most spectacular event, namely "mutual recognition." Yassir Arafat's letter, addressed to the Israeli prime minister, says the following: "The PLO recognizes the right of the State of Israel to exist in peace and security," and "accepts UN Security Council Resolutions 242 and 338." The most important of these resolutions, 242 (November 1967), which the State of Israel has accepted from the beginning, had been rejected by the PLO for a long time, because it made no mention of the right of the Palestinians to return and to self-determination and ratified the principle of "secure borders," interpreted by the Israelis as justifying their redrawing of borders and their territorial demands.[48] In exchange for this concession, the PLO obtained no mention of the right of the Palestinians to self-determination or to return—one finds only, in the accords, the vague formula of "legitimate rights."

The Arafat letter affirms that "the PLO renounces the use of terrorism and other acts of violence and will assume responsibility over all PLO elements and personnel in order to assure their compliance, prevent violations, and discipline violators." Because it applied only to the personnel of the PLO, this repudiation of violence and the commitment to repress it in the face of a continuing occupation was not enough for the Israeli government. In a second letter, addressed to the Norwegian minister Holst and annexed to the first, "the PLO encourages and calls upon the Palestinian people in the West Bank and Gaza Strip to take parts in the steps leading to the normalization of life, rejecting violence and terrorism."

Through the first affirmation of his letter to Yitzhak Rabin, Arafat repudiated the PLO's basic program (the *liberation of Palestine*). Logically enough, he concluded that "those articles of the Palestinian Covenant which deny Israel's right to exist and the provisions of the Covenant which are inconsistent with the commitments of this letter are now inoperative and no longer valid." This amounted to say, in reality, that the Covenant itself was no longer valid. The tiger had indeed transformed itself into a horse; it could now be mounted. Rabin's letter, for its part, addresses itself to the Norwegian minister and not to Arafat: "In light of the PLO commitments... the Government of Israel has decided to recognize the PLO as the representative of the Palestinian people"—without any mention of rights.

The Declaration of Principles aims "to establish a Palestinian Interim Self-Government Authority, the elected Council for the Palestinian people in the West Bank and the Gaza Strip, for a transitional period not exceeding five years, leading to a permanent settlement based on Security Council Resolutions 242 and 338" (Art. 1). The Palestinian "Self-Government" Authority will exercise its prerogatives in the territories that the Israeli army will choose to withdraw from. *The accords specify that these territories will be determined according to the principle of the withdrawal from the territories with a strong Arab population density, which is at the heart of the Allon Plan:* "A redeployment of Israeli military forces in the West Bank and the Gaza Strip will take place.... In redeploying its military forces, Israel will be guided by the principle that its military forces should be redeployed outside populated areas." (Art. 13)

East Jerusalem, officially annexed by Israel since 1967, is not covered.[49] Moreover, not only does the accord not envisage the dismantling of any settlements, but it guarantees to the settlers and other Israelis a veritable regime of extraterritorial rights under which they will not come under the jurisdiction of the Palestinian Authority on its own territory. The Authority is responsible only for controlling Palestinians, and this by means of its police. It will have no army, its external defense being assured by Israel (*sic*) whose army can circulate freely in the "self-government" territory.[50]

> In order to guarantee public order and internal security for the Palestinians of the West Bank and Gaza Strip, the Council will establish a strong police force, while Israel will continue to carry the responsibility for defending against external threats, as well as the responsibility for overall security of Israelis for the purpose of safeguarding their internal security and public order. (Art. 8)

The first phase of the application of the accords affects the Gaza Strip and the region of Jericho, and it is stipulated in the Agreed Minutes that "subsequent to the Israeli withdrawal, Israel will continue to be responsible for external security, and for internal security and public order of settlements and Israelis. Israeli military forces and civilians may continue to use roads freely within the Gaza Strip and the Jericho area." (Annex 2)

Thus, *the general framework envisaged by the Washington accords is much that of the Allon Plan: Israeli withdrawal from the populated Arab areas, except for East Jerusalem, and redeployment in the rest of the Palestinian territories occupied in 1967, with the maintenance of the settlements; the constitution of the evacuated enclaves as an autonomous Palestinian entity without full state powers, and without military means other than those necessary for internal repression; Israeli control of access to these enclaves, in particular the crossing points to Egypt and Jordan* (confirmed by the accords signed later in Cairo).

Admittedly, these are for the moment interim arrangements, in expectation of a permanent status that is to be defined within five years at the latest. But this, like the interim settlement, will depend on a balance of forces—which speaks for itself. One would really have to believe in miracles to imagine that at the end of five years of implementation of the framework envisaged by the Allon Plan—and it was obvious during the negotiations on Gaza and Jericho that the Israeli regime had no intention of giving anybody any presents—the Zionist state, out of sheer charity, would decide to evacuate the rest of Gaza and the West Bank, including East Jerusalem, to allow the creation of an "independent and sovereign" Palestinian state. This is, nonetheless, what Arafat is promising to anyone prepared to believe him. In reality, if the PLO ever manages to obtain even the dismantling of some of the settlements that the Israeli government considers to be "strategic" (that is, those that fall outside the framework of the Allon Plan), it should count itself lucky.

Meron Benvenisti, a well-known Israeli specialist on the 1967 territories, states that the PLO negotiators have already accepted two principles: "no Israeli settlement will be evacuated" and "settlement blocs—constituting a continuous expanse—will be under Israeli authority."[51] According to Benvenisti, "These settlement blocs, which include the majority of the existing settlements, will be hooked up to Israel by far-reaching road networks, along which Israel will possess the authority to perform autonomous security activities." They will divide the West Bank into "three cantons linked to each other by narrow corridors." Moreover, "The road network serving these settlement blocs will turn the Palestinian cantons into a puzzle that will not permit the [Palestinian] administration any real authority." The author concludes that the Palestinians will not be able to contest these principles, because they have already accepted them.

What is more, the peace treaty currently being negotiated between Israel and Jordan envisages agreement on a border between the two states running along the Jordan River and the Dead Sea. This treaty could, then, remove all international legitimacy from the demand for Israeli withdrawal from the whole of the West Bank, which was under Jordanian sovereignty before June 1967. The Palestinian entity being new, its frontiers with the state of Israel remain to be defined, as the Declaration of Principles stipulates.

The Allon Plan is, then, well on the way to getting the consecration it expected: international and Arab recognition of the Israeli *fait accompli* in the West Bank and Gaza; peace in exchange for a "territorial compromise" allowing Israel to exercise direct or semi-direct sovereignty over the whole of British Mandate Palestine; the solution—some would say the liquidation—of the Palestinian problem, at little cost, and the preservation of the "Jewish and democratic state," with yet more favorable front-page headlines.

## "PEACE OF THE BRAVE" OR SURRENDER?

Nonetheless, the historic context in which these accords have been concluded gives a specific meaning to the role allotted to Yassir Arafat's PLO, a meaning which was no more than a secondary consideration for Yigal Allon. For Allon, the main argument was demographic, in relation to the composition of the

Israeli population. True, it did not escape the clear-sighted Zionist strategist that controlling the Arab population of the 1967 territories could ultimately pose a problem.[52] But the fact is that until 1987, that is, until the outbreak of the Palestinian Intifada, the tensions inside these territories had been kept at an acceptable level for the Israeli occupier.[53]

The main problem during the elaboration of the Allon Plan was the Palestinians in exile organized by the PLO, as well as "Arab rejection," which remained steadfast in the wake of the "Six Day War."[54] The Labor Party's program of "territorial compromise" appeared, at best, as the policy of an active waiting game. Time played in favor of Israel and its territorial strategy of requisitions and settlements, faced with the impotent Arab demand for the complete restoration of the territories occupied in 1967. When King Hussein crushed the Palestinian armed movement in Jordan in 1970–71, he became a potentially valuable partner for Labor's project, having largely proved himself in the matter of control of his subjects. It was then that he formulated his project of the "United Arab Kingdom," involving his recovery of the West Bank as a federated province. However, the Arab context hardly permitted him to enter into a separate peace with the Zionist state on its own conditions, the only option that Israel ever offered to its neighbors.

The affair became more complicated when the Jordanian monarch found himself still more isolated following the 1973 war, in which he did not take part. The PLO had succeeded in reconstituting its quasi-state in Lebanon and replaced its initial nationalist maximalism with the program of the independent Palestinian state in the West Bank and Gaza.[55] The Rabat summit of Arab heads of state in 1974 approved this new program of the Palestinian leadership and recognized it as "sole legitimate representative of the Palestinian people." The Israeli-Arab negotiations (International Conference at Geneva, bilateral military negotiations), which followed the Yom Kippur/Ramadan war, had raised the perspective of a "negotiated settlement" but then got bogged down. The second attempt to crush the PLO degenerated into a fifteen-year war in Lebanon.

The coming to power of Likud in Israel, in 1977, ruled out any perspective of a comprehensive settlement. It was out of the question that the Zionist Right would envisage any kind of compromise on the Golan or the Palestinian territories. Only the Sinai fell out of its political mystique; the neutralization of the Egyptian front under a U.S. guarantee could strengthen Likud's annexationist ambitions. Thus, the defection of Sadat led to a separate peace and the restoration to Egypt of this vast desert expanse, except for the Gaza Strip. Israeli preconditions—demilitarization and alert mechanisms under U.S. control—assured perfect security for this enormous "buffer zone." Likud proceeded to officially annex the Golan, emptied in 1967 of most of its Arab population; demographic considerations prevented them from doing the same in "Judea and Samaria" and Gaza.

The Zionist Right nonetheless worked toward annexation: intensification and extension of the settlement process; pressures of every kind for a creeping expulsion of the indigenous inhabitants; the project of extraterritorial Palestinian self-government and attempts to set up a network of collaborators to this end; efforts to increase the flow of Jewish immigration to Israel, so as to consolidate the Jewish demographic majority in the whole of Palestine. However, the 1982 invasion of Lebanon discredited Likud and led to worsened relations between Israel and its U.S. godfather. This war had nonetheless considerably weakened the PLO, just as the peace with Egypt had opened the road to the Israeli-Arab settlement.

Having left Lebanon, Yassir Arafat had praised Ronald Reagan's policies, reconciled himself with King Hussein, and quickly fallen out with Syria. After his second departure from Lebanon by sea (1983), he went to Cairo, thus breaking the official Arab boycott of Egypt. Then in 1985 he concluded an agreement with the Jordanian monarch for common participation in negotiations with Israel, leading to dissidence among the PLO left-wing factions. The conditions for a settlement on the Jordanian-Palestinian front seemed to be ripening rapidly on the Arab side.

Having returned to power in the context of a coalition government with Likud, the Israeli Labor Party led by Shimon Peres had made overtures to King Hussein. Hussein increased his pressure on the PLO to accelerate the process, and believed himself strong enough to go forward without it. At the 1987 Arab summit in Baghdad the PLO was more marginalized than it had ever been. But at the end of this same year the intifada exploded in Gaza and the West Bank, overturning the basics of the situation. For the first time in twenty years, the Palestinians of the interior became uncontrollable and placed Israel in an extremely embarrassing situation. King Hussein, acknowledging his defeat, announced officially the abandonment of his claim to the West Bank. The PLO found itself once more in a position of strength.

Shimon Peres waged his electoral campaign in 1988 under the slogan of "territorial compromise," with an open invitation to the PLO to negotiate with Israel.[56] He was, however, defeated, while the Palestinian leadership, on its side, bent itself to the requirements of negotiations with the United

States, being unable to negotiate with an Israeli government dominated by the Likud. The situation once more got bogged down, despite U.S. efforts, when the Gulf crisis blew up. By considerably reinforcing the weight of the United States in regional politics, the 1991 war opened the road to the peace conference inaugurated in Madrid, including for the first time direct negotiations between the Israeli government and a delegation officially sponsored by the PLO.

For Likud, led by Yitzhak Shamir, it was just a matter of temporizing so as to obtain the U.S. green light for a $10 billion loan. Israel needed this sum to be able to absorb the million Jewish immigrants expected to arrive as a consequence of the collapse of the USSR. For Shamir, this heaven-sent immigration would allow the annexation of the 1967 territories without any demographic worries. But the Bush administration was not stupid. It kept in hand its means of financial pressure, which was a key argument in the victorious electoral campaign of the Israeli Labor Party in 1992 under the leadership of Yitzhak Rabin.

Meanwhile, the traditional forms of struggle of the intifada were running out of steam, giving way to Palestinian radicalization marked by the irresistible rise of the Islamic fundamentalist Hamas movement and a multiplication of the violent actions it advocated. These attacks succeeded in seriously disturbing the Israeli sense of security on both sides of the 1967 border. Rabin first tried to repress the Palestinian fundamentalists by expelling several hundred of them to Lebanon in December 1992. The operation boomeranged, strengthening considerably the prestige of Hamas.

Yet Rabin was convinced, with good reason, that the Palestinians of the interior, those of the Palestinian delegation at the Peace Conference, under the pressure of a population in the process of radicalization, were not disposed to bend themselves to the demands of the Allon Plan, and still less to commit themselves to repress the struggle of the fundamentalists. Only the Palestinian bureaucracy of the PLO in exile would be prepared to meet these conditions, all the more so in that it was on the verge of bankruptcy, the Arab oil monarchies having ceased to finance it because of its favorable attitude toward Iraq during the Gulf crisis. This was why Rabin and Peres decided to engage in direct secret negotiations with Arafat, who did not ask for anything more. These negotiations would quickly lead to the Washington accords.

This summary of the historic context allows us to clarify the specific role allotted to the PLO in the current implementation of the final phase of the Allon Plan. The intifada, then the expansion of Hamas and its violent struggle in the interior—whereas the armed Palestinian exile organizations had long since ceased to seriously threaten Israeli security—have given a capital importance to a function that seemed relatively minor during the first twenty years of Israeli occupation of the West Bank and Gaza: *the maintenance of order in these territories and the repression of the armed anti-Zionist struggle.* The bet of the Israeli Labor Party is that Arafat and his men are best suited to carry out this task.

This explains, in particular, the novel turn made by the Rabin government in relation to what one could call the Zionist law of the "non-return" of the Palestinians in exile. Rather than negotiating with the Palestinians of the interior about what was supposed to be their *self-government,* the Zionist regime has decided the fate of the 1967 territories with a small group of leaders based in Tunis, behind the backs of the delegates from the interior. It accepted that a part of the PLO bureaucracy, this little state apparatus in exile, could install itself in the West Bank and Gaza to be responsible for the local population. In addition, it agreed that some thousands of exiled Palestinians, soldiers of the units of the regular PLA (Palestine Liberation Army), would accompany the bureaucracy of the PLO to constitute the backbone of the Palestinian police force.[57]

The smallest details concerning "the Palestinian authority" are moreover subject to the agreement of the Israeli government: "the structure of the Council, the number of its members," its legislative and executive authority (Art. 7), as well as "the system of elections" and even "rules and regulations regarding election campaign" (Annex I). The meaning of this tight control of the Palestinian electoral procedure was obvious to Elias Sanbar: "Israel, a democratic state for its own citizens, is betting on an authoritarian Palestinian self-government that will muzzle its own opposition and avoid any surprise effect resulting from an always possible change of mind on the part of Palestinian public opinion."[58]

If the Rabin government has chosen to begin with "Gaza-Jericho first," it is obviously so as to test in the powder keg of Gaza, bastion of Palestinian radicalism, the PLO's real capacity to master the situation and repress the anti-Zionist struggle—a struggle that Hamas and its allies have of course no intention of halting voluntarily.[59] The PLO must prove its repressive capacities in Gaza before being allowed to run other enclaves on the West Bank. If not, as Rabin has unceasingly stated, the accords will be abrogated. Noam Chomsky expressed the feeling of many observers when he said, alluding to a statement by the Israeli prime minister: "Yitzhak Rabin is obviously right:

the Palestinian mercenaries can govern the population without fearing recourse to the Supreme Court ... or the beautiful souls of every kind." [60]

*

In the light of the Zionist strategy defined by the Allon Plan and the mission of repressing the anti-Zionist struggle devolved to the PLO, the Israeli-Arab peace takes on a quite different appearance to that presented by the dominant idyllic presentation. Rather than a "peace of the brave" and reconciliation between peoples, it appears as a peace between governments, concluded essentially on the conditions laid down by the Israeli victor— a Pax Sionista, one could say. From the point of view of the Arab peoples who have been receptive for several decades to the nationalist discourse, today exploited by the Muslim fundamentalists, this peace has every chance of being perceived as surrender, the culmination of America's crushing of Iraq.[61]

But is this not the case? Is there any possible doubt about the direct link between the Gulf war and the process of settling the Israeli-Arab conflict, inaugurated by George Bush at Madrid and sealed by Bill Clinton in Washington? How can one not see in the current arrangements the establishment of the "New Arab Order" announced as the local variant of the "New World Order"? The cycle that began in 1947 with the Arabs' rejecting the award to the "Jewish state" of half of Palestine is concluding today with Arab recognition of this same state, now in control of all of Palestine— without any hope of return for the majority of its original inhabitants.

This is what Yigal Allon called "acceptance of reality."[62] When this acceptance follows forty-five years of rejection of this same reality because of its injustice, it amounts to capitulation. Lucid to the end, Allon knew that this would not amount to a "revolution in people's hearts." Such a revolution is not yet on the agenda, far from it. Israel and the United States will, however, have succeeded in displacing the tension from the confrontation between the Zionist state and its Arab neighbors, toward the internal confrontation in the Arab countries between states and popular opposition movements. So long as this conflict is not definitively resolved, the peace between governments will rest on shaky ground.

SEPTEMBER 8, 1994; first published in English in *New Politics* 5, no. 3 (Summer 1995).

## CHAPTER FIFTEEN

# Hezbollah's Victory

*Israel's withdrawal in the spring of 2000 from most of the southern Lebanese terri-
tory it had kept under occupation after 1985 appeared as a victory for the Lebanese
organization Hezbollah. It formed a stark contrast with the many rebuffs that the
Palestinian Authority had swallowed from the signature of the Oslo-Washington
accords up until the deadlock of the Camp David negotiations in July 2000. This
contrast would play an important role in strengthening Palestinian Islamic fundamentalist currents and inspiring their more and more frequent recourse to suicide bombings after the "Second Intifada" began in September 2000. I wrote the
following text in April 2000, shortly after the Israeli army's withdrawal, in
response to questions posed by Tikva Honig-Parnass for* News from Within, *a
publication of the Alternative Information Center in Jerusalem.*

Hezbollah's victory gives a broad blueprint of a comprehensive strategy
(military, political) in defeating Israeli occupation. Can you evaluate the
possibility of its reproduction elsewhere?

In order to do so, one has to separate the various elements of this "broad
blueprint," as you call it. Let us start with the military aspect, since you mention it: I would say that the peculiarities of the Lebanese terrain should be as
obvious to anyone in the Arab world as the peculiarities of the Iraqi terrain
are now to anyone in Washington who took the 1991 Gulf war as a "broad
blueprint" for further U.S. interventions. I mean that, just as the desert is
the ideal terrain for taking full advantage of the superiority in airpower (as
proven by the great contrast between the six weeks of carpet-bombing the
Iraqi troops in 1991 and the poor results of NATO's air campaign against the
Federal Republic of Yugoslavia in 1999), the mountainous and populous
character of southern Lebanon should be taken into consideration before
generalizing its experience into a "broad blueprint."

This being said, what should be emphasized in the first place is that the victory in southern Lebanon was not a "military" victory. The Israeli army has not been defeated militarily: it was much less exhausted than the U.S. forces in Vietnam, and even in the latter case it would be quite improper to talk of a "military defeat." In both cases, the defeat is primarily a political defeat of the governments, against a background of an increasingly reluctant population in the invader country. In that regard, the military action finds its value in its political impact, and not primarily in its direct military impact. The guerrilla actions of the Lebanese resistance against the occupation—which , even proportionally, was far from matching the scale of the Vietnamese resistance—were mainly effective through their impact on the Israeli population, just as the coffins of GIs landing back in the United States were during the Vietnam War. In both cases, the population of the invader country became more and more opposed to a war effort that was clearly devoid of any moral justification.

This had already been experienced by Israel since the beginning of its full-scale invasion of Lebanon in 1982. The withdrawal from Beirut in 1982, and later on from most of the occupied Lebanese territory in 1985, were mainly motivated by the fact that the Israeli population could not endorse a situation in which Israeli soldiers were facing death every day for the sake of an occupation which could hardly be justified, even from a mainstream Zionist view. So the key issue is that of the balance between the cost and benefits of an occupation: whereas in the Golan the benefits for Israel exceed the present costs, in southern Lebanon the reverse was obviously true.

Let us now extrapolate to the Palestinian occupied territories: during twenty years the benefits clearly exceeded the costs from the viewpoint of Israeli "security." The desperate "guerrilla" operations of the Palestinian resistance could not counterbalance the feeling of enhanced security stemming from the extension of the border to the Jordan River. The situation began to change dramatically with the mass mobilization of the intifada. This made the cost nearly intolerable for the moral of the Israeli army and for the reputation of Israel in its backer countries. The pressure mounted within the Israeli army, up to its highest ranks, in favor of a withdrawal of the troops from the populated areas, and their redeployment in those strategic parts of the West Bank where no Palestinians are concentrated.

It is precisely this pressure from the military that Rabin was responding to when he entered the Oslo negotiations. He tried to get the highest possible price for the implementation of this withdrawal from a PLO leadership that had been accumulating concessions and capitulations for many years.

And he got what he wanted, to a degree that he could not had even imagined when he started the talks with the Arafat leadership! Instead of building on the impetus of the intifada, and doing everything possible to sustain it until they got the withdrawal of the Israeli army from the entire populated areas—without betraying anything of what they stood for previously and with minimal accommodations, negotiated not by the PLO but by the leadership of the intifada within the territories—the Arafat leadership went into what even some Zionist commentators described as an ignominious surrender, leading to the execrable situation prevailing now.

Hezbollah acted differently: they kept up the pressure uncompromisingly. They forced the unconditional and total withdrawal of the Israeli army from the Lebanese territories occupied since 1978 (the remnant goes back to the 1967 war). A tremendous victory, indeed! And surely a feat that the Palestinian population will meditate over and from which they will draw some inspiration.

To what extent is the Hezbollah victory a slap in the face for the imperialist agenda in the region? What might we expect from it in the future?

The Lebanese victory is certainly a defeat for the U.S. agenda, which, like that of its Israeli ally, foresaw the insertion of this withdrawal into an overall peace agreement with Syria including all sorts of conditions, concessions, and guarantees obtained for Israel. Besides, Israel is the "most brilliant" proxy of the U.S. armed forces, the one always quoted as an example to follow. Here is a withdrawal, taking the shape of a debacle, evoking irresistibly the images of the U.S. debacle in Vietnam, in 1975—incidentally, just at the time of the twenty-fifth anniversary of that withdrawal! This is a new vindication of the famous "dare to struggle, dare to win" that inspired so bravely the Vietnamese resistance. It can be expected that it will contribute to reversing the winds of defeatism that have swept through such a big part of those who once used to fight imperialist domination.

However, with regard to the U.S. agenda in the Middle East, I think that the main change in the Israeli agenda—which will certainly be integrated in the agenda of the next U.S. administration—is that the prospect of a peace treaty with Syria is pushed back indefinitely. The Zionist establishment is definitely not eager to relinquish the Golan for the sake of just establishing relations with Syria, relations that will never be "normal" anyhow. And they are all the less eager to do so in that the Syrian dictator Hafiz Al-Assad is on the verge of death and that the political future of the country is highly uncertain.

Why has the Lebanese victory been claimed by Hezbollah alone? Were not other forces—Palestinians, Lebanese Left—involved in the resistance movement? If not, why not?

The reason Hezbollah appeared as the only father of victory (as the saying goes, victory usually has several fathers, whereas defeat is an orphan) is that they did everything they could to monopolize the prestige of the resistance movement. After the 1982 Israeli invasion, you had an uneasy coexistence and competition between two tendencies in the fight against the occupier: the Lebanese National Resistance, dominated by the Lebanese Communist Party, and the Islamic Resistance, dominated by Hezbollah. The Palestinian forces had been wiped out from southern Lebanon by the invaders; those remaining in the refugee camps were not really a match for Hezbollah, especially since some Lebanese forces like the Shiite communalist militias of Amal were keen on preventing them from spreading out of the camps again. Amal are still there—they are among those who recuperated the stretch of land abandoned by Israel and its local proxy. But they were never a key force in the resistance movement: they lost their impetus long ago to the benefit of the Hezbollah, and turned into a purely conservative and patronage-based party.

Hezbollah conducted all sorts of operations to establish their monopoly of the resistance movement, up to repeated onslaughts against the Communists, murdering some of their key Shiite cadres in particular. The CP behaved in a most servile manner, not daring to retaliate and instead calling on the "brothers" in the Islamic Resistance to behave in a brotherly manner—a call that has no real chance of being heard if it is not backed by decisive action to show the damage that could result, precisely, from the alternative behavior! Such an attitude contributed greatly to the progressive shift in the balance of forces to the advantage of Hezbollah. Many of the most militant members of the Lebanese left among the Shiites were attracted to Hezbollah.

We should recall that at the beginning of the Lebanese civil war in 1975 there was no Hezbollah and the CP was the major militant force among the Shiite population in southern Lebanon. The party started losing ground to the advantage of Amal first, and Hezbollah later, after 1982. In both cases the lesson was the same: all these movements were appealing to the same constituency, that is, the traditionally militant Shiite population of southern Lebanon. In such a competition, the shyest is doomed to lose inevitably, all the more so when you don't even dare to put forward your own radical program and you end up tail-ending the dominant communalist forces. Here again you need to dare to struggle and dare to win!

Hezbollah have been very effective on that score. They were definitely "daring" in their actions, inspired by their quasi-mystical views of martyrdom. And they also knew how to win the souls and minds of the population, by making clever use of the significant funding they got from Iran, thus organizing all kinds of social services to the benefit of the impoverished population. To be sure, they also took advantage of the ideological winds, which blew much more in their direction than in the direction of a left that became utterly demoralized by the collapse of the Soviet Union.

**What are the implications of the Hezbollah victory on the relationships between the political forces in Lebanon? For the Palestinian refugees there? And for the entire region?**

One thing is sure. This victory will greatly enhance the appeal of Hezbollah in Lebanon and of Islamic fundamentalists in the whole region. In Lebanon, Hezbollah faces an objective limitation due to the composite religious character of the population. Hezbollah is inherently unable to win over Christians, Druzes, or even Sunni Muslims in any significant numbers. They are no threat to the Palestinian refugees, since their Islamic universalism make them champions of the Palestinian cause. In that sense, they are actually competitors of the Palestinian forces in Lebanon, whether Arafat loyalists or left dissidents; at best, they can contribute to strengthen the Palestinian Islamic fundamentalist tendencies.

In that sense, too, their victory is a bad omen to Arafat, obviously, as I have already explained. Among Palestinians in the West Bank and Gaza, Hamas members are the only ones likely to be boosted by Hezbollah triumphalism. More generally, we can say that this victory will be precious for the whole Islamic fundamentalist movement in countering the negative impact of the recent events in Iran. Those who thought they could already bury Islamic fundamentalism (a French "Orientalist" recently produced a book heralding the terminal decline of this phenomenon) are blatantly refuted. As long as they have no real competitor for the embodiment of the aspirations of the downtrodden masses, and as long as the social effects of globalization are with us, the fundamentalists will also be part of the picture, with ups and downs naturally.

First published in *News from Within*, Jerusalem, May 2000

## CHAPTER SIXTEEN

# Israel's Military Onslaught and U.S. Interests in the Middle East

*I wrote this text in 2002 in response to questions framed by Tikva Honig-Parnass and Toufic Haddad, the editors of the Jerusalem bulletin* Between the Lines. *Their questions focused mainly on two issues: first, the relationship between Ariel Sharon's offensive—particularly Israel's reoccupation of Palestinian territories that it had withdrawn from under the terms of the Oslo-Washington accords—and U.S. regional strategy in the Middle East; and second, the consequences of Sharon's offensive for the Arab world.*

Israel has traditionally been a key component of U.S. strategy in the Middle East. As everyone knows too well, this strategy has evolved primarily around the issue of oil: the leap in the importance of oil in general and Middle Eastern oil in particular to Western economies since World War II explains the increased involvement of the United States in the area. This centered on the tutelage over the Saudi kingdom—a tutelage established since 1945, before the creation of the state of Israel. The latter would become the watchdog of U.S. regional interests: since Israel is congenitally a militarized state—that is, a state with a high degree of military readiness, a high ratio of military spending to its GDP and a high ratio of military mobilization to its population—and could not be otherwise due to its colonial origin and its hostile relationship with its environment, it was predestined to play that role.

Thus it would become a threat to any neighboring Arab regime challenging U.S. interests in the area, and chiefly U.S. control of Saudi oil. In this sense, the Saudi kingdom and Israel are two complementary key pieces of U.S. regional strategy.

However Israel's importance to U.S. regional interests only became vital in the late 1950s; before then there was no serious challenge to U.S. interests in the Middle East. Rising Arab nationalism was still weak and oriented primarily against traditional Western European colonialism. Its radicalization subsequently took place under Nasser, who was to become the chief enemy of the Saudi monarchy. Nasser's project of unifying the Arab nation under his leadership, and the alliance that he established with the Soviet Union giving it access to that part of the world are the factors that elevated Israel to the rank of a decisive regional ally of the United States.

This shift found expression in the change of U.S. attitude from the 1956 war to the 1967 war. In 1956, Israel attacked Nasser's Egypt in alliance with the two traditional representatives of European domination in the region: France and the UK. This was opposed by the United States, not only because the United States dissociated itself from traditional colonial interests, but also because the tripartite aggression could only inflame anti-Western sentiments among the Arabs at a time when the United States still hoped to maintain friendly relations with Egypt. In 1967, however, Arab nationalism was at the peak of its "socialist" radicalization, whether in Egypt since the early 1960s or in Syria since 1966, and the hostility of both states to the Saudi kingdom was intense. The United States feared that a Cairo-Damascus radical alliance, along with Iraq where Arab nationalists were already in power, could establish a powerful vise around the Saudis. The green light was given to Israel therefore to launch its aggression on June 5, 1967.

In this war, the key watershed in the region after 1948—the Middle East is still coping with the direct results of the 1967 war—two different but converging sets of interests were at stake. On the one hand, U.S. interests as explained, and on the other, the interests of the Israeli state, which was never a mere "puppet" of the United States but always had its own distinct agenda, as was obvious in 1956 and remains true to this date. For Israel, the accomplishment of the U.S. mission of dealing a mortal blow to the two regimes of Cairo and Damascus matched perfectly its own agenda of finishing the work started in 1948 by occupying the West Bank up to the Jordan River, as well as the Gaza Strip.

As a reward for its military feat, the United States would lend Israel support for two claims the Zionist government made on its Arab neighbors: redrawing Israel's borders in light of Israel's "security" and recognition by the Arab regimes of the state of Israel, thus ending the state of belligerence that had existed since 1948. These claims were at the center of UN Security

Council Resolution 242 approved by the United States in November 1967, whether openly (recognition and peace) or implicitly (the famous "the" missing from the mention of Israeli withdrawal from "occupied territories").

Israel's territorial claims were all the more palatable to the United States given that the Palestinian population went into sharp radicalization after June 1967 and it became clear that any straightforward return of the West Bank to Jordan would put the Hashemite monarchy at risk. Thus the Israeli government could work on implementing the Allon Plan of establishing strategic footholds in the West Bank in order to control the territory, with a view to relinquishing its populated areas later on. This plan was to remain the major architectural conception of Zionist peace offers, including the Oslo agreement up to Barak's offers in the 2000 Camp David negotiations. And it was and still is backed by the United States.

Many observers thought that Israel's strategic importance to the United States would diminish sharply after 1991: this was the year of the Gulf War, involving massive U.S. direct military intervention in the region and the establishment of a permanent U.S. military presence in the Gulf Arab states, as well as the year of the demise of the USSR. Actually one could even consider that the turning point was Egypt's shift in allegiance from the Soviet Union to the United States in 1972, under Sadat, which explains the "more balanced" attitude of Washington in brokering a peace between Egypt and Israel after the 1973 war.

True, both 1972 and 1991 were major turning points, inciting the United States to exert greater pressure on Israel for concessions in order to establish a Pax Americana. This is how the peace treaty between Begin's Israel and Sadat's Egypt could be concluded, and this is why the United States exerted high pressure on the Shamir government in 1991 in order to join the "peace process." However, Israel's importance as a strategic asset to the United States did not wane to the point of vanishing. Given the highly volatile and explosive character of the social and political situation in the Arab countries, the United States knows too well that it cannot bet on the stability of any alliances there. Compared to that, the strategic dependence on the United States of Israel as a political entity makes it the most stable of allies. The United States knows that there are narrow limits to the number of troops it can station in the region, as was well illustrated by the heavy cost already paid for keeping 5,000 U.S. soldiers in the Saudi kingdom, which include the September 11, 2001, attacks. It knows moreover that it takes time to get troops to the area and it is not granted that it would always be as easy as during the military buildup of 1990 against Iraq. In this sense, Israel's role as a forward positioned military base in this part of the world is still precious, and the $5 billion it costs the U.S. taxpayer annually is a sound investment compared to what could be achieved if the same amount were added to the huge U.S. military budget instead.

Which brings us to the present situation. The Israeli military onslaught against the Palestinian-controlled territories in the West Bank is the product of a convergence among several factors. The first is the dead end in the implementation of the Allon Plan framework known as the "peace process"; it became clear that the Palestinian population would not accept what increasingly appeared as a fool's bargain after the first illusions of 1993–94. It became clear as well that Arafat would not take the risk of confronting his people for the sake of what increasingly looked to him as monkey business and a deadly trap. Both aspects were closely related: it is only if the Palestinian population had been submitted to a harsh dictatorship that it could have been brought to swallow the bitter pills of U.S.–Zionist medicine.

The second factor is obviously Sharon's accession to power in Israel, as an expression of a quasi-unanimous decision by the Zionist establishment to settle scores with the Palestinians. With the support of the Laborites, Sharon is doing what they could not have done themselves without jeopardizing their specific political capital at home and in the West.

The third factor is obviously September 11 and its aftermath. By making the "war against terrorism" the new headline of U.S. worldwide interventionism, the attacks on Washington and New York gave Sharon the needed political cover for his own design.

We are now reaching a point where this convergence will probably come to an end and the occasional allies will part ways. Sharon's own agenda is not to destroy the "terrorist infrastructure" in order to pave the road for a renewed attempt at setting up a Palestinian Bantustan. His real agenda is destroying the "Palestinian Authority" in order to establish a coercive direct grip on the Palestinian population that would compel them to leave the West Bank, thus achieving the "transfer" project that he has always shared with his assassinated friend Zeevi.

The United States, and their faithful Israeli allies in Zionist Labor, are aiming at a restored Palestinian Authority presiding more repressively over a much weakened Palestinian population, in the framework of a peace based more or less on Barak's 2000 offer at Camp David, combined with the Saudi offer of "normalizing" relations between Israel and the whole

Arab world. The latter offer was actually designed by the U.S. State Department as a means to reinvigorate the agonizing "peace process"; it contains nothing new basically, except that it is formulated by the Saudi kingdom, which had preferred to remain out of the picture until now from fear of the political spillovers of such a chaotic "peace process."

The huge problem, however, is that Sharon's onslaught against the Palestinians has created such a sharp and bitter resentment against Israel and the United States in the whole Arab world that it became in itself a serious impediment facing any resumption of the "peace process." That this is Sharon's goal is beyond doubt.

The same does not hold true for Bush or Peres, however, but both of them share political shortsightedness and lack of intelligence. What they have let Sharon accomplish, with a mixture of connivance and indulgence, might very probably prove to be a historical turning point destroying any prospect of U.S.-sponsored Arab-Israeli peace and causing a destabilization of the whole region highly detrimental to U.S. interests, as shown already by the huge mass mobilizations that occurred in all the Arab countries with almost no exception.

This would not be the first time—or the last to be sure—that the US sows the seeds of rebellion against its own interests. Bush and Sharon are preparing future disasters for the United States and Israel, which might well make September 11 appear in retrospect as a mere starting point.

First published in *Between the Lines*, Jerusalem, May 2002.

# PART IV

# Iraq: From One War to the Next

## CHAPTER SEVENTEEN

# The Long Tragedy of the Iraqi People

*This article was written in March 1991, a few days after the U.S.-led coalition's offensive drove Saddam Hussein's troops out of Kuwait. At that moment the forces of the Iraqi regime had turned to bloodily repressing the popular uprising that had broken out after the Iraqi defeat, with the obvious and cynical complicity of coalition forces. The Iraqi people, particularly in southern Iraq, bitterly resented the coalition's complicity in the bloodshed. Their resentment contributed to the attitude of defiance tinged with hostility that U.S. and British troops encountered during their invasion of Iraq in 2003. The domestic, regional and international political factors analyzed in this article still seem amazingly timely twelve years later.*

What an absurd, indecent spectacle America is showing the world—as proud and surprised at its victory as if it were David's over Goliath! The commander of the coalition troops, Norman Schwarzkopf (known as "The Bear") is difficult to classify as a David, though, weighing in as he does at 240 pounds. After having brilliantly and heroically distinguishing himself against mighty Grenada seven years ago, he is now playing a starring role in the upsurge of self-satisfaction over the brave deeds of American arms in the Gulf. The greatest prowess shown in this feat of arms will long be remembered: the massacre of horrifying numbers of soldiers and civilians retreating or fleeing along the highway leading from Kuwait City to Basra.

Apart from the stomach-turning display of vanity—fueled by Hollywood-style staging, as in the return of the U.S. ambassador by helicopter, sixteen years after another U.S. ambassador fled Saigon by the same means—the extent of the carnage wreaked by the "surgical war" in Iraq and Kuwait is only slowly coming to light. This sledgehammer surgery has been a horrible operation; the destruction it has caused will take many years to heal, leaving behind ugly, deep stigmata. And to complete the image of what amounts (minus the radioactivity) to the equivalent of an atomic bomb attack, terms like artificial night and nuclear winter are being used to describe the effects of the huge toxic cloud produced by the burning Kuwaiti oil wells, already considered one of the worst ecological disasters in history.

The dimensions of the slaughter and disaster, the terrible devastation left in Kuwait and Iraq by the clash between two criminal madmen—the Nero of Baghdad and the Truman II of Washington—makes the rush by the worthy representatives of world capitalism, laying siege to the holders of the petrodollars so as to grab the postwar contracts, all the more revolting. Bush, crowned *imperator* by the U.S. Congress and the imperialist media, is now turning his attention to "winning the peace" after having won the war, to use the fashionable phrase. Or to put it another way, the U.S. administration is hoping to strike while the iron is hot to forge a regional Pax Americana, without which the military victory will soon lose its luster. In the aftermath of the great battle, politics is becoming in turn the continuation of war by other means.

## FEAR OF AN IRAQI POWER VACUUM

Washington's first big political problem is, of course, Iraq itself. The extent of Washington's cynicism is showing in the most obvious way on this point. All those in the West who believed, or claimed to believe, in the "antifascist" character of this war are now being very much put out of countenance.[1] The situation when George Bush ordered the cease-fire on February 28 is well-known. What remained of the Iraqi army in southern Iraq was in such disorder that the fighting had turned into a killing game with human targets. The coalition troops could have easily continued their advance to Baghdad, or at least to the gates of the capital, in order to bring about the overthrow of Saddam Hussein.

This they chose not to do—and certainly not out of respect for the UN Security Council's mandate! In Grenada and Panama, for much less serious causes than the invasion of Kuwait, and against regimes that were almost democratic compared with Iraq's, Washington's troops did not hesitate to depose the existing regime and replace it with another one on the U.S. payroll. But in these two countries pro-U.S. alternatives with a minimal degree of legitimacy and stability existed. This was not and still is not the case in Iraq.

The White House and its Saudi protégés are far more frightened of a power vacuum in that country than of Saddam Hussein. The spectacle offered by the Iraqi opposition at its meeting in Beirut from March 10 to 13, 1991, was not one that the supporters of the new regional order—a subdivision of the "new world order"—could view with relish. This mosaic of tendencies with nothing in common except their hostility to the tyrant in Baghdad, distinguished or divided by everything else, would find it difficult to establish a minimum of stability in Iraq, if they had to set up their government on the rubble of the Saddam regime's military-police apparatus.

Ba'athist totalitarianism, especially in the last decade, has been the kind that seems to leave either chaos or the partial or complete maintenance of the ruling apparatus as the only two alternatives. Even worse from the point of view of Washington and its protégés, the main forces likely to emerge from this chaos are tied to Damascus, Tehran, or Moscow, which means they would be difficult to integrate into the projected Pax Americana. Thus Bush's appeals to the Iraqi people—and to "the Iraqi soldiers," we must not forget—to get rid of the tyrant can only be understood as appeals to the Ba'athist leaders to sacrifice Saddam Hussein on the altar of the supreme interest of their regime and its stability.

The Saudis have built up ties to the Iraqi opposition bloc with the sole aim of softening the blow of whatever might happen. Furthermore, they have been promoting dissident Ba'athists who could contribute to the maintenance of the regime once it has gotten rid of some of its leaders. But all in all Riyadh, like Washington, would find it a hundred times more preferable to deal with a weakened and "tamed" Saddam Hussein (in the apt phrase of a top U.S. official) than risk the big leap in the dark that a total collapse of the regime would entail.[2] This is the political calculation that is determining their concrete military attitude to developments in Iraq.

Other reasons could perhaps be found to explain why the coalition troops did not march on Baghdad when the road lay open before them. But this is the only explanation for the six weeks of intensive air and missile attack that largely spared the Iraqi forces massed in the north of the country, in Kurdistan, and even in the capital. Washington's—explicit—objective was never to destroy and dismantle the whole of the Iraqi armed forces, but to cut them down to an "acceptable" size, around 200,000 to 300,000 men, incapable of threatening their neighbors but strong enough to dissuade neighbors who might have their own hegemonic ambitions, and to crush Shiite, Communist, or Kurdish oppositions at home.

## CAUSES OF THE IRAQI UPRISING

The U.S. troops' attitude in Iraq illustrates perfectly the basic choice that has been made; the events that have been taking place there since the coalition offensive ended follow naturally and logically from this basic choice.[3] The bulk of Baghdad's military forces has been smashed in the south of the country, creating a power vacuum. The lid was taken off the pressure cooker, and a mass uprising ensued, an uprising of a population subjected for many years to a terrible, unbearable tyranny—a population that had also borne the brunt of Saddam's two insane wars.[4]

According to several sources, this uprising was essentially spontaneous. Soldiers from the routed army joined in, particularly soldiers originally from this region. The fact that the southern Iraqi cities have Shiite majorities and are close to the Iranian border was bound to lead Tehran to intervene. Iraqi refugees from the pro-Iranian Shiite fundamentalist current were thus smuggled in toward Basra. But that does not mean that we can describe the revolt as such as Shiite, in the sense of a communalist uprising. Still less can we describe it as fundamentalist or pro-Iranian, as the imperialist media have deliberately done.

In fact, the main pro-Iranian fundamentalist current, led by Mohammad Baqer al-Hakim, has avoided putting forward its basic program and has been sticking to general democratic demands, as seen at the Beirut gathering, which are much more popular even among Iraqi Shiites than the call for an "Islamic republic." Tehran is also well aware that the Arab population—whether Shiite or Sunni, let alone the Kurds—is unlikely to install its men in power. The mullahs' regime also fears the appearance in Iraq of a "chaos" that would foster a free Kurdistan, the resurgence of a powerful Communist movement and the appearance of liberties long suppressed in Iran itself, all of which could be a source of subversive infection for Tehran.[5]

From this point of view, the West has largely misinterpreted Iranian President Rafsanjani's proposals of March 8, 1991. The media presented Rafsanjani's appeal to Saddam Hussein to step down as a show of support for the insurgent masses. The reality was quite different. In fact, the Iranian president was calling on the Ba'athist Party to get rid of the despot and rule in alliance with the (pro-Iranian) opposition.[6] This appeal came after an offer of cooperation from Saddam Hussein himself, who had sent his Shiite lieutenant Saadun Hammadi to Tehran for the purpose. Saddam has also made a similar offer to the Kurds, proposing to reactivate the March 1970 accords on Kurdish autonomy.[7]

The hand extended by the despot was rejected owing to intransigent opposition not to his regime, but to his person. Tehran and its supporters as well as the Kurds linked to Iran demand Saddam Hussein's withdrawal, which they see as the minimum they need to make their collaboration with the Ba'athists credible. This means that the Iranians' calculations, or at least the Rafsanjani faction's, are similar to U.S. and Saudi calculations—they are all looking toward a partial retention of the Ba'athist regime, minus its chief. There is an obvious rivalry between the two camps, however: each side wants Iraq to swing over to its side and cut out the other.

In consequence each of the two camps—Tehran on the one side and Washington/Riyadh on the other—is trying to put spokes into the other's wheels. The more-anti-United States-than-thou rhetoric coming out of Tehran during the last days of the coalition offensive, preceded by the offer of a safe haven for Iraqi planes on Iranian soil, was meant to keep the possibility open of an alliance with Baghdad against the coalition. In return, U.S. forces in southern Iraq have given the green light for Saddam Hussein's regime to drown the Tehran-backed uprising there in blood.

## THE UNITED STATES GIVES SADDAM FREE REIN

As a matter of fact, on top of the two military choices cited above, there is a third, even more blatant one. The U.S. army could have blocked the road to the south from northern and central Iraq to all troop and tank reinforcements without the slightest difficulty. It could have simply included a prohibition on troop and tank movements in the cease-fire conditions, since the Iraqi regime, exclusively concerned once more with crushing its own people, docilely accepted all the conditions set by Bush in Washington and New York and Schwarzkopf in Safwan.[8] Similarly, Baghdad could have been prohibited from using its airspace for military ends, so as to stop Iraqi army helicopters from intervening against the popular rebellion.

But the U.S. forces' actual choice was just the opposite. They allowed Saddam Hussein to move his soldiers, tanks, and helicopters throughout Iraqi territory, including toward Basra. They allowed and continue to allow him to crush the popular uprising in southern and central Iraq in a gruesome bloodbath. The scant information that filters out through the Iraqi iron curtain that the Ba'athists have lowered again, here too with the complicity of the coalition, includes reports of massacres with heavy arms and mass executions of hundreds of insurgents—reports in keeping with the known fact that Saddam heads one of the world's most bloodthirsty regimes.

In the face of protests in the United States from those who had believed in the myth of the democratic crusade against a new Hitler, Bush felt obliged on March 13 to "confess to some concern" (*sic*) on the subject of the use of helicopters. Yet a few days earlier General Brandtner had declared at the Pentagon that the United States would even allow Saddam Hussein to use his planes against the rebellion if he could get them back from Iran, as long as they did not threaten coalition troops.[9]

Bush's "concern" on the subject of helicopters, ludicrously restrained compared to the concern he expressed the same day about "instability" in Iraq, followed his warning to Baghdad against using chemical weapons. Faithful to the "conventional" model established by the Pentagon, the Iraqi regime restricted itself to bombing the rebel areas with napalm!

U.S. forces are doing more than just letting the Ba'athist dictatorship repress the popular uprising in its own fashion. They are offering it the services of their "Desert Shield," by directly or indirectly dissuading Iran from stepping up aid to the rebels. According to the *International Herald Tribune*: "The United States, Saudi Arabia and other countries in the coalition form an imposing deterrent to any Iranian attempt to gain a foothold in Iraq, particularly if Tehran violated Iraqi territorial integrity."[10]

In the same way, Turkey, Washington's ally to the north, is energetically dissuading the Kurds from going too far in their fight with Baghdad. Turkish President Türgut Özal has more than once threatened to intervene in Iraqi Kurdistan if the Kurds show separatist impulses. From the start of the coalition offensive, the parliament in Ankara granted the government special war powers authorizing sending Turkish troops into northern Iraq if considered necessary. The limit to Kurdish aspirations in Iraq set by Özal is no different from the autonomy that Baghdad, on paper, already granted them twenty-one years ago, and that Saddam Hussein is offering to reactivate today.

## PLAYING THE ARMY OFF AGAINST THE KURDS AND SHIITES

The issue on which everyone in the region seems to agree most is opposition to the Kurdish people's right to form its own state. The United States, Iran, Syria, and Saudi Arabia all loudly proclaim their support for "the territorial integrity of Iraq." Speaking to journalists who asked him what the

Kurds could hope to get out of the "new world order," French Foreign Minister Roland Dumas could only respond, "The Kurds are desperate."[11] Saddam Hussein is well aware that the danger from the Kurdish side is limited. He knows equally well that whatever advances the Kurdish forces make, they cannot force him to grant more than he had already accepted in 1970. He also understands that the Kurds, as a national minority, cannot hope to take power in Baghdad.

The danger in the regions inhabited by Shiite Arabs, the majority in Iraq, is much greater, particularly because of Tehran's intervention on the side of the insurgents. This is why the Baghdad tyrant, profiting from the safe conduct granted by the U.S. forces, has chosen for the time being to strip the north of his elite troops in order to wipe out the rebellion in the center and south. He knew that he was exposing his remaining troops in the north to defeat, which ensued rapidly under pressure from the rebellious masses joined by Kurdish nationalist guerillas. He had to parry the most dangerous threat and leave the settling of accounts with the Kurds until later, as he appears to have begun doing now.

## SOLIDARITY WITH THE IRAQI PEOPLE

In this battle for the survival of his dictatorship, Saddam Hussein is relying first of all on his praetorian Republican Guard and his police and para-police services, which are the target of terrible popular vengeance wherever the uprising has even temporarily got the upper hand. The despot's next concern is to try to stop the rest of his army from disintegrating. To this end, he has decreed an amnesty for deserters and granted monthly bonuses to all his troops, in particular to the soldiers of the Guard who are highly privileged anyway in terms of pay, equipment, social advantages, and so on. The rest of the army is held together, with only limited success, by the same Ba'athist terror that holds down the population. Soldiers' families are taken hostage, thus limiting the possibility of rebellion by those whose relatives live on territory under Ba'athist control. The systematic execution of rebels, finally, dissuades the troops from revolting themselves.

The outlook for the rebellion is also dimmer thanks to the de facto support that the United States has given the Baghdad regime. As a figure from the Iraqi bourgeois democratic opposition has rightly protested in the *Washington Post*: "The United States, behind a fig leaf of noninterference, is waiting for Saddam to butcher the insurgents in the hope that he can be overthrown later by a suitable officer."[12] A commentary in the U.S. Senate reported in *Newsweek* turns Bush's Saddam/Hitler analogy back on its author: "The position of the administration is precisely that we want to get rid of Saddam, but not his regime.... It is like getting rid of Hitler but leaving the Nazis in power."[13]

The peoples of other Arab countries, when they are not actually hostile to the Iraqi rebels for reactionary reasons such as anti-Shiite communalism or anti-Kurdish chauvinism, are showing a glaring lack of solidarity with Iraq's Arab and Kurdish rebels against the Ba'athist tyranny. This is tragic confirmation of our apprehensions about the serious illusions present among the Arab masses, including on the Left, about the real meaning of the Iraqi despot's actions.

In symmetrical fashion, the noble souls in the West who supported the "antifascist" democratic crusade of the imperialists have fallen silent today, on the pretext that there are forces even more "fascist" than Saddam: the "fundamentalists" who threaten to take power in Baghdad. Both sides, people who sided with the United States as well as those who sided with Iraq in the six-week war, view the rebels in Iraq with suspicion if not hostility. The importance of having fought the imperialist aggression without giving the least support to Saddam Hussein's regime or his annexation of Kuwait is now absolutely clear.

Today, just as yesterday, genuine support to the people of Iraq requires a struggle for:

· Immediate withdrawal of the imperialist troops, who first committed the crime of the pitiless blockade and bombardment of the Iraqi people and are now committing a further one by supporting the Saddam regime against them.
· An end to all embargoes, sanctions, and war reparations imposed on the Iraqi people.
· Support to the Arab and Kurdish peoples of Iraq in their struggle against the Ba'athist tyranny, for democratic liberties and the election of a constituent assembly.
· Support to the Kurdish people in its struggle for national emancipation and for its right to self-determination, including forming its own state.

MARCH 14, 1991; first published in English in *International Viewpoint*, no. 203 (April 1, 1991).

## CHAPTER EIGHTEEN

# Operation Oil:
# Why the United States Wants a War

*In the fall of 2002 a powerful antiwar movement got under way, roused by Washington and London's avowed intention of taking over Iraq. This interview with Anthony Bégrand dealt with the key questions raised in building the movement, starting in particular from the French case.*

How do you analyze the reasons that the Bush administration gives to justify a "preventive war" against Iraq?

The attacks on September 11, 2001, gave the Bush administration an excellent pretext to implement policies that they had already thought up much earlier to defend vital interests, which are much more important to it than responding to a terrorist attack. Since September 11 it has set a strategy in motion of extending the U.S. military presence around the world, starting in Central Asia. Using the Afghanistan war as a pretext, it built military bases in two ex-Soviet Central Asian republics, Uzbekistan and Kyrgyzstan; negotiations are under way with other countries in the region. The United States has extended its military presence as far as Georgia. It is establishing a lasting presence in the Caspian Sea basin, which is considered one of the most promising regions for hydrocarbon wealth (oil and gas)—outside the Arab-Persian Gulf area—and a region where U.S. oil companies are already very much present.

As for Iraq, the specious character of the reasons given is even more flagrant than the pretext for the "war against terrorism" was in Central Asia. The war on Iraq cannot be seen as a response to any attack anywhere. The Bush administration quickly gave up trying to do much with the argument of a supposed direct link between the Iraqi regime and the Al-Qaida network.

Today its main arguments focus on two themes: first of all, the dictatorial nature of the Iraqi regime and the fact that it is guilty of abominable acts. But this is a piece of boundless hypocrisy. The Iraqi regime committed most of these acts with Washington's blessing, at a time when the United States viewed Iraq's war against Iran very favorably. Furthermore, who are they trying to fool into thinking that Washington is against dictatorships? We need only note that the Central Asian countries where the United States is now setting up bases, which it is giving hundreds of millions of dollars in aid, are some of the worst despotisms on the face of the earth. The Pakistani regime, Washington's loyal vassal, born of a coup d'état against an elected government, is now creating a constitutional basis for its dictatorship. In reality, when the U.S. administration decides to change a regime, its reason is not replacing a dictatorship with a democracy but replacing a recalcitrant or hostile regime with a regime loyal to Washington—dictatorial or democratic according to its needs in each case.

But the argument that carries the most weight today, particularly with the U.S. people, is that the Iraqi regime is a "terrorist threat" to the United States because it is trying to acquire weapons of mass destruction. The argument that Iraq is on the verge of getting weapons of mass destruction is not backed up by any evidence. This country was subjected to inspections for years. True, the inspections have been interrupted for a few years, but the country has remained under strict surveillance. If there were any concrete evidence, the United States would not have hesitated to put it on display. In reality, the campaign being prepared against Iraq is motivated by quite different considerations.

So what are the Bush administration's real motives?

In part the motives are the same ones that led to U.S. military expansion into Central Asia. Central Asia lies at the heart of the continental mass formed by Russia and China, so there strategic considerations supplemented the economic prize of hydrocarbons. By controlling Iraq, similarly, the United States would strengthen its hold over the whole Gulf region. It would also considerably ratchet up the pressure on Iran and Syria, two regimes that the United States considers refractory. But the stakes in this particular case are not warding off the emergence of a rival power like Russia or China; they are essentially economic, meaning oil.

The chief figures in the Bush administration are tightly linked to the oil industry, and oil motivates their actions in this case. They know full well that United States oil reserves will be exhausted in about ten years, so that their country will become wholly dependent on imports. Moreover, according to current projections, world oil reserves will be running dry about halfway through this century. In other words, the oil market is going to get tight in the middle term, and demand will increasingly, structurally tend to exceed supply. Oil, the fuel of the world economy, will become even more crucial than it is today. So the United States wants to be in control of the bulk of world oil reserves, beginning with the two-thirds that lie in the Arab-Persian Gulf.

Can the UN and European countries be a hindrance to Bush's military ambitions?

In 1991 the United States waged its first war against Iraq under a UN mandate, because the administration of Bush Senior needed the UN then to convince U.S. public opinion, which was still traumatized by Vietnam and therefore hesitant about foreign military interventions. It used the UN as a domestic political argument. Afterward Washington sidestepped the UN and the Russian and Chinese vetoes on carrying out bombing in Bosnia and then wage war in Kosovo, through NATO.

The United States considers the UN an obsolete organization based on an out-of-date relationship of forces. Four countries are treated as equals of the United States as permanent members of the Security Council, with veto power; in the eyes of U.S. leaders, this no longer corresponds to the reality of the contemporary, unipolar world. The U.S. hyperpower prefers not to be hindered by any legal or institutional constraint that might limit its freedom of action.

The Bush administration has taken this position far, raising unilateralism to the level of doctrine. George W. Bush did nonetheless address the UN on the subject of Iraq, but only because he was put under very great pressure inside the United States. Warnings that unilateral intervention could heighten the risks of destabilizing the Middle East rained down on him from all sides, including from the Republican ranks and his own father's entourage. This induced him to go to the United Nations, but with an ultimatum: you do what we want or we'll go it alone! Having gone to the UN, Bush can demand a blank check from Congress for military action against Baghdad. He absolutely needs a green light from Congress. A green light from the UN is a bonus, but it's not indispensable.

In order to obtain this bonus, which would be politically convenient, Washington is negotiating with the Russians and French, genuinely wheeling and dealing over who will get what in Iraq after Saddam Hussein. But if he has to, Bush will not hesitate to go to war without a UN stamp of approval, counting on legitimation of his action after the fact by an explosion of joy from the Iraqi people when the regime's decapitation is announced—which is entirely possible. The only function that Bush can still see for the UN is to organize the postwar administration in the countries that the United States devastates militarily on its own unilateral decision, as in Kosovo and Afghanistan.

As for the attitude of European countries that are dragging their heels, there are differences in kind. German Chancellor Gerhard Schroeder came out against the war for obvious electoral reasons, taking advantage of Germans' pacific sentiments. With the French things are different and more serious. France was Iraq's supplier in chief for a long time, and continues to have major interests there (debts, oil, and contracts) as well as special ties to Baghdad. This explains why Paris is dragging its heels on the war. If Washington replaces Saddam Hussein's regime with a regime under its control, French interests will inevitably suffer. This is why the French government is calling to continue disarming Iraq while leaving the regime in place. France even hopes in this way eventually to get the embargo lifted, which would enable it to enjoy the full benefit of its special ties with the current regime.

But the United States insists that it will overthrow the Baghdad regime whatever else happens. So if France and Russia want to save anything of their Iraqi interests, they have to go along with the United States. In these conditions I wouldn't bet a cent on Jacques Chirac's determination to oppose the U.S. war drive to the bitter end. Though if we manage to build a big antiwar movement in France, that will certainly have an impact on Chirac.

How should we build this antiwar movement? And what should our attitude be toward Muslim currents inside it?

We have to take into account that public opinion is much more critical of the coming war than it was of the two previous wars, in Afghanistan and Kosovo. So this is the moment to invest as much as possible in building an antiwar movement in France—I'd even say rebuilding it, because the French anti-imperialist movement has been at its lowest ebb for many years now and is lagging behind the rest of Europe. The U.S. administration's current super-arrogant course is creating a very favorable climate for rebuilding the movement.

This movement is dealing primarily with wars where Islam is involved, from Palestine to Iraq by way of Afghanistan. It can therefore mobilize sections of Muslim communities in France. There are two opposite excesses that must be avoided in doing so. We must not accommodate fundamentalist groups that raise reactionary calls and slogans, anti-Western or anti-Jewish slogans rather than anti-imperialist or anti-Zionist ones. Going along with them would facilitate their growth inside Muslim communities, confuse the general message of the antiwar movement, and hinder participation by other sectors of the public. The opposite excess would be to see a fundamentalist under the bed of every Muslim who affirms his or her Muslim identity. In France the racism that permeates the media and certain kinds of confused discussion of "Islamism" contribute to this attitude. There have always been Christians in antiwar movements who affirm their religious identity. There is no reason to be less tolerant of people with other religious identities.

Translated from *Rouge*, 10 October 2002.

## CHAPTER NINETEEN

# The Empire Prepares to Strike

*This interview by Anthony Bégrand in February 2003 updated my analysis at the moment when preparations for the war against Iraq were all but complete.*

What do you think of the argument advanced by Bush as a justification for the war that Iraq possesses weapons of mass destruction?

It is obviously a pretext and not an argument, in the sense that the accusation has been made from the beginning without proof. Since the start of the UN inspections, a number of U.S. leaders (Donald Rumsfeld in particular) have said on several occasions that the inspections were pointless and that they could not demonstrate the nonexistence of weapons of mass destruction. This comes on top of a surprising logic that demands that Iraq demonstrate that it does not have any. But obviously this is completely impossible.

The entire UN inspections operation was then intended to win time for the deployment of troops and equipment and give the impression to U.S. public opinion that the United States had taken the trouble to go through a legal procedure bearing some relation to international law before going to war.

In other words, the result was known in advance. If the inspectors discover that there is a violation, the United States will consider it has the right to go to war, and if they discover nothing, that proves nothing. Because if you can't find something, that doesn't prove it doesn't exist.

Colin Powell, before the UN Security Council, also sought to show that the inspections had no point, claiming that equipment was moved whenever the inspectors arrived somewhere. It is obvious, then, that this is only a pretext for a war that has long been decided on in principle.

As for the heart of the accusation, we should always remember that so far as the supreme weapons of mass destruction, nuclear arms, are concerned, even Washington does not claim that Baghdad possesses them. Bush, in his September 2002 speech to the UN General Assembly, said that if Iraq procured fissile material (uranium) it could have nuclear weapons within a year. This amounted to an admission that Iraq has neither a nuclear weapon nor even fissile material. This is a striking illustration of this particular notion of a "preventive war," which involves not preempting an adversary that has shown its intention to attack, but rather attacking an adversary to which one attributes the intention of wanting to acquire weapons that it still does not have. The most total absurdity reigns.

As for chemical or biological weapons, Iraq has possessed them for many years and has even used them against the Kurds in the North and against Iranian troops during the Iran-Iraq war. At the time this evoked no indignation from Western capitals. The necessary material for these weapons had moreover been provided by Western companies with the knowledge of the Western powers. Since then the country has been subjected to seven years of UN inspections, which destroyed the stocks. Even supposing that something remains in Iraq, if one takes account of the fact that the country has no delivery vehicles (missiles), it cannot constitute a threat to its environment and still less to the United States, which, like Israel, holds huge arsenals of weapons of mass destruction.

The argument that the war will establish democracy is one more bad joke, given that most of the region's despotic Arab regimes are closely linked to Washington.

So if all that is just hypocrisy, then what are the real aims of the Bush administration?

The real aims have been stressed several times. First and foremost, there is oil. Iraq holds the world's second largest oil reserves, after the Saudi kingdom. Moreover, Iraq's oil production is currently a third of its objective production capacity, and in the coming years it will be necessary to increase it to avoid sharp price hikes. But to increase Iraqi oil production, the embargo has to be lifted so that the infrastructure can be rebuilt and modernized.

Washington considers regime change, at the same time canceling the concessions granted by Baghdad in recent years to French and Russian oil interests, an indispensable condition for lifting the embargo. This is about ensuring that the lion's share of the exploitation of Iraqi oil goes to the United States.

Then there is the enormous market for the reconstruction of Iraq, a country that was utterly ruined in 1991 and has not really been able to rebuild because of the embargo.

These are the real aims. Beyond that, this step forward in U.S. control of world oil reserves is a significant boost to its world hegemony in the face of all their potential rivals, including the vassal powers of Western Europe and Japan, who are even more dependent on oil from the Gulf region than the United States is.

**Bombs alone are not enough to install a new regime. So what are the Bush administration's plans?**

We have known since the war preparations began that the United States is planning to establish a lasting military presence in Iraq.

Some months ago, they envisaged coupling a military occupation with the establishment of a puppet government, but one made up of a sort of representation of the various Iraqi ethnic groups. However, the Iraqi opposition they have tried to organize offers a far from brilliant spectacle. The apparently dominant force among the opposition groups that are ready to deal with Washington—the Supreme Council of the Islamic Revolution of Iraq—is closely linked to Tehran. So the United States seems to be headed now toward a direct military government of the country while it takes the time to set up a government that is at all inclined to manage the situation in a way that suits it.

This is the big difference between the first Gulf War in 1991 and the current situation. If the United States did not overthrow Saddam's regime in 1991, it was because the world situation and the U.S. domestic situation stood in the way of a military occupation. Washington preferred to keep Saddam Hussein in power to avoid the Iraqi situation's escaping from its control and destabilizing the region. From then on Washington deliberately spared the Republican Guard, the praetorian guards assigned the task of maintaining order.

Faced with the insurrection that set Iraq ablaze after the war's end in March 1991, the United States allowed the regime to drown the rebellion in blood in its two main centers, the South and the North. In the South the U.S. army even withdrew to allow the Republican Guard to come through, and the United States authorized the Iraqi regime to use helicopters to suppress the southern and northern rebels. There were tens of thousands of deaths.

Today the United States has set itself the goal of overthrowing Saddam Hussein because it believes the world situation has changed—the U.S. lead over the rest of the world has grown, especially militarily—as well as the domestic situation. Washington sees the political climate following September 11 as openly allowing a long period of virtually unlimited military interventions using the pretext of the war on terror.

With Afghanistan and now Iraq, it seems the United States has embarked on a period of military deployment across the entire planet.

Absolutely. Since September 11 the United States has begun to finish covering the whole of the planet with a network of military bases, whether directly or through alliances or the two combined. Using the pretext of the war in Afghanistan, they built military bases in the heart of the last area where Moscow still had a sort of veto power: Central Asia. They have established themselves in the Caspian Basin, which is also a significant region in terms of hydrocarbon supplies, but also a region of considerable strategic importance since it is situated at the heart of the continental land mass stretching from Russia to China, two countries that Washington considers potential rivals.

There has also recently been a new round of NATO enlargement, which has involved former Soviet Republics. If one adds to that the whole program of military intervention proposed by the Bush administration, we have today an unrivaled degree of military expansion by the United States, which is already intervening militarily in the Philippines, Colombia, the Horn of Africa, and Yemen. It is threatening Iran and North Korea, two countries lumped together with Iraq in Bush's "Axis of Evil." It is also trying persistently to overthrow the Chávez regime in Venezuela.

Washington has set as its objective since the end of the Cold War increasing the military gap between the United States and the rest of the world, to the point that it now accounts for 40 percent of world military expenditure. We are approaching a situation where it will soon spend as much as all the other countries on the planet combined.

However, this hyperpower is not all-powerful. It has an Achilles' heel; there is a power capable of blocking the war machine and reversing this militarist drift: the U.S. people. The people of the United States already showed during the Vietnam War its ability to stop the war machine, preventing U.S. administrations from carrying on the slaughter and forcing the withdrawal of U.S. troops from Vietnam. This mobilization had the effect of jamming the U.S. war machine, preventing its massive use until the first Gulf war.

There is a basis for hope, then, in the remarkable growth of the antiwar movement in the United States in these last several months. Nobody imagined barely a year after September 11 that the movement would surpass in breadth anything seen since Washington began its large-scale military operations again. The antiwar movement is still growing. It is linking up with the youth radicalization that we see, particularly in the movement for a different globalization.

That said, given the time constraints, it is highly improbable that the war against Iraq can be stopped. But we should realize, also so as to avoid any demoralization, that the target now should be building an antiwar movement for the long haul, given that we are facing a long-term program of military interventions. Washington has said that the "war on terror" is meant to last several decades. We have to build a movement to jam this machinery and halt the aggressive course of U.S. policy.

First published in English in *International Viewpoint*, no. 348, March 2003.

## CHAPTER TWENTY

# Washington and London's Problems Have Only Just Begun

*I wrote this short article at the beginning of the U.S.–British offensive launched on March 21, 2003, for the conquest of Iraq.*

The Bush administration committed itself to this war without any certainty regarding its outcome, betting like a poker player on drawing a lucky card. Or should we say: trusting to divine intervention—judging by the religious devotion commonly attributed to the U.S. president, a visionary who has so much in common with Osama bin Laden.

It is basic common sense always to plan for the worst-case scenario. But Washington based its campaign against Iraq from the beginning on an arrogant gamble on an easy victory in which the occupying forces would control the country, welcomed as an army of liberation. One of the keys to this scenario, promised by the pro-U.S. fraction of the Iraqi opposition to its all too credulous audience, was a turnabout by the Iraqi army, which would then become the principal support of a new regime under Washington's thumb.

But so far things have turned out differently. The first reason for this is that the political difficulties of the Bush-Blair tandem—above all the massive upsurge of the worldwide antiwar movement, in particular in Britain and the United States—forced Washington to delay launching its offensive and to reinforce its deployment even more for fear of a protracted war. The delay, especially given the climatic difficulties that are expected during April, precipitated the ground offensive, launched almost at the same time as the bombing campaign. In 1991, by contrast, Washington subjected the Iraqi army to more than five weeks of intensive bombardment before it sent in ground troops.

This meant that forces of the Iraqi regime were still inclined to fight when the ground offensive started—infinitely more than in 1991, when those who had survived the air campaign were exhausted and stupefied and surrendered en masse to coalition troops. The Iraqis for their part surprised the occupying forces by not being terribly friendly when they are not overtly hostile. What the rulers in Washington and London had not grasped is that the Iraqi people—which has so many reasons to hate Saddam Hussein—has even more reasons to hate them. The Iraqis remember the way in which the coalition delivered them up to Saddam Hussein in 1991. They are still suffering the pangs of twelve years of a genocidal embargo imposed by Washington and London with the complicity of their partners in the UN Security Council. And how could they welcome as liberators an alliance of the former British colonial power with the sponsor of the Israeli state and the main oppressor of the Middle East?

Many Iraqis will certainly greet the fall of Saddam Hussein's regime with relief. But they are sensible enough to realize that occupation by Britain and the United States is nothing to yearn for either, and that Washington and London are motivated by their desire to lay their hands on Iraq's resources, not by concern for the happiness of its people. So it will probably be difficult for Washington to set up an Iraqi government devoted to its interests and able to control the Iraqi domestic situation with its own indigenous forces—even if the United States establishes military bases in the country for a long-term occupation, as it intends to. And everybody understands how dangerous it would be for U.S. and British troops to be stationed for a long time in the cities.

Washington and London's problems have only just begun. It is up to us, to the antiwar movement, to make them much worse. George W. Bush, Tony Blair, and all their supporters must be made to pay a very high price for their war of aggression.

The battle for immediate, total, and unconditional withdrawal of coalition troops from Iraqi territory already looks promising. It must be combined with the demand for free and democratic elections for the Iraqi people, without occupying troops, and for self-determination for the Kurds of Iraq—as well as of Iran, Syria, and Turkey.

MARCH 24, 2003; first published in English in *Resistance*, April 2003.

## CHAPTER TWENTY-ONE

# The War in Iraq and the Establishment of a "New Imperial Order"

*Jean-Marc Lachaud did this interview with me in April 2003 on the regional consequences of the U.S. –British occupation of Iraq.*

As we speak U.S. and British troops have entered Baghdad. Why do you think the United States wanted this war?

First of all, I understand why people are a bit skeptical when direct economic explanations are given for a war. This is often indeed a reductionist approach. But the economic explanation cannot be ruled out a priori. In the case of the two wars against Iraq, economic motives were fundamental.

The issue in 1990–91 was expelling Iraq from Kuwait, a country rich in oil with major investments in the West. The goal was to stop Saddam Hussein from carrying out his hegemonic projects in the region. The United States didn't overthrow him at that time because the conditions, both from an international and a U.S. domestic political point of view, did not allow Washington to occupy Iraq and take full control of the country. This is why the United States, faced with a choice between keeping the Iraqi leader in power and letting a popular insurrection overthrow him, opted for Saddam Hussein and let him crush the rebellion that had broken out in March 1991. The United States preferred to keep him in power, even if it meant having to contain him, rather than deal with a regime born of a popular uprising. A criminal embargo was imposed on Iraq (which according to UN agencies caused over a million deaths). This situation was entirely satisfactory from the point of view of the world oil market, where supply exceeded demand and cutting Iraqi oil production thus suited the dominant players.

But this situation could only be temporary. Given the steady growth of demand and the objective limits of global resources, the oil market has a fatal tendency to tighten up. From Washington's point of view, however, restoring and developing Iraq's capacity to produce oil is inconceivable if it does not increase U.S. profits.

September 11, 2001, provided George W. Bush with the political conditions he required in order to occupy Iraq. So the United States threw itself into the operation. Its objective is a government in Baghdad under its control, enabling it to cancel the concessions that the Iraqi regime gave French and Russian oil companies in order to encourage Paris and Moscow to work to get the embargo lifted. The prize is securing U.S. and British companies the lion's share in exploiting Iraqi oil. An enormous amount is at stake, since Iraq sits on at least 12 percent of the world's oil. In addition, the United States seeks to strengthen its hegemony in the Gulf region, where two-thirds of world oil reserves are concentrated, as well as its control over OPEC. It also wants to safeguard the role of the dollar (Iraq, Iran, and Venezuela were considering pricing their oil in euros). Control over Iraqi oil would mean considerable leverage for the United States over its potential enemies (above all China) and its partners (which, like the European countries and Japan, are also its economic competitors). Finally, we must mention the importance for the United States of the market for Iraqi reconstruction, the biggest rebuilding project since the Second World War—all the more because Iraq has the resources to pay the bill!

In what sense can this conflict lastingly destabilize the Gulf region?

This second Iraq war and its aftermath can only fuel the strong resentment that already existed against the West in general and the United States in particular (due to the Israeli-Arab conflict, the Iraq embargo, stationing of U.S. troops in the Saudi kingdom and elsewhere, etc.). For the peoples of the Middle East, this war is one more proof that the U.S. will to domination is the modern equivalent of the colonial enterprises of earlier times. This war, and the military occupation of Iraq that will likely follow it, are bound to exacerbate this resentment greatly. Outbursts of resentment will at the same time be directed, even more than they are now, against despotic Arab regimes that are carrying out antisocial domestic policies under U.S. tutelage.

Not only the Middle East is threatened with destabilization, however. The rest of the world is threatened, too, as we saw on September 11. There is in fact a strong temptation to take the war to the heart of the dominant powers in the form of terrorist actions, inasmuch as the imbalance of forces on the ground is obvious and a frontal war seems impossible. Faced with such overwhelming military force, increasing recourse to what are called in the United States "asymmetric means"—weapons or tactics that target the most vulnerable spots of the powers under attack—is inevitable.

Other than the growth of Islamic fundamentalism, may we see a revival of anti-imperialist resistance in the Middle East?

For historical reasons Islamic fundamentalism, especially in its most radical forms, has been the privileged form of expression of popular resentment over the past twenty years. Progressive expressions failed and have been throttled. A new kind of fundamentalist current, in opposition to the West (which was *not* a prominent characteristic of Islamic fundamentalism when it was opposing the rise of progressive nationalist movements), has filled the void. This is still the situation we are in. The only gleam of hope for rebuilding a left-wing anti-imperialist movement in this part of the world seems to depend on what happens in the rest of the world.

The advance of the global justice movement, born a few years ago in the struggle against neoliberalism, has already captured people's attention in the Middle East. The spectacular growth of the antiwar movement in the West has meant even more to Arab public opinion. Remember, this antiwar movement could never have reached the size it did so quickly if it hadn't benefited from the growth of the global justice movement. The global justice movement has explicitly adopted this antiwar dimension as its own, as the World Social Forums in Porto Alegre have shown. This global movement is the only force capable of eventually counterbalancing U.S. hyperpower and thus of blocking the dangerous course that the country is following, which risks plunging the whole world into still more barbarism. This also shows the rest of the world that there is a big part of the population in Western countries, even majorities in Europe, that opposes this kind of imperialist policy. This can only help people in Muslim countries to view events through a different prism from the "clash of civilizations." It allows people to understand what is really going on and, displacing religious perspectives, regain some progressive political consciousness. But this is only a hope today, far from a certainty.

Is it plausible to think that there will be movement toward a political settlement of the Israeli-Palestinian conflict?

That depends on the way the Iraqi situation develops after the overthrow of Saddam Hussein, the way in which the United States manages to control Iraq. It would certainly be in the U.S. interest to consolidate its regional hegemony by imposing terms for a settlement of the Arab-Israeli conflict, which is a source of anti-U.S. feeling. We might see more energetic intervention by Washington now as a result, as we did after the first Gulf war, including pressure on Ariel Sharon. Washington has already imposed a new type of political representation on the Palestinian people.

But if the question is whether a "just and lasting" settlement is now plausible, then my answer is a categorical "no." No credible settlement can conceivably emerge from the current state of affairs. If the Oslo process didn't lead to a heartfelt peace, how could anyone think that a Pax Americana could be perceived in this postwar period of heightened rancor as anything other than one element of a U.S. matrix of control over the Middle East?

APRIL 7, 2003; translated from *Mouvement* no. 22, May 2003.

## CHAPTER TWENTY-TWO

# Letter to a Slightly Depressed Antiwar Activist

*The impressive growth of the antiwar movement in the months leading up to the offensive, and the military resistance that the U.S.–British forces encountered in the offensive's first days, gave rise to some illusions among activists. As a result, a stiff breeze of demoralization blew through the movement when the invaders took Baghdad. This "letter," written in the heat of events in April 2003, was meant as a response. It was very widely distributed, in many countries and languages. Clearly it responded to a need.*

Dear Friend,

I don't think that the disappointment you've felt at the news of the Iraqi regime's collapse is warranted.

Of course, I can understand it. The main thing that saddened you was that this collapse has enabled the vultures in Washington and London to deck the carrion-filled halls. This was a semi-colonial war that the tandem Bush and Blair (let's call them B2—it suits them well to call them after a bomber!) waged in defiance of a clear majority of world public opinion. Yet now they can declare it a "war of liberation" inspired by democratic ideals. Yes, that's infuriating!

But remember the predictions that we've been making for months and months. They can be summed up in a few hypotheses:

1) That B2's easiest task would be overthrowing Saddam Hussein's regime, which they could defeat without too much trouble.
   Their real problems would begin afterward.
2) That they dared to defy public opinion because they counted on the spectacle of Iraqi crowds celebrating Saddam Hussein's fall to win

over public opinion. We had to be prepared for this spectacle.
Given how hated the Ba'athist dictatorship was—with good reason—
it was inevitable.

3) B2 are adventurers, gamblers; they went to war betting on a best-case
scenario. They bet on taking over the bulk of the Iraqi state apparatus,
particularly the army, on its turning against Saddam Hussein,
and on their being able to use it to control Iraq after their victory.
But the most likely outcome was that their intervention—which
would begin with an attempt to liquidate Saddam Hussein and the
occupation of the Iraqi oil fields—would lead to the collapse of the state
apparatus and result in a vast chaos marked by bloody score-settling.

All these hypotheses have been verified. Nothing that has happened, in the
last analysis, should have surprised you; everything was predictable. Let's
take a closer look at the events of the last few days:

### 1. THE "VICTORY"

On one side we had a "coalition" between the world's main military power,
which accounts on its own for more than 40 percent of world military
expenditures, and a major vassal power. On the other side we had a Third
World country, two-thirds of whose armed forces had been destroyed in
1991, the other third of which had been worn away through the ensuing
years by an embargo that interfered with maintaining its weaponry, and all
this further aggravated by several years of UN-supervised disarmament.
How could anybody be surprised in these circumstances at an Iraqi rout?

This same regime had already suffered a crushing defeat in 1991 with
the collapse of Iraqi forces in Kuwait and southern Iraq. True, this time
Washington's goal was to take the cities and occupy the whole country;
admittedly, that was a harder goal to achieve. But in the meantime the
country had been bled white, exhausted by more than twenty years of wars,
bombings, and embargo. This is the country that Washington set out to
conquer. And in 2003 as in 1991, the great majority of the Iraqis who were
supposed to carry out the orders from Baghdad hated the Ba'athist regime.
How could anybody expect a popular mobilization in conditions like these?

What was surprising was not the rapid victory by U.S. and British
troops, but the resistance that the Iraqi regime's troops put up in the first
days of the offensive. Remember, all the commentators joined at first in

sneering at the predictions of a speedy victory. Many believed that the quagmire predicted in 1991 was now finally becoming reality. They were mistak-
en about the reasons for the initial resistance. It was due to the fact that the
ground offensive was launched at the same time as the intensive bombing
campaign, whereas in 1991 Washington had subjected the Iraqi army to
more than five weeks of savage bombing before sending its troops into
action. This meant that the regime's forces were still ready to fight at the
moment when the ground offensive began—much more than in 1991,
when the Iraqi troops that had survived the bombings were exhausted and
dazed, and surrendered en masse to the coalition troops.

The *regime*'s forces, nothing more! Anyone who confused what happened
in Iraq with genuine popular resistance, anyone who confused the regime's
troops' defense of Baghdad with the people's defense of Beirut during the
Israeli army siege in 1982, made a big mistake about the military prospects as
well as about the Iraqi people's relationship to Saddam Hussein's tyrannical
regime. The main setback for the Pentagon's plan was in any event that the
"opportunistic" bombings on the offensive's first day missed their target:
Saddam Hussein. And the end of Saddam Hussein's role as commander in
chief probably directly provoked the sped-up collapse of the defense of Baghdad, whether he was killed by a bomb or sneaked off. In such a centralized,
personalized dictatorship, getting rid of the dictator is enough to destroy the
regime's foundations once they are put under intense pressure.

## 2. THE REACTIONS IN IRAQ

How could anybody be surprised at the Iraqi people's relief and joy when
they learned of the dictatorship's fall? I felt genuine relief myself, even
though I had never experienced what the Iraqis did. The Iraqi Ba'athist dictatorship took power in July 1968, when I was in the midst of my own radicalization, like much of my generation in many parts of the world. The new
regime's first priority was to crush the Iraqi expression of that radicalization, whose catalyst in the Middle East had been the Arab regimes' defeat
by Israeli aggression in June 1967.

The reign of terror established in Baghdad proceeded to ruthlessly
crush the guerrilla front opened in southern Iraq by the Guevarist Khaled
Ahmed Zaki as well as the left-wing split from the Iraqi CP. The new junta
quickly earned a reputation as the region's most vicious regime. Iraqi militants knew that they were better off dying in combat with the regime's

forces than being arrested and dying under torture of unrivalled cruelty. The Ba'athist regime crushed the Iraqi Left, the largest component of the Arab Left, in blood and gore. It thus contributed in its way to preparing the ground for the hegemony of Islamic fundamentalism over Middle Eastern popular protest movements. Of all the dictators who have been compared to Hitler in the past half-century, generally in the most tendentious way and for propagandist ends, Saddam Hussein is the one who most closely fit the bill—not only in terms of his regime's domestic characteristics (minus Nazism's ideologically mobilized mass base) but also in terms of an expansionist drive fuelled by blind megalomania.

For thirty-five years I have been waiting and hoping for the fall of this hateful regime! So I was relieved when it finally fell, as were millions of Iraqi men and women. Nor was the Iraqi people's relief surprising; it was completely predictable. What was surprising, at least for Washington and London, was the lukewarm welcome, often edged with hostility, that Arab Iraqis gave their troops—including in the Shiite south, which they thought they had won over.

This is not hard to understand either. What Washington and London failed to grasp is that this people, which had so many reasons to hate Saddam Hussein, has even more reasons to hate them. Iraqis remember how the coalition abandoned them to Saddam Hussein in 1991. They are still suffering from the twelve years of genocidal embargo imposed by Washington and London with the complicity of their UN Security Council partners. And they could not welcome as liberators the United States, the main oppressor of the Middle East and sponsor of the state of Israel, or the tag-along British colonizers of yesteryear who had left such bitter memories behind them.

As a result, the Iraqis' expressions of joy were quite restrained. Washington had to resort to propaganda tricks in order to give the impression that the U.S. –British coalition troops were being welcomed as "liberators." Hailed they were, but above all by the looters, who with their booty in hand had the most reason to find "Bush very good." The occupation troops deliberately "liberated" these looters' instincts, on the orders of "unlawful commanders" who thought they were securing the occupation against popular hostility and in the end increased it considerably. (The only public building in Baghdad that was well guarded was the Ministry of Oil, just as the only "secured" areas in Iraq were the oil fields.) The new invaders became responsible for a sack of Baghdad that will linger in historical memory as the modern equivalent of the thirteenth-century sack of Baghdad during the Mongol invasion.

The only part of the Iraqi population that allied with the occupied troops and massively expressed joy at their presence has been the Kurds. Once more the leaderships of Iraqi Kurdistan have demonstrated their sempiternal short-sightedness, having so often cast their lot with poor allies: Israel, the Shah of Iran, the Turkish government, the Iranian mullahs—even Saddam Hussein! They have not had the sense to avoid compromising themselves with an occupation force destined to become an object of resentment for Arab Iraqis, the only ally that will make a decisive difference in the end to the future of Iraqi Kurdistan. It would be disastrous for the Kurds for their leaders to confirm their image as devoted partners of the occupying powers. The United States and Britain have no intention of defending the Kurdish people's right to self-determination. They will not hesitate to sacrifice Iraq's Kurds if that serves their purpose of consolidating their hold on the country.

## 3. CONTROLLING IRAQ, DOMINATING THE WORLD

The small-scale looters of Iraq's cities have at this early date already singularly complicated the task of the big-scale looters, the occupying powers. Each passing day confirms how difficult it will be for B2 to control Iraq in face of a population that cordially detests them. Confidence man Ahmed Chalabi and his handful of mercenaries brought along in the U.S. troops' baggage are certainly not capable of changing this situation.

The United States' problem is that—to a far greater extent than in Germany or Japan after 1945, when it could make use of whole layers of the old regime's state apparatus (including in Japan the emperor himself)—it will find nothing more reliable in Iraq than the leftovers from Saddam Hussein's apparatus. Only the servants of the old regime have in sufficient numbers the degree of moral degradation required to put themselves at the occupiers' devoted service. They alone will be inclined to serve the country's new masters, with all the more enthusiasm because they will be saving their skins while slaking their thirst for power. This will make the occupation all the more hateful for the great majority of Iraqis.

As it extends its presence in the Arab world further and further, the United States is stretching its troops too thin. The hatred that it evokes in all Middle Eastern countries and throughout the Islamic world has already blown up in its face several times; September 11, 2001, was only the most spectacular, deadliest manifestation so far of this hatred. The occupation of Iraq will push the general resentment to extremes; it will speed up the decomposition of the regional order backed by Washington. There will be no Pax Americana. Rather there will be another step downward towards barbarism, with the chief barbarism of Washington and its allies sustaining the opposite barbarism of religious fanaticism—as long as no new progressive forces emerge in this part of the world.

The project of building a global empire dominated by the United States by means of brute force is inexorably doomed to failure. In this respect Washington has at this early stage already suffered major political reverses, contrary to the impression that its military victory in Iraq might temporarily offer. Never since the end of the Cold War has U.S. hegemony been so widely challenged in the world; never has the consensus around this hegemony been so lacking. This is the case at the level of international relations: the grumbling and fractiousness of countries that Washington considered its loyal allies have never been so widespread. Even the Turkish government refused to let U.S. troops pass through its territory. Washington failed to buy it, just as it failed to buy enough members of the UN Security Council to get nine measly votes for its war on Iraq!

Admittedly, the existing states are not reliable allies for the antiwar movement, nor its allies at all—particularly when, like France and Russia, they behave just as brutally and hatefully in their own imperial domains as the United States does in its. But this cacophony in the system of states associated with the great empire ruled from Washington has in a way reflected the other major reverse for the imperial project. I refer, of course, to the emergence of the other superpower, "world public opinion,"—or rather, the real movement—as the *New York Times* rightly labeled it after the demonstrations on February 15, 2003, the biggest day of worldwide popular mobilization in history. "World public opinion" was embodied in the real movement, the antiwar movement; polls do not demonstrate.

During the 1990s many thought that this movement was fated never to overcome its notorious weakness. They thought that the Vietnam years had essentially been well and truly buried, particularly since Washington had learned the lessons of Vietnam and applied them in its later wars, starting in Panama (1989). But beginning in the fall of 2002, we have seen the breathtaking rise of a new antiwar movement, which has quickly set new historic records in several countries and even engulfed the United States. This fact is absolutely decisive; the key mobilization is the one that takes place in the United States itself. The U.S. antiwar movement has not yet the level of its peak in the Vietnam years, but it has already distinguished itself by reaching a mass scale, in spite of the trauma of September 11 and the Bush administration's exploitation of that trauma.

Carefully selected images of the so-called liberation of Iraq and the Pentagon's scripted scenes have impressed many opponents of the war. But each passing day shows how right the antiwar movement was. The countless deaths, the massive destruction, and the pillage of Iraq's national wealth constitute a huge tribute imposed on the Iraqi people to pay for a "liberation" that is ushering in a foreign occupation. As Washington bogs down in a country that cannot be hidden from the world—unlike Afghanistan, more chaotic today than ever—the antiwar movement will be able to rise to new heights.

This movement's spectacular growth has only been possible because it rested on the foundations of three years of progress by the global movement against neoliberal globalization, which was born in Seattle. These two dimensions will continue to fuel each other, to strengthen people's awareness that neoliberalism and war are two faces of the same system of domination—which must be overthrown.

APRIL 14, 2003; published wholly or in part on ZNet, *L'Humanité* (Paris), *Liberazione* (Rome), *La Libre Belgique* (Brussels), *Le Courrier* (Geneva), etc.

# NOTES

## PREFACE

1   Gilbert Achcar, *The Clash of Barbarisms: September 11 and the Making of the New World Disorder*, trans. Peter Drucker (New York: Monthly Review Press, 2002).

2   The article "The Tragedy of the Iraqi People" in the present book was published in that earlier collection: André Gunder Frank and Salah Jaber, *The Gulf War and the New World Order* (Amsterdam: IIRE, 1991).

3   The subtitle of this book is inspired by the title of one of Maxime Rodinson's articles, a critical review of Marxist works on Egypt, "L'Égypte nassérienne au miroir marxiste" [Nasser's Egypt in a Marxist mirror], in *Marxisme et monde musulman* (Paris: Seuil, 1972), pp. 603–32. The abridged English version of this book, *Marxism and the Muslim World* (New York: Monthly Review Press, 1981), does not include the article in question. I also mean this as a tribute to Rodinson's undogmatic Marxism, which has inspired my own thinking and my own critical relationship to "Marxism."

## INTRODUCTION

1   " Sir Maurice Hankey, the extremely powerful secretary of the War Cabinet, wrote to Foreign Secretary Arthur Balfour that, 'oil in the next war will occupy the place of coal in the present war, or at least a parallel place to coal. The only big potential supply that we can get under British control is the Persian and Mesopotamian supply.' Therefore, Hankey said, 'control over these oil supplies becomes a first-class British war aim.' " Daniel Yergin, *The Prize: The Epic Quest for Oil, Money and Power* (London: Pocket Books, 1993), p. 188. On how Middle East oil was divided up after World War I, see chap. 10 of Yergin, " Opening the Door on the Middle East: The Turkish Petroleum Company. "

2   This account leaves Calouste Gulbenkian's interests out of the story.

3   Raymond Aron, *The Imperial Republic: The United States and the World, 1945–1973*, trans. Frank Jellinek (Englewood Cliffs, NJ: Prentice-Hall, 1974), pp. 186–87.

4   These two last companies merged to form ExxonMobil, the world's biggest oil company.

5   On the alliance between the United States and the Saudi kingdom see Gilbert Achcar, *The Clash of Barbarisms: September 11 and the Making of the New World Disorder*, trans. Peter Drucker (New York: Monthly Review Press, 2002), esp. pp. 30–35.

6   George Lenczowski, *The Middle East in World Affairs*, 4th ed. (Ithaca, NY: Cornell University Press, 1980), pp. 581–82.

7   On this subject see Stephen McFarland, "The Iranian Crisis of 1946 and the Onset of the Cold War," in Melvyn Leffler and David Painter, *Origins of the Cold War: An International History* (London/New York: Routledge, 1994), pp. 239–56.

8   Yergin, *The Prize*, p. 416.

9   On this subject see Marc Gasiorowski's instructive article, " U.S. Foreign Policy Toward Iran During the Mussadiq Era," in the very interesting collection edited by David Lesch, *The Middle East and the United States: A Historical and Political Reassessment*, 2nd ed. (Boulder, CO: Westview Press, 1999), pp. 51–65.

10  A raid carried out by the Israeli Army's Unit 101, commanded by Ariel Sharon. See Amnon Kapeliouk, " Les antécédents du général Sharon," *Le Monde Diplomatique*, November 2001.

11  Officially a deal with Czechoslovakia in which Egyptian cotton was bartered for weapons.

12  On this period see Peter Hahn's article, " National Security Concerns in U.S. Policy Toward Egypt, 1949–1956, " in Lesch, *Middle East*, pp. 89–99, as well as Peter L. Hahn, *The United*

*States, Great Britain, and Egypt, 1945–1956: Strategy and Diplomacy in the Early Cold War* (Chapel Hill, NC: University of North Carolina Press, 1991).

13  See Lesch, " The 1957 American-Syrian Crisis: Globalist Policy in a Regional Reality," in Lesch, *Middle East*, pp. 128–43.

14  See Erika Alin, " U.S. Policy and Military Intervention in the 1958 Lebanon Crisis," in Lesch, *Middle East*, pp. 144–62.

15  Incidentally Truman's partiality for Israel coexisted with anti-Jewish sentiments on his part, revealed in his recently opened personal papers. The revelation came as a blow to Truman's great admirer—and unconditional supporter of Israel—columnist William Safire (see his article " Truman on Underdogs," *New York Times*, 14 July 2003).

16  These people have been surprised to see a Republican president, George W. Bush, who got a narrow minority of the Jewish vote in 2000 and a big majority of the Muslim vote, show unprecedented complicity with the most extremist government in the history of the state of Israel.

17  This is a much more accurate name than "Jewish lobby." The American Israel Public Affairs Committee (AIPAC) calls itself incidentally "America's Pro-Israel Lobby."

18  Noam Chomsky, *Fateful Triangle: The United States, Israel and the Palestinians*, 2nd ed. (Cambridge, MA: South End Press, 1999), pp. 17, 22.

19  Figures cited in Cheryl Rubenberg, *Israel and the American National Interest: A Critical Examination* (Chicago: University of Illinois Press, 1986), pp. 67, 96.

20  Ibid., p. 91. Rubenberg's work is a good critical history of U.S.-Israeli relations up to the eve of the first intifada, although she has an idealist conception of U.S. "national interests," far removed from the real interests that dictate Washington's foreign policy.

21  Ibid., pp. 112–13.

22  The East Bank of the river Jordan, the area that is called Jordan today.

23  See in this collection, chap. 10, "The PLO: The Long March Backwards."

24  See chapter 9, "OPEC and the U.S.: One Struggle," in Pierre Terzian, *OPEC: The Inside Story*, trans. Michael Pallis (London: Zed Press, 1985), pp. 188–202. See also the debate between Ernest Mandel and Salah Jaber in *Critiques de l'Economie Politique*, no. 22 (October–December 1975): 41–108.

25  See chapter 7, "Participation versus Nationalization," in Terzian, *OPEC*, pp. 147–62.

26  On Islamic fundamentalism see Part 1 of this collection and Achcar, *Clash of Barbarisms*.

27  Gary Sick, "The United States in the Persian Gulf: From Twin Pillars to Dual Containment," in Lesch, *Middle East*, p. 280.

28  See chapter 6, "The Implications of Soviet Troop Withdrawal."

29  See chapter 17, "The Tragedy of the Iraqi People."

30  See chapter 15, "The Hezbollah Victory."

31  See chapter 12, "The Dynamic of the Intifada."

32  See chapter 14, "Zionism and Peace: From the Allon Plan to the Washington Accords."

33  See chapter 10, "The PLO: The Long March Backwards."

34  On the Beilin–Abu Mazen agreement as well as the road traveled from Oslo to Sharon, see Tanya Reinhart's excellent *Israel/Palestine: How to End the 1948 War* (New York: Seven Stories, 2002).

35  Articles as lucid and honest as Joshua Hammer's "Words & Deeds," *Newsweek* (international edition), 9 June 2003, are rare in the big U.S. media.

36  Elected leader of the Labor Party for one year in June 2003, Shimon Peres reportedly aspires to negotiate his return to government through a new coalition with Sharon.

37  Rumsfeld, Wolfowitz, Abrams, Armitage, Bolton, Dobriansky, Khalilzad, Perle, Rodman, Schneider, and Zoellick.

38  This is not the place to prove this assertion. We mention only that the Rockefeller group has played a central role in U.S. foreign policy. David Rockefeller was for many years president of the Council

on Foreign Relations, the main U.S. foreign policy think tank. His company finances the Council together with other companies like Bechtel, the huge construction firm that has managed to ingest all sorts of contract tidbits in the oil-producing countries and is now in charge of rebuilding Iraq.

39  OPEC Reference Basket price.

40  OPEC, *Annual Statistical Bulletin 2001*, p. 119.

41  The nominal price dropped back again the following year (to $23.12) while remaining above the 1990 price, but it rose once again in 2002 (to $24.36) and reached $27.87 a barrel on 16 July 2003, despite record Russian oil exports.

42  See Michael Klare, *Resource War: The New Landscape of Global Conflict* (New York: Henry Holt, 2002).

43  CSIS Panel Report, "Executive Summary," *The Geopolitics of Energy into the 21st Century*, vol. 1, *An Overview and Policy Considerations* (Washington: CSIS, 2000), p. xvi.

44  Ibid., p. xix.

45  The kingdom has an unused, installed capacity today of 3 million barrels a day, without counting its much more considerable potential capacity.

46  Edward Morse and James Richard, "The Battle for Energy Dominance," *Foreign Affairs* 81 no. 2 (March–April 2002), p. 20. See also the debate around this article, "Does Saudi Arabia Still Matter?," *Foreign Affairs* 81, no. 6 (November–December 2002), pp. 167–78.

47  See in this collection, chaps. 18 and 19, "Operation Oil," and "War Drive." See also Achcar, " Le nouvel ordre impérial ou la mondialisation de l'empire états-unien," in Achcar, ed., *Le nouvel ordre impérial* (Paris: Actuel Marx, 2003), pp. 15–24, as well as John Bellamy Foster, Harry Magdoff, and Robert McChesney, "U.S. Military Bases and Empire," *Monthly Review* 53, no. 10 (March 2002).

48  On this aspect of the situation, see Achcar, "The Strategic Triad: The United States, Russia and China," and "Rasputin Plays at Chess: How the West Blundered into a New Cold War," in Tariq Ali, ed., *Masters of the Universe?: NATO's Balkan Crusade* (London: Verso, 2000). See also Achcar, "A Trio of Soloists," *Le Monde Diplomatique*, December 2001.

49  CSIS Panel Report, p. xvi.

50  OPEC, *Annual Statistical Bulletin 2001*, pp. 10, 12.

51  The current situation is quite similar to the situation after the mujahedin overthrew the Najibullah regime in 1992; see in this collection, "The 'Lebanonization' of Afghanistan."

52  See chapter 20, "Washington and London: The Problems Have Only Just Begun," and chap. 22, "Letter to a Slightly Depressed Antiwar Activist."

53  Niall Ferguson, "The Empire Slinks Back," *New York Times Magazine*, 27 April 2003.

54  Thom Shanker, "Officials Debate Whether to Seek a Bigger Military," *New York Times*, 21 July 2003.

55  Samuel Huntington, *The Clash of Civilizations and the Remaking of World Order* (New York: Touchstone, 1998), p. 94.

56  See chapter 3, "The Arab Despotic Exception."

57  George W. Bush, "Remarks by the President in Commencement Address at the University of South Carolina," Washington, D.C.: Office of the Press Secretary, White House, 9 May 2003.

58  Richard Mably and Tom Ashby, "Iraqis Agree on Role for Oil Majors, OPEC," Reuters, 5 April 2003.

## CHAPTER ONE

1  [General Mohammad Zia Ul-Haq overthrew Bhutto in a 1977 coup, and was president of Pakistan from 1978 until his death in an accident in 1988.]

2  Karl Marx and Friedrich Engels, *Manifesto of the Communist Party*, in Marx and Engels, *Collected Works*, vol. 6 (New York: International Publishers, 1976), p. 494.

3   Ibid.

4   A different description of the role of the petty bourgeoisie is in Marx and Engels' celebrated *Address to the Communist League* of 1850, but its rallying to the proletariat is not envisaged.

5   In Tunisia and Lebanon, the profound "westernization" of society handicaps the progress of the Islamic fundamentalism, which is no less real.

6   [Zulfikar Ali Bhutto, first president and later prime minister of Pakistan from 1971 until his overthrow in 1977, was executed in 1979.]

7   Gaddafi, contrary to what one might think, is not a fundamentalist in the strict sense of the term. He was a fundamentalist up to a certain point during the first years of his petty bourgeois dictatorship, becoming a sort of precursor to the current resurgence and even one of its main instigators. His subsequent radicalization extended even as far as Islam, which he now claims to be reforming. The "Muslim Brotherhood" exists in Libya and is repressed there.

8   The gains made by different currents of the fundamentalist movement inside the same country differ as well, but we cannot take account of these distinctions in the framework of these general theses.

9   [These lines were written before an Islamic fundamentalist activist assassinated Anwar al-Sadat in October 1981. The Egyptian Left was crushed in the 1980s, while the radical fringes of the fundamentalist current put up violent opposition to the regime.]

## CHAPTER TWO

1   Despite the sexist etymology of the word "hysteria" (from the Latin *hystera*, "uterus"), the hysterical crowds were mostly male.

2   See chapter 1, "Eleven Theses on the Resurgence of Islamic Fundamentalism."

3   See the description of the clergy given in Chapour Haguiguat's excellent, concise book, *Iran: La Révolution Islamique* (Brussels: Editions Complexe, 1985).

4   [Ayatollah Khomeini appointed Bazargan, who had been Mussadiq's deputy prime minister, provisional prime minister in February 1979. Barzagan resigned in November 1979 and died in 1995.]

## CHAPTER THREE

1   See Alain Gresh, "Fragile New Order for the Middle East," *Le Monde Diplomatique*, English ed., November 1996.

2   In Lebanon in 1996 there was a shutdown of political pluralism in radio and television, and a recrudescence of the kind of political arrests that the country had not known for a long time.

3   "Islam and Democracy Simply Aren't Compatible," *International Herald Tribune*, 21 January 1992.

4   1993 figures. Saudi Arabia ranks ninth in the world for military spending, behind the five permanent members of the UN Security Council, plus Germany, Italy and Japan.

5   *International Herald Tribune*, 1–2 February 1997.

6   See Olivier Roy, "Between Sharia and Pipeline," *Le Monde Diplomatique*, English ed., November 1996.

7   Obviously the reasons cited here are not the full story. They combine with various other, more or less endogenous factors, which are well outlined in Ghassan Salamé, ed., *Democracy Without Democrats?: The Renewal of Politics in the Muslim World* (London-New York: I. B. Tauris, 1994), a work that argues firmly against the cultural determinist thesis. The main reservation about this book is that it keeps silent about the responsibility of the West, which has been demonstrably fundamental.

## CHAPTER FIVE

1   V. I. Lenin, "Report on the Party Programme" (19 March 1919), in *Collected Works*, vol. 29 (Moscow: Progress Publishers, 1965), p. 172.

2   See the works of Alexander Bennigsen, particularly his article in *Le Monde*, 15 November 1984.

3   Cited by Fred Halliday in "War In Afghanistan," *New Left Review*, no. 119, January–February 1980.

4   Detailed descriptions of the Khalq regime's measures will be found in most of the studies devoted to Afghanistan since 1978.

5   In fact, a large number of the refugees in Pakistan and Iran are there for economic reasons rather than political ones.

6   Estimates of the number of victims of the Afghan war vary between 100,000 and a million, the figure advanced by the mujahedin, which, judging by the number of Soviet soldiers they claim to have killed is rather fantastical. If you consider that the Soviet army has limited itself to controlling the "useful part of the country" and the arteries of communication and has not used big bombers of the B-52 type, the real number of the dead must be between 100,000 and 200,000, including those killed by the mujahedin, who have not been inactive either.

7   Babrak Karmal, message of 29 December 1979.

8   See the description of the regime's measures by Jonathan Steele in *The Guardian*, 15–17 March 1986. These articles were reprinted in *MERIP* 16, no. 4, July-August 1986.

9   Peshawar, the mujahedin "capital," is located in the heart of the Pushtun area of Pakistan.

10  On this subject see the article by Ahmed Rashid in *The Nation* , 31 January 1987.

11  Henry Kissinger's article in *Newsweek*, 2 March 1987.

12  In this vein, Iran has proposed that its troops participate in an "Islamic force" that would replace the Soviet troops in Afghanistan.

13  The following quotations come from the translation published in *Le Monde*, 18–19 January 1987.

14  See *Le Monde*, 12 March 1987.

## CHAPTER SIX

1   See chapter 5, "Afghanistan: Balance Sheet of a War."

2   A sampling of such views by "specialists" such as Helene Carrere d'Encausse can be found in the special feature published in *Défis Afghans* no. 13 March/April 1987, "Que veut Gorbatchev?"

3   Graham Fuller, in the *Washington Post*, reprinted, *International Herald Tribune*, 8 March 1988.

4   *La Nouvelle Revue Internationale*, no. 353, January 1988.

5   Shevardnadze interview given to the Bahktar News Agency, 6 January 1988.

6   [Mikhail Gorbachev received the Nobel Peace Prize in 1990.]

7   Good racist that he is, Kissinger describes Thieu's methods as "detestably Vietnamese"!

8   See chapter 5, "Afghanistan: Balance Sheet of a War."

9   *Comrade Najib's Speech at the Plenum of the PDPA CC* (Kabul: Afghanistan Today Publishers, June 1987).

10  [Contrast George W. Bush's famous statement after September 11, 2001: "You're either with us or against us." Delivered in a joint news conference in Washington with French President Jacques Chirac, 6 November 2001.]

11  Correspondents stationed in Peshawar have noted a sharp rise in the value of the Afghan currency on the local market, a clear sign of people preparing to return.

12  *Newsweek*, 9 May 1988.

13  *Le Monde diplomatique*, April 1988.

14  *Défis Afghans*, no. 15, November 1987.

15  Among others, *Newsweek*, 18 April 1988, and *Le Monde*, 19 April 1988.

16  It is significant that the rally called in Peshawar by the Islamic Alliance to denounce the Geneva accords drew only 25,000 men (*Le Monde*, 19 April 1988), considering that the three million Afghan refugees in Pakistan are tightly regimented by the organizations in the Alliance.

17  *Défis Afghans*, no. 16, December 1987/January 1988.

18  *Le Monde*, 22 April 1988.

19  See chapter 5, "Afghanistan: Balance Sheet of a War."

20  *Le Monde Diplomatique*, June 1988.

21  See chapter 5, "Afghanistan: Balance Sheet of a War."

22  *Newsweek*, 30 May 1988.

23  *Newsweek*, 1 February 1988.

24  The new, watered-down constitution of the Republic of Afghanistan still nonetheless includes Article 14, which stipulates that "men and women have equal rights in all economic, political, social, and cultural spheres." In an Islamic country this is a revolutionary assertion.

## CHAPTER SEVEN

1   See chapter 6, "The Agreement on Soviet Withdrawal."

## CHAPTER EIGHT

1   On the Allon Plan, see chap. 14, "Zionism and Peace: From the Allon Plan to the Washington Accords."

2   *Le Monde*, 2 January 1988.

3   [Ibid.]

4   [Reserve general Rehavam Zeevi, later minister of tourism (*sic*) in Ariel Sharon's government before the Popular Front for the Liberation of Palestine (PFLP) assassinated him on October 17, 2001.]

5   The mere decision to banish nine Palestinian "agitators" has cost Israel strong criticism (as well as a vote against it in the UN) from its U.S. tutor, which is anxious to calm things down in the Middle East. A massive deportation of Palestinians would immediately set the whole region ablaze—a real disaster for Washington. It should be pointed out, moreover, that international condemnation of the banishments—although Israeli governments have used this practice for a long time, almost constantly—shows to what extent rights are won only through struggle. The rights of the Palestinian people have never been so self-evident in the eyes of the whole world as since the current uprising began.

6   *Newsweek*, 31 August 1987.

7   [Excerpt from a report that I drafted for an international meeting, published as "The Crisis of the PLO", *International Marxist Review* 2, no. 2 (Spring 1987): 80–81. The report analyzed the 1985 split in the PLO; on this same subject see in this collection, chap. 10, "The PLO: The Long March ... Backwards."]

## CHAPTER NINE

1   *International Herald Tribune*, 26 January, 1988.

2   *Le Monde*, 21–22 February 1988.

3   Quoted by Glenn Frankel of the *Washington Post* in the *International Herald Tribune*, 26 January 1988.

4   *Newsweek*, 25 January 1988.

5   Speech made at the University of Tel Aviv on October 17, 1972.

6   Ronald Reagan's statement on September 1, 1982.

## CHAPTER TEN

1   The Gaza Strip passed under Egyptian administration in 1948 without being formally annexed.

2   Chapter 11 will explain why governments must be pressured to recognize the Palestinian state.

3   *Al-Hayat* (London), 12–13 November 1988. Published in the journal of the Sons of the Country Movement (Abna' El-Balad), printed in Nazareth: *Al-Raia*, 25 November 1988.

4   This faction was ousted from power in Syria and repressed by Hafez El-Assad in November 1970.

5   Resolution on "The Arab revolution" published as an IMG *Red Pamphlet* (London). It foresaw, after the destruction of the Zionist state in the context of a socialist revolution in the Middle East, recognition of the right to self-determination of "the Jewish national minority in Palestine, including their right to form an independent state on a part of Palestinian land," under the condition that the exercise of this right in no way harms the Palestinian Arab people.

6   PDFLP, *Hawla azmat harakat al-muqâwama al-filastînyya* On the crisis of the Palestinian resistance movement (Beirut: Dar at-Talia, 1969), p. 78, translated from the Arabic original.

7   [I first formulated the thesis of the bureaucratic bourgeois transformation of the PLO in 1974 in an article in Arabic that appeared in English translation in *Inprecor* (English ed.), no. 19, 13 February 1975.]

8   French translation published in *Revue d'Etudes Palestiniennes* no. 21, Autumn 1986.

9   This demand appeared in the 1974 program of Middle Eastern Trotskyists (see note 5), linked to the perspective of a "Palestinian or Jordanian/Palestinian government, as a national revolutionary workers' and peasants' government" in these territories.

10  *Al-Hadaf*, no. 892, special issue, December 1987.

11  *Al-Yom Assabeh*, 23 November 1987.

12  *Jerusalem Post*, 28 June 1998.

13  *Le Monde*, 23 September 1988.

14  [Khalil Al-Wazir, whose nom de guerre was Abu Jihad, was one of Fatah's founders and main leaders. An Israeli commando squad led by Ehud Barak assassinated him in Tunis.]

15  *Le Monde*, 25 October 1988.

16  [Reference to the popular uprising in Algeria in October 1988.]

17  *Al-Yom Assabeh*, 28 November 1988.

18  *International Viewpoint*, no. 153, 12 December 1988.

19  *Le Monde*, 13–14 November 1988.

20  According to the poll already cited, only 22 percent of West Bank inhabitants approved of a confederation with Jordan.

21  *Le Monde*, 16 December 1988.

22  *Al-Yom Assabeh*, 2 January 1989.

23  [Abu Iyad was assassinated in January 1991.]

24  *Al-Qabas*, reprinted in *Al-Raia*, 5 August 1988.

## CHAPTER ELEVEN

1   At the time we retorted, "The timescale of a 'peaceful settlement' could be brief or long, but it would be absurd to build a political line on the hypothesis that this settlement is impossible. Those who adopt such a hypothesis find a cozy pretext for undertaking no action against the 'peaceful settlement' and those who are preparing it." *Al-Munadel* (Beirut), no. 30, March/April 1975.

2   *Al-Yom Assabeh*, 2 January 1989.

3   *Le Monde*, 2 January 1988

4   *Le Monde*, 25 February 1988.

5   *Le Monde*, 2 June 1988.

6   *Newsweek,* 6 June 1988.

7   *Le Monde,* 19 October 1988.

8   *Newsweek,* 12 September 1988.

9   *New York Times,* 2 January 1989.

10  *Al-Yom Assabeh,* 28 November 1988.

11  See chapter 10 in this collection.

12  V. I. Lenin, "Left-wing" Communism—An Infantile Disorder," in *Collected Works,* vol. 32 (Moscow: Progress Publishers, 1966), p. 68.

13  Ibid., p. 69.

14  *International Herald Tribune,* 27 May 1988.

15  Manifestly even someone like Jerome Segal could envisage proclaiming the state well before the king of Jordan took the initiative on July 31, 1988.

16  See chapter 10 in this collection.

17  Leon Trotsky, "The Chinese Revolution and the Theses of Comrade Stalin" (7 May 1927), in *Leon Trotsky on China,* ed. Les Evans and Russell Block (New York: Monad Press, 1976), pp. 182–83.

18  *Al-Hadaf,* no. 892, special issue, December 1987.

19  Leon Trotsky, *The Third International After Lenin,* trans. John G. Wright (New York: Pathfinder Press, 1970), p. 218—emphasis in the original.

20  Abu Iyad, *My Home, My Land: A Narrative of the Palestinian Struggle* (New York: Times Books, 1981), p. 65.

21  *Revue d'Etudes Palestinians,* no. 25, autumn 1987, p. 207.

22  *Al-Hadaf,* no. 892, special issue, December 1987.

## CHAPTER TWELVE

1   See chap. 11, "Where Is the PLO Going?: The Long March ... Backwards."

2   The inhabitants of Gaza, which Egypt had washed its hands of and which had been included since 1972 in the Jordanian project for a "United Arab Kingdom," also rejected the prospect.

3   *Le Monde,* 15 September 1987.

4   Abu-Lughod, et al., "A Profile of the Palestinian People," *Journal of Palestinian Studies,* 1984. [Reprinted in Said and Hitchens, eds., *Blaming the Victims: Spurious Scholarship and the Palestinian Question* (London-New York: Verso, 2001), p. 278.]

5   *Newsweek,* 25 January 1988.

6   According to the study in Abu-Lughod, et al., "A Profile of the Palestinian People."

7   *Haaretz,* 11 September 1988.

8   Of all the bodies described, only the "shock committees" as a general rule exclude women. Feminists in the occupied territories, men and women, have to fight to change this situation, which is both unfair and wrong.

9   The PCs have received little coverage in the Western media, which are much more interested by the most insignificant statement from "moderate" Palestinians, who are good at expressing themselves—literally as well as metaphorically—in Hebrew and/or English.

10  See chap. 10, "Where Is the PLO Going?: The State, the PLO, and the Palestinian Left."

11  *Al-Qabas,* reprinted in *Al-Raia,* 5 August 1988.

## CHAPTER FOURTEEN

1   This article was originally written in French and published in October 1994 in the French sociological journal *L'Homme et la Société,* no. 114. The author wishes to thank Bernard

Gibbons in London, who has kindly translated the article into English, and Peter Drucker in Amsterdam, who has edited the American version, as well as Tikva Honig-Parnass in Jerusalem and Michael Löwy in Paris, who have read the first draft and given their friendly suggestions. However, none of the friends mentioned here bears any responsibility for the views expressed in the article.

2   "We hold these Truths to be self-evident, that all Men are created equal, that they are endowed by their Creator with certain unalienable Rights, that among these are Life, Liberty, and the Pursuit of Happiness," proclaimed the U.S. Declaration of Independence in 1776. Blacks and Indians were excluded de facto from the ranks of men, by "the white, or European, the MAN preeminently so called" (Alexis de Tocqueville, *Democracy in America*).

3   The universalism/particularism antithesis belongs to the vocabulary of Christian theology. The affinities between the universalist doctrine of Redemption and that of the rights of the human person are, moreover, to be counted among the contributions of Christianity to political humanism.

4   Florence Gauthier vigorously stressed this point at the time of the bicentennial of the 1789 revolution. See "Le droit naturel en révolution," in Étienne Balibar et al., *Permanences de la Révolution* (Paris: La Brèche, 1989).

5   "Wanting to create a purely Jewish, or predominantly Jewish, state in an Arab Palestine in the twentieth century could not help but lead to a colonial-type situation and to the development (completely normal sociologically speaking) of a racist state of mind, and in the final analysis to a military confrontation between the two ethnic groups." Maxime Rodinson, *Israel: A Colonial-Settler State?* (New York: Monad Press, 1973), p. 77.

6   Theodor Herzl, *The Jewish State: An Attempt at a Modern Solution of the Jewish Question* (London: H. Pordes, 1972). The reference to colonists is on p. 46.

7   Ibid., p. 71. "We should there [in Palestine] form a portion of the rampart of Europe against Asia, an outpost of civilization as opposed to barbarism" (p. 30).

8   Shabtai Teveth, *Ben-Gurion: The Burning Ground, 1886-1948*( Boston: Houghton Mifflin, 1987), pp. 542, 544. Rather than rehabilitating the Zionist far right, one discredits still more its democratic professions of faith in recalling, as Alain Dieckhoff does, that "the various proclamations by the Irgun [the Zionist Revisionist armed organization] always mentioned, like that published in July 1946, that the aim of the political struggle was to found an independent democratic society where equality of rights would be guaranteed for all whatever their origin and their belief." (*The Invention of a Nation: Zionist Thought and the Making of Modern Israel*, trans. Jonathan Derrick [London: Hurst & Company, 2003], p. 229). [Interestingly, the English translation of Dieckhoff's book published in 2003 omitted the sentence that followed in the original French version: "It even made reference to drawing up a constitution based on the United States Declaration of Independence." (*L'invention d'une nation: Israël et la modernité politique* [Paris: Gallimard, 1993], p. 264)]

9   Nearly 55 percent of the territory of British Mandate Palestine was attributed to the "Jewish state," whereas the Jewish residents of this territory only constituted one third of its total population. Even allowing that all the residents—newly arrived immigrants, like indigenous inhabitants—would have enjoyed equal rights to sovereignty in the territory, the partition plan was manifestly iniquitous. In effect, the UN took up the Zionist thesis of the right of the Diaspora Jews to sovereignty in Palestine. "The authors of this partition saw this demographic relationship in a dynamic perspective: the expected immigration would very quickly allow the constitution of a Jewish majority." Jean-Paul Chagnollaud, "Palestine: l'enjeu démographique", in *Revue d'Etudes Palestiniennes* no. 7, (Spring 1983): 27–29.

The victors of the Second World War, Truman's United States in particular, sought to rid themselves of the troublesome burden of the survivors of the Holocaust by diverting them to Palestine, in concert with the Zionist movement. Recall the vehemence with which the Zionists had previously opposed the Roosevelt plan to admit the refugees to other countries, including the United States (see Morris Ernst, *So Far So Good* [New York: Harper, 1948], and Alan Taylor, *Prelude to Israel* [New York: Philosophical Library, 1959]). During the Holocaust, Roosevelt himself had failed to come to the aid of the Jews of Europe, as has been shown by David Wyman (*The Abandonment of the Jews: America and the Holocaust, 1941-1945*, New York: Pantheon, 1984). The same author admits, however, although in an apologetic fashion, that the Zionists deliberately chose to privilege their Palestinian project to the detriment of saving the Jews of Europe (pp. 175-177).

This was Ben-Gurion's choice, as his biographer Shabtai Teveth explains: "In spite of the certainty that genocide was being carried out, the JAE [Jewish Agency Executive, presided by Ben-Gurion] did not deviate appreciably from its routine.... Two facts can be definitively stated: Ben-Gurion did not put the rescue effort above Zionist politics, and he did not regard it as a principal task demanding his personal leadership..." op. cit., p. 848. Teveth attributes this attitude to what he called a "philosophy of the beneficial disaster" (p. 850), quoting Ben-Gurion who said: "The harsher the affliction, the greater the strength of Zionism" (ibid.). In this respect, Ben-Gurion was only taking after his inspirer, Theodor Herzl, who stated in the prologue to his book-manifesto: "the present scheme... includes the employment of an existent propelling force... And what is our propelling force? The misery of the Jews." (op. cit., p. 8)

Recently again, the Zionist movement has been inciting the departure of the Jewish population of the ex-USSR and has sought to channel them towards Israel, contrary to the wish of the great majority of emigrants to go to North America. "Mr. Shamir, the Israeli prime minister, complained that the [US] administration offered them the freedom to choose their country of destination. This free choice, in effect, is unfavorable to Israel. Ninety percent of Soviet Jews prefer to go to the United States." *Le Monde*, 4 October 1989.

10 This debate is today dominated by the work of the Israeli historian Benny Morris, *The Birth of the Palestinian Refugee Problem, 1947-1949* (Cambridge: Cambridge University, 1987).

11 Ibid., p. 31.

12 On the odd debates in Israel on the definition of Jewish identity, see Akiva Orr, *The UnJewish State: The Politics of Jewish Identity in Israel*(London: Ithaca, 1981). See also on this subject, Nathan Weinstock, *Le Sionisme contre Israël* (Paris: Maspero, 1969), pp. 310-19.

13 To the point that the teaching of the Jewish religion is even imposed on Arabs: "At the end of his studies, the Arab high school student knows much more of the history of the Jewish people than that of the Arabs. The Koran is less studied than the Torah." Doris Bensimon and Eglal Errera, *Israéliens: Des Juifs et des Arabes* (Brussels: Complexe, 1989), p. 443.

14 See the note by Claude Klein in the preface to his French translation of Herzl's manifesto, *L'État des Juifs* (Paris: La Découverte, 1989), pp. 5-12.

15 "In fact, there is an identity between the emergence of Yiddish, that is its passage, or its *promotion*, from the status of 'jargon' to that of language, and the appearance of Jewish national sentiment," wrote Claude Klein (p. 135) in his excellent *Essai sur le sionisme*, published as an appendix to his translation of Herzl (op. cit., pp. 117-186).

16 Herzl, *The Jewish State*, p. 71.

17 Ibid., p. 54. The phrase that we stress here conceals, and for good reason, the specificity of Yiddish, which the overwhelming majority of Jews in Central and Eastern Europe spoke.

Alain Dieckhoff, in his previously-mentioned *The Invention of a Nation*—a brilliant work not, however, free from ambiguities and contradictions in his attempt to stress the "political modernity" of Zionism—stumbles in explaining the patent inadequacy of this ideology so far as secularism is concerned. He attributes this inadequacy principally to the persistence, in Zionism, of an "ardent longing for community life" (p. 96)—a quasi-tautological explanation. The author shows nonetheless how this inadequacy is inherent to the Zionist doctrine of the "Jewish nation," to the "invention" of which his book is devoted *without for all that ever questioning the pos-*

*tulate.* Indeed only the pan-Jewish postulate explains why "the religious criterion was in the last resort the only one that could precisely define the contours of the Jewish nation, all the other parameters—cultural, subjective, etc.—being too vague or inapplicable" (p. 131). And it was the insufficiency of this same criterion to cement a nationalism that impelled Zionism to "invent" a veritable new nation, the *Israeli nation* (which Dieckhoff does not even mention), founded on a new-old language—modern Hebrew—and on the destruction, for the purposes of assimilation, of the original national particularities of the immigrants, the Yiddish language in the first place.

Thus one can understand the paradox of Zionist nationalism, at the same time anti-assimilationist and strongly assimilationist, which considered the French model of national integration "unsuitable when applied to the detriment [*sic*] of the Jews (as in France in 1789), but perfectly valid when it enabled the Jews to rediscover a collective substratum." ( p. 99). Perhaps one can thus keep in mind the fact that "Zionism also included an element of protest against, even rejection of republican modernity which had assumed for the Jews the form of civic emancipation and integration in the host societies" (p. 73).

18  A convergence that, since Herzl, has been reflected by the alliance between the two currents inside the World Zionist Organization.

19  Hannah Arendt, "The Jewish State: Fifty Years After—Where Have Herzl's Politics Led?," in Gary Smith, ed., *Zionism—The Dream and the Reality: A Jewish Critique* (New York: Barnes & Noble, 1974), pp. 67–80.

20  See Teveth, *Ben-Gurion: The Burning Ground, 1886-1948,* chap. 26 in particular. The Ben Gurion-Jabotinsky meetings and their 1934 agreement (aborted by the opposition of the Zionist Left) were the occasion for the two men to note their "like-mindedness" ( chap. 29, p. 482). It was Ben-Gurion's Rafi that insisted in 1967 on including Menachem Begin's Gahal in the government of national unity. On the convergence between Ben-Gurion and Jabotinsky-Begin, see Mitchell Cohen, *Zion & State: Nation, Class and the Shaping of Modern Israel* (New York: Basil Blackwell, 1987).

21  This is eloquently explained by Alain Dieckhoff: "In all this an essential question arose: was building a Jewish national home compatible with scrupulous respect for democratic rules? Jabotinsky's reply was unhesitatingly negative, for an obvious reason. If the British Mandatory power applied the democratic (i.e., majority rule) principle in its full rigor, political power would automatically go to the Arabs, the largest community in numbers, and they would make haste to ban Jewish immigration and put a stop to consolidation of the sociopolitical infrastructure of the Yishuv [the Jewish community in Palestine]. So the national objective required non-application of the majority rule principle.... As usual Jabotinsky proclaimed without unnecessary flourishes the cold facts on which his left-wing opponents preferred to maintain hypocritical silence" (*The Invention of a Nation,* p. 182).

Astonishingly, the same author shortly afterward takes as good coin the democratic proclamations of the Irgun (see n. 7): he uses them as an argument to refute the anathemas hurled against this organization by Hannah Arendt, who characterized it as terroristic and chauvinist, similar to fascism and Nazism. One of the main ambiguities of Dieckhoff's work is his attempt to absolve Jabotinsky of the accusation of fascism (to be distinguished from any comparison to Nazism, which would be excessive certainly in his personal case, although justified for a number of his comrades). The main argument invoked by the author is the proclaimed "liberalism" of the founder of Revisionism, which supposes an antinomy between economic liberalism and Mussolini's fascism (a debatable postulate: see Cohen, *Zion & State,* pp. 170-174). Moreover, Dieckhoff obscures the full extent of the relationship between Jabotinsky and fascist Italy, which he shunts aside later in a few lines (*The Invention of a Nation,* pp. 242-243). As to the alleged "contempt" held by Jabotinsky for the cult of the Fuehrer and the Duce (p. 209), anybody familiar with the trajectory of the "Rosh Betar" can judge its worth.

22  Judah Magnes, "A Solution through Force?," in Smith, ed., *Zionism—The Dream and the Reality*, pp. 109–18.

23  Simha Flapan, *The Birth of Israel: Myths and Realities* (New York: Pantheon, 1987, p. 37).

24  An allusion to the case of the burial of Joseph Steinberg, son of a Jewish father and a Christian mother, which made the news in 1958.

25  Quoted in Smith, *Zionism—The Dream and the Reality*, p. 131.

26  In the sense in which Élise Marientras describes *Les mythes fondateurs de la nation américaine* (Brussels: Éditions Complexe, 1992). Moreover the founding myths of the Israeli nation clearly imitate U.S. founding myths, to the point that one could detect a narcissistic dimension in the mutual admiration between the two nations.

27  Flapan, *The Birth of Israel*, p. 234.

28  Ibid., p. 236. The emphasis is the author's.

29  See Theveth, *Ben-Gurion: The Burning Ground, 1886-1948*, chaps. 34 and 35, as well as p. 853. Chaim Weizmann shared the same opinion (see Norman Rose, *Chaim Weizmann: a Biography* [New York: Viking, 1986], pp. 320–30); the aim was, he said, "to get a fulcrum on which to place a lever... leaving the problems of expansion and extension to future generations" (p. 323).

30  To the argument of *Lebensraum* and the references to the Bible, there was added, after 1949, the security or "strategic" motivation that predominated in the eyes of the Israeli political-military establishment, and whose key argument turned around the narrowness of the strip of territory between the Mediterranean and the old Jordanian frontier (the "Green Line") where the majority of Israelis lived.

31  Saul Friedländer has summed up the concerns of the Ashkenazi Labor establishment with admirable frankness:

"Faced with the presence of a vast Arab population inside Israel, one can conceive the reinforcement of Jewish extremist tendencies inspired as much by economic as by religious or national motives, to demand the expulsion of all the Arabs or the application of an 'apartheid' regime. If these elements succeeded in imposing themselves, the Jewish state would be cut off from the world and the Jews of the Diaspora themselves. Finally, if it is probable that in contact with a vast Arab population the 'Oriental' Jews would tend to integrate themselves more rapidly inside the 'western' population to distinguish themselves from the Arabs, it is not entirely excluded that the poorest elements among them would be attracted by the Arab proletariat on both the social and cultural levels. The Arab population could then become an active element in the disintegration of Jewish society." *Réflexions sur l'avenir d'Israël* (Paris: Seuil, 1969), p. 146.

32  As this article is devoted to the solution that finally imposed itself, this is not the place to go into the different points of view expressed in Israel, on the debate on the fate of the territories occupied in 1967. On this subject see, for the immediate post-1967 debate: Éli Lobel, "Palestine and the Jews," in Ahmad El Kodsy and Eli Lobel, *The Arab World and Israel*, trans. Brian Pearce and Alfred Ehrenfeld (New York: Monthly Review Press, 1970), pp. 63-137; Peretz Merhav, *The Israeli Left : History, Problems* (San Diego/London: A.S. Barnes/Tantivy Press, 1980), chaps. 24 and 25. For a review of the more recent debates, see Louis-Jean Duclos, "La question des frontières orientales d'Israël," in *Revue d'études palestiniennes* 9 (Fall 1983): 17–31. Moreover, since this article deals with the Israeli-Palestinian settlement, we have not gone into the debates concerning the non-Palestinian Arab occupied territories.

33  See Yigal Allon, *Israël: la lutte pour l'espoir* (Paris: Stock, 1977). The Allon Plan met with the approval of the United States and, remarkably, François Mitterrand (see the extracts from Yeruham Cohen's book in Hebrew on the Allon Plan, reproduced in the appendix to Allon's book, pp. 243-247). Allon died in 1978.

34  Allon, *Israël: la lutte pour l'espoir*, p. 180. Emphasis by the author.

35  Ibid., p. 184.

36  For a detailed description of the Allon Plan, see Jean-Paul Chagnollaud, "Palestine: l'enjeu démographique,"and Alain Dieckhoff, *Les Espaces d'Israël* (Paris: FNSP, 1989) pp. 28-33. The Likud in turn divided the northern enclave (Samaria) into two sections. This is what Alain Dieckhoff calls a *"strategy of segmentation* of the territory and of demarcation between human groups" (p. 79).

37  Allon, *Israël: la lutte pour l'espoir*, p. 189.

38  Allon was already in 1948 a partisan of the conquest of the whole of Palestine up until the Jordan river, as he himself recalled: "...I say it openly: I disagreed with the way in which the war ended... I was already convinced that we should go as far as the Judean desert and the Jordan to create the conditions of a stable defense... while finding a solution to the problem of the Arab population." (p. 37) Allon had certainly conceived this "solution" well before presenting it to the Israeli cabinet. In 1967, he was the leader of Ahdut Haavodah (Unity of Labor), which laid claim to the whole of Palestine, as well as of the Hakibbutz Hameuhad movement, which pioneered the creation of strategic settlements in the aftermath of the "Six Day War." It is also significant that he was in charge of the ministry of absorption of immigration, from 1967 to 1969.

39  See Merhav, *The Israeli Left*. In the debate that raged inside the Labor Party in 1969, Allon's faction, Ahdut Haavodah, allied itself to Rafi, the rightist faction led by Moshe Dayan and Shimon Peres, against the "doves" of the party (Abba Eban, Pinhas Sapir, allied to Mapam).

40  Lobel, "Palestine and the Jews," p. 85. Subsequently, the drift to the right of Israeli society revealed by the electoral victory of the Likud would make Allon appear as a dove. Simha Flapan, former leader of Mapam, could not fall victim to this optical illusion. In his posthumous work, he recalled that "the first settlements in the West Bank were constructed at the instigation of Yigal Allon," and that "it was again Allon who gave his agreement to the attempts of the fundamentalist rabbi Moshe Levinger to establish a Jewish community in the heart of Arab Hebron" (Flapan, *The Birth of Israel*, p. 239—one of the Hebron settlers carried out the massacre in the Tomb of the Patriarchs/Mosque of Ibrahim in February 1994).

41  Alain Dieckhoff gives a remarkable analysis of this process of partial annexation and the strategies that underlie it in his already cited work, *Les Espaces d'Israël*. See also Michel Foucher, "L''intersection' jordanienne," in *Maghreb-Machrek* (Paris), no. 108, April 1985.

42  "Peace will not come as a result of a 'revolution of hearts' among them [the Arabs], but as the corollary of the balance of forces and cold political realism. It will be lucidity and the acceptance of reality which will lead them to reconciliation, negotiation and peace." Allon, op. cit., p. 179.

43  Ibid., p. 257 (from a speech made by Yigal Allon to the Central Committee of the Israeli Labor Party in 1972, reproduced as an appendix to the book).

44  Here again it is important not to be taken in by appearances. The stress placed on the distinction between the Palestinian West Bank and the Jordanian kingdom is not in itself indicative of the attitude of a dove. Initially, it was the right wing of the Labor Party—Dayan and Peres, in particular—who rejected the idea of returning it to Jordan, whereas the left defended the idea of a territorial continuity between the two banks of the Jordan (see Merhav, *The Israeli Left*, chap. 24). The Likud, partisans of the annexation of the whole of the West Bank, supported all the more strongly Palestinian "autonomy" (purely administrative in the framework of Israeli sovereignty), which it placed at the heart of the Camp David agreement with Sadat's Egypt.

45  Ibid., p. 204.

46  See Edward Said, "The Morning After," in *London Review of Books*, vol. 15, no. 20, 21 October 1993; Noam Chomsky, "The Israel-Arafat Agreement," in *Z Magazine*, October 1993; as well as Meron Benvenisti's article in the Israeli daily *Haaretz* of 19 May 1994.

47  See on this subject articles by Sara Roy, "La prospérité ou l'affrontement," and Mahmoud Abdel-Fadil, "Une coopération économique déséquilibrée en faveur d'Israël," in *Le Monde diplomatique*, August 1994.

48  See Duclos, "La question des frontières orientales d'Israël," p. 21.

49  Annex 1 (point 1) stipulates nonetheless that "Palestinians of Jerusalem who live there will have the right to participate in the election process" (the elections to the Palestinian "Council"). That is to say, the Arab inhabitants of the old city—who have refused Israeli citizenship—will have, in some way, the status of foreign residents in their own city, holding citizenship in territories where they do not live. So far as the holy places are concerned, recall that Herzl had envisaged "a formula of extraterritoriality coming under international law" (*The Jewish State*, p. 47).

50  Nathan Weinstock commented on this type of status in 1969: "The Israeli plans for the constitution of a Palestinian entity explicitly envisage that the diminished sovereignty of the Arab state would not cover any essential questions. As the Pretoria government has written in relation to Transkei: 'So far as defense, foreign affairs and certain judicial questions are concerned, the guardian republic of the new state must remain responsible for the moment'... in other words, it amounts to the creation of an indigenous protectorate under the authority of the dominant nation: a Bantustan." (*Le Sionisme contre Israël*, p. 520).

51  Benvenisti, "An Agreement of Surrender"; quotations taken from the monthly bulletin *News from Within*, Alternative Information Center, Jerusalem, June 1994.

52  "I understood that it was neither politically nor morally necessary to control the Arabs of this territory. Moreover, even if we wanted to, we could only do it at the point of a bayonet, and that only for a time—we are well placed to know it." Allon, *Israël: la lutte pour l'espoir*, p. 174.

53  See Dieckhoff, *Les espaces d'Israël*, pp. 195–97.

54  Maxime Rodinson, *Israel and the Arabs* (New York: Pantheon, 1968). The title of the French original is *Israel and the Arab Rejection*.

55  Alain Gresh's *The PLO: The Struggle Within: Toward an Independent Palestinian State*, trans. A.M. Berrett (London: Zed Press, 1985), is devoted to this programmatic evolution. See also Nadine Picaudou, *Le Mouvement national palestinien: genèse et structures* (Paris: L'Harmattan, 1989).

56  See his article published in *Le Monde*, 23 September 1988: "The PLO must, in the final analysis, choose between two options: support from Syria ... or dialogue with Jordan.... It is only with Jordan that the PLO can work out a policy of negotiation with Israel."

57  The Palestinian police force will consist of "police officers recruited locally and from abroad (holding Jordanian passports and Palestinian documents issued by Egypt). Those who will participate in the Palestinian police force coming from abroad should be trained as police and police officers." Annex 2 of the Declaration of Principles, point 3c.

58  Eliaf Sanbar, "L'autogouvernement palestinien: premiers défis," p. 107, in Ghassan Salamé, ed., *Proche-Orient: les exigences de la paix* (Brussels: Complexe, 1994), pp. 101–10. See also the article by Alain Gresh, "Israéliens et Palestiniens sur un terrain miné," in *Le Monde diplomatique*, January 1994.

59  The choice of Jericho, a small and relatively peaceful town, is purely symbolic: it is close to the Allenby bridge—the crossing point to Jordan, prefiguring a Jordanian-Palestinian confederation—and is also on the edge of the "sovereign corridor" envisaged by the Allon Plan.

60  Quoted from a French translation of an article by Noam Chomsky, "L'accord d'Oslo, vicié au départ," in *Courrier International*, 3 March 1994. The same opinion was recently expressed by Amos Perlmutter, who formulated this prediction as to the key instrument of the new regime: "Arafat will have to rely heavily on his security services, *Mukhabarat*, the old terrorist machine that has protected him from the Israelis, dissident Palestinians and Arab foes for so long. As a result, the police will have some military functions, while the security services, rather than the political parties, human rights organizations or other institutions, will become the foundation of Arafat's political power and administrative domination." ("Arafat's Police State," *Foreign Affairs*, July–August 1994, p. 10).

61  In an article with a revealing title—"An Agreement of Surrender," in *Haaretz*, 12 May 1994—Meron Benvenisti writes: "one can clearly recognize that Israeli victory was absolute and Palestinian defeat abject," adding: "It is also easy to understand the depth of disappointment of those Palestinian leaders from the Territories who considered the Agreement shameful to the point of discrediting their people as a whole."

62  See quote in note 42, above.

## CHAPTER SEVENTEEN

1   Including people who see themselves as on the Left—not only naive people ignorant of the facts but also "experts" such as Fred Halliday in Britain. Halliday has written, "The military action against Iraq was legitimate, just as in the 1930s and '40s it was justified to support the war against fascism." *The New Statesman and Society*, 8 March 1991.

2   *International Herald Tribune*, 11 March 1991.

3   The Arab members of the coalition have restricted themselves to Kuwaiti territory.

4   Southern Iraq was in the front line of the Iraq-Iran war as well as the Kuwait war.

5   The Iraqi Communist Party can take advantage of Moscow's non-involvement in the military coalition, the credit won by the Kremlin from its last-minute attempts to stop the war, and the fact that any regime in Baghdad will inevitably be largely dependent on the USSR. The fact that Moscow has maintained its 1972 Friendship and Cooperation Treaty with Iraq and has refused to promise not to deliver arms to it, as British Prime Minister John Major asked when he met Gorbachev in Moscow at the beginning of March (see *International Herald Tribune*, 7 March 1991), is also very revealing of the Kremlin's calculations.

6   "It is impossible for the Ba'ath Party to govern alone, especially under the leadership of someone no longer wanted by the world, the region or the Iraqi people" (*International Herald Tribune*, 9–10 March 1991).

7   *International Herald Tribune*, 8 March 1991.

8   The site of the meeting on Iraqi territory between the Iraqi military chiefs and those of the coalition.

9   *International Herald Tribune*, 11 March 1991.

10  *International Herald Tribune*, 6 March 1991.

11  *Le Monde*, 12 March 1991.

12  *International Herald Tribune*, 13 March 1991.

13  *Newsweek*, 18 March 1991.

# INDEX